J.A. Mitchell

You: The Greatest Good

AN EXPLORATION OF HISTORY, MORALITY, AND AUTHORITY

You: The Greatest Good
Copyright © 2024 J.A. Mitchell

No part of this publication may be reproduced, distributed, or transmitted in any form or by any means, including photocopying, recording, or other electronic or mechanical methods, without the prior written permission of the author.

www.ja-mitchell.com

First published in 2024

ISBN: 978-1-7382482-1-6

First Edition

*To all those throughout history engaged in
the tireless pursuit of liberty*

Contents

Introduction	1
PART I: THINKERS	
Chapter 1 - Overview	6
Chapter 2 - A Brief History of Western Utilitarianism	9
Chapter 3 - Ideas Aligned with Utilitarianism	35
Chapter 4 - A Brief History of Western Natural Law	42
Chapter 5 - Ideas Aligned with Natural Law	67
Chapter 6 - Anarchism and Natural Law	76
Chapter 7 - On the Shoulders of Giants	83
PART II: THEORIES	
Chapter 1 - Overview	86
Chapter 2 - Core Concepts of Utilitarianism	88
Chapter 3 - Core Concepts of Natural Law	104
Chapter 4 - Natural Rights	112
Chapter 5 - Notes on Natural Law	120
Chapter 6 - Ethics & Justice	130
Chapter 7 - Putting the Theories to the Test	138
Chapter 8 - Unravelling the Ideas	150
PART III: ETHICS IN ACTION	
Chapter 1 - Welcome to the Real World	154
Chapter 2 - Utilitarianism in Practice	157
Chapter 3 - Natural law in Practice	180
Chapter 4 - The Gap between Theory and Practice	229

PART IV: GREATEST GOOD

- Chapter 1 - Arguing Morals 234
- Chapter 2 - Opposing Natural Law 236
- Chapter 3 - The Case for Natural Law 242
- Chapter 4 - The Case for Utilitarianism 251
- Chapter 5 - Opposing Utilitarianism 256
- Chapter 6 - Escalating Arguments 269
- Chapter 7 - Utilitarian Variants 283
- Chapter 8 - Distilling the Theories 290
- Chapter 9 - Moral Triumph 300
- Chapter 10 - The March Towards Utility 305
- Chapter 11 - The Greatest Good 325
- Chapter 12 - Restoring Natural Order 328

Conclusion 333

References 336

About the Author 343

Introduction

The year was 1926. It was a snowy Christmas weekend in New York, and millions of residents were gathering with their families, singing, feasting, and celebrating the holiday season. The roaring 20s had seen unprecedented growth and prosperity in the wake of WWI, and New York was considered one of the greatest cities in the world. But across the city, sombre events were unfolding, and for some, the holiday weekend would end only in tragedy. By the time Monday morning rolled around, dozens of people lay dead at New York's Bellevue Hospital, alongside hundreds of others across the country.

At the height of Prohibition, during the period now called the "Chemist's War," the US government mandated that industrial alcohol should be mixed with toxic substances like methanol, hoping to make it undrinkable. Over the course of that holiday season and the entire duration of the Chemist's War, it is estimated that over 10,000 people died from consuming the poisoned alcohol. In the end, the public outrage from the policy helped lead to the eventual repeal of Prohibition in 1933.

In retrospect, it's rather ironic that the intended goal of President Hoover's "Noble Experiment" of Prohibition was the *betterment* of society. Hoover and company sincerely believed that outlawing alcohol – and eventually *poisoning* it – would reduce crime and corruption, help solve social problems, decrease the tax burden of prisons, and improve overall health and hygiene in America. The results of these actions, no matter how well-intentioned, were only a tiny bit short of disastrous. Alcohol consumption increased in many parts of the United States alongside increases in crime and corruption, and the legal system was overwhelmed with millions of peaceful Americans who had been turned into criminals by a victimless crime.

Of course, grand political and social schemes like Hoover's Prohibition are nothing new to us. We've all heard the infamous phrase, "The road to hell is paved with good intentions," and many of us have seen this phrase play out. But behind these intentions there's something much deeper going on. Beneath the historical hindsight and witty sayings that deliver conventional wisdom there is an *ethical* bedrock. No, not "ethics" in the sense of some stringent corporate memo or company code of conduct, rather ethics as a foundational framework through which all human decisions reach the world. It is these ethical structures that this book aims to explore and, if possible, separate from the bland connotations they've accumulated in recent times.

Throughout this book, we will explore two titans of moral philosophy that have been struggling in an unseen tug-of-war for the better part of two centuries – *utilitarianism* and *natural law*. Even though these systems aren't alone in the ethical landscape, they are the two systems that have risen to the top, influencing moral, legal, and political decision-making across the Western world. But before we get there, the first part of this book will take us back to the start – a journey through the thinkers and the formation of their ideas. From ancient Greece to modern-day America, we will see the ideas coalesce, form, and be applied to the real world.

In the utilitarianism tradition, we chart the ideas of personalities like David Hume, a Scottish philosopher well-known for being a thorn in scientists' sides with his still-unanswered "problem of induction"; Cesare Beccaria, the Italian criminologist and founder of the larger-than-life literary society, "the Academy of Fists"; and Jeremy Bentham, an eccentric prodigy whose last request was to have his body mummified and put on display for eternity.

From the annals of natural law theory, we encounter Cicero, a literary genius and Roman statesman who is said to have authored more than three-quarters of the Latin literature known to have existed in his lifetime;

St. Thomas Aquinas, a faithful 13th-century friar and priest whose handsome face still features on stained glass windows across the world; and Lysander Spooner, a man born on a farm and named after a Spartan general, who is perhaps the most staunch and sophisticated legal opponent of slavery the world has ever encountered.

As we explore these thinkers (in Part I) and their ideas (in Part II), we will see how these concepts stack up against each other – both in theory and practice.

In Part III, "Ethics in Action," we look into how these theories laid out by some of the world's best thinkers actually hold up when theory encounters reality – millennia worth of philosophy brought to bear against the problems of our time. From September 11th to COVID-19, the past several decades of global history have been a hard test of our moral decision-making tools. Many forces have stepped up, professed a "better way forward" and offered (or imposed) rules and regulations to purportedly help humanity overcome crises. But, as we saw with Hoover's "Noble Experiment" above, a lot can go wrong in between great intentions and delivering a better world, and clever schemes can often lead to tragic results. So, then comes the natural question – how do we make decisions that avoid the trap of utopian intentions with dystopian results?

In a word – *ethics*.

This is the ethics that guides human action, and the ideas on moral philosophy that have been compounding for thousands of years. In today's world we have the good fortune of having simple and easy access to the breadth of human knowledge, experience, and reasoning. As we weave our way through the wealth of themes, thinkers, and implementations of these two theories, utilitarianism and natural law, a fundamental shift in Western morality is unearthed – a change reflected in culture, politics, and law.

The final part of this book, Part IV, captures and aims to reinvigorate concepts that have spent too long consigned to academic corners and out of the public eye. With a fresh perspective on ethical problems, we will discuss brand new ideas on chaos and unpredictability, the siren song of intuition, and how Schrödinger's cat applies to moral action.

From the first word to the last, this book aims to both reveal and consider the growing gap between our moral roots and present-day policy – touching on a range of policies from vaccine mandates to international trade to restrictions on free speech. Together we will discover how intuition, human nature, and optimal outcomes intertwine across history, a dance between opposing forces that each claim to be the only moral guide for humanity. In the end, I hope to show that every person is their own end, not simply the means to achieve a better world.

With that in mind, let's take the first step in the journey towards demonstrating that YOU are the greatest good.

PART I

THINKERS

1

Overview

Utilitarianism and Natural Law. Two theories that capture two unique sets of ideas, ideas which — whether you know it or not — have changed the course of billions of lives.

Utilitarianism is a theory that falls into the "consequentialist" school of ethics, a group of theories that in their simplest form judge the morality of actions based on outcomes – or consequences. For utilitarianism specifically, one consequence is held to the highest value: *human happiness*. In essence, this means that every action should be judged based on the total collective happiness it brings.

Even though ideas on the common good and maximizing social well-being have been around in some capacity for thousands of years, modern utilitarian concepts are rooted in the work of several prominent philosophers that we will explore in the following chapters. These thinkers who developed utilitarianism into the driving force it is today each had their own unique twists on the core ideas, but most variations ultimately share at least one common thread: *maximizing happiness.*

So the question becomes, how do we measure happiness in order to choose between different available actions? The answer lies in the concept of "utility," co-opted and refined by Jeremy Bentham, which represents the sum of every good and every bad outcome of an action. For example, if an action results in more good than bad, it can be said to have positive net utility – the criteria that is used to determine morality, and where utilitarianism got its name. Later variations of the theory made efforts to tweak utility calculations, with some focusing on personal preferences, harm reduction, or even moral rule following instead of simply maximizing happiness.

Overall, the focus on collective happiness has – understandably – made the theory quite a powerful and attractive tool for people and policymakers, offering a practical, convenient, and intuitive framework for making moral decisions, at least on its face.

Natural law, on the other hand, has ideas that can be traced back to the very beginnings of human society, a school of thought which believes the moral principles that guide us are encoded into human nature. According to the theory, because morality is embedded in nature, its principles are universal and are applicable to humans around the world.

So what do these universal rules look like? And how do we see them in nature? The primary way that natural law is typically expressed is through the concept of natural rights. According to theorists like St. Thomas Aquinas, Locke, and others, these rights can be discovered in nature through reason, observation, and the study of human behaviour. An example of one of these natural rights is the *right to life*. Natural law argues that because humans are naturally social beings and – like most living organisms – have a drive for self-preservation, that respect for the lives of others is necessary for cooperation, harmony, and social cohesion. As a result, everyone has a right to life that cannot be violated without harming the fabric of social order and natural justice.

Because these rights are believed to be a result of immutable human nature, they are considered to be absolute and inviolable, regardless of the context, the decision-maker, or the people being affected. This leads to natural law being categorised as a morally absolute theory, and the idea that actions that violate these rights are immoral, no matter the situation.

As you can imagine, since utilitarianism doesn't care about the morality of actions as long as they have a positive outcome, and natural law *only* cares about the morality of actions, these two theories are generally in complete opposition to one another. While these differences in both theory and practice will be expanded on in later parts of the book, we will start to see these conflicting principles arise through the ideas of the thinkers outlined in this section. Here, we will take a peek at some of the major contributors to both of these concepts over time, charting the evolution of the ideas, and later the formal theories that they became. With that, let's dive into the first theory: utilitarianism.

2

A Brief History of Western Utilitarianism

Like many of the other prominent philosophical ideas in Western tradition, utilitarianism's influences originate back in the days of ancient Greece. In particular, some of the first concepts in line with utilitarian thinking can be traced back to the hedonistic school of thought associated with Epicurus, who emphasized the pursuit of pleasure and the avoidance of pain. But formally, it wasn't until thousands of years later, during the Enlightenment, that utilitarianism really took shape as an ethical theory, organized and presented in the works of British philosophers Jeremy Bentham and John Stuart Mill.

Bentham, often considered the founding father of utilitarianism, introduced a twist on David Hume's concept of utility with his "principle of utility," which requires that actions be judged based on their ability to maximize overall happiness or pleasure. Mill, a prominent philosopher and political economist in the 1800s, expanded on Bentham's ideas and developed the theory much further, introducing an approach based on rules, the obligation to act, and distinguishing between higher and lower pleasures, arguing that intellectual pleasures were more valuable than physical ones.

Throughout the 19th and 20th centuries, utilitarianism continued to grow in popularity, influencing many aspects of society, especially within the realm of public policy and economics. Today, it has risen to become a dominant decision-making tool that continues to exert a greater and greater impact on our collective understanding of moral action.

Over the following chapters, we will take a look at the backgrounds and history of some of the thinkers whose ideas inspired, paralleled, or overlapped with utilitarianism throughout history. Although the people included here each contributed or shared ideas with utilitarianism, this is certainly not an exhaustive list.

Epicurus, the garden philosopher
(341-270 BCE)

Our journey into utilitarian ideas begins over 2,200 years ago with a Greek philosopher named Epicurus. Although he is not considered a utilitarian by direct comparison, his ideas share many similarities with its core principles, not to mention his influence on future philosophers, including figures like Nietzsche and Karl Marx.

In 341 BCE, while Alexander the Great was busy expanding the Macedonian Empire, Epicurus was born in Greece on the island of Samos, which was at the time a colony of Athens. His father, Neocles, was a schoolteacher, and his mother, Chaerestrate, was born to a noble family. Epicurus was introduced to philosophy at a young age, and he studied under a variety of philosophers, including Nausiphanes, a follower of Democritus – an ancient pioneer of atomic theory. After spending some time in Asia Minor, he returned to Athens in 306 BCE, where he set up his own school of philosophy, known as "The Garden."

It was at the Garden that Epicureanism was developed, a philosophy centred on the idea that the pursuit of pleasure was the highest good. This philosophical community was unique for its time because it allowed both men and women, even slaves, to participate in discussions and learning. Unlike hedonism in the modern sense, which is all about chasing physical pleasures, Epicurus advocated for the importance of inner peace and freedom from physical pain. He suggested living a modest life, cultivating friendships, and participating in philosophical discussion – his goal? To better understand the nature of the world and the human experience.

Inspired by his teacher Nausiphanes, Epicurus was an early materialist, holding the idea that everything was made up of both *atomos* – or atoms – and void. He was also widely considered to be among the first atheists, proposing that the gods, if they did exist, were not interested in humans. This idea was summed up in his famous argument that the existence of natural evil proves that: God either doesn't know about human suffering (not all-seeing), doesn't care about human suffering (not all-loving), or is not able to save us from suffering (not all-powerful).

Epicurus believed that empirical knowledge – our senses and feelings – were a reliable source of information about the world, and that we should trust our experiences to guide our beliefs and actions. The focus on materialism and the senses led to his conclusion that happiness was the ultimate goal of life, and that living a life based on reason and moderation would lead to the highest form of happiness.

Even though only a relatively small number of his writings survived over the millennia, many of his ideas were preserved and passed on by his followers and later philosophers. Epicureanism was influential up until the Roman era, but eventually experienced a significant decline with the rise of Christianity. The ideas of Epicurus would spend more than 1,500 years in the background until they made a comeback during the Enlightenment, with a resurgence that still influences modern philosophy today.

–

Even though they are separate philosophical theories, the influence of Epicurus's ideas on the development of utilitarianism during the enlightenment are visible in some of the following core concepts.

Pursuit of Happiness: Epicurus believed that the ultimate goal of every person's life should be to achieve happiness or pleasure. Unlike utilitarian ideas on collective happiness, he argued that people should seek to maximize their own happiness.

Hedonism: Since Epicurean philosophy treats pleasure as the highest good, it is usually described as hedonistic. Epicurus's ideas were different from those of other hedonists who focused on physical pleasure, concentrating instead on chasing mental pleasures and avoiding physical pain.

Differentiation of Pleasures: According to Epicurus, the greatest pleasure comes from inner peace and freedom from fear and pain. He believed that not all types of pleasure were equal. This distinction between pleasures influenced future utilitarian thinker John Stuart Mill, who built on these ideas.

Prudence in Decision-making: Inspiring future utilitarian ideas on outcomes, Epicurus advocated for the virtue of prudence – or being cautious – when making decisions. He suggested that people should consider the potential consequences of their choices, and that sometimes sacrificing short-term pleasures would lead to greater long-term happiness.

Lack of Social Focus: In contrast with utilitarianism's focus on the social collective, Epicurean philosophy – like many of the ideas of the time – focused more on individuals and their purpose.

Even though Epicurus is not considered to be a utilitarian, the influence of his ideas on later philosophers and ethical thinkers was sizeable. His ideas on the pursuit of happiness, the emphasis on caution and the consideration of consequences, and his beliefs on different types of pleasures, are all concepts that are found in different variations of utilitarianism today, more than 2,000 years later.

Claude-Adrien Helvétius, the moral institutionalist
(1715-1771 CE)

Our next thinker whose ideas can be seen as an early form of utilitarianism is French philosopher Claude-Adrien Helvétius. He was born in Paris in 1715, just eight months before the death of King Louis XIV. His father Adrien Helvétius was a physician who would later become the personal physician to Queen Marie Leszczyńska, the wife of the next king, Louis XV. Helvétius's childhood was spent mostly in the company of French nobility, exposing him to many of the era's prominent intellectuals.

Following in his father's footsteps, Helvétius pursued a medical education at the University of Paris. During his time at university he was influenced by the writing of French materialist, hedonist, philosopher, and physician Julien Offray de La Mettrie. La Mettrie's work on the mechanical nature of human beings and the importance of the physical experience in shaping knowledge left a lasting impact on Helvétius.

Over the next 13 years Helvétius worked as farmer general – effectively a tax collector – at the request of Queen Marie, while spending time with the intellectual community in Paris, including philosophers like Jean-Jacques Rousseau and Montesquieu. In his position as a tax collector he became wealthy, and at the age of 36, he retired to his lands in Voré with his wife.

In 1758, he published his incredibly controversial book *De l'Esprit* (On the Mind), where he combined the influences of La Mettrie, Locke, and other Enlightenment thinkers in order to develop his own materialist philosophy. His book explored the role of the senses and experience, self-interest, and the value of education as a tool to promote social welfare and the greater good. However, its attacks on religious morality quickly led to the book being burned in public, as well as criticism from Voltaire, Rousseau, and others.

—

Even though Helvétius's views generally focused on self-interest in his pursuit of happiness, his work on social welfare was inspirational to future thinkers in the utilitarian tradition. Helvétius's views on the greater good can be summarized as follows.

> **The Pursuit of Pleasure**: Helvétius's views centred around the idea that people's motivations are primarily driven by self-interest and the pursuit of pleasure. These ideas of pleasure as a universal goal resonated with later thinkers, helping inspire the development of the utilitarian objectives.
>
> **Education and Social Institutions**: Helvétius believed that proper education and setting up social institutions was the best path towards a greater good, a way to align people's self-interest with what was best for society. With education playing a vital role in shaping people's values, he thought that governments should encourage and reward actions that benefit the well-being of society.
>
> **Empiricism and Consequentialism**: Influenced by his exposure to La Mettrie and John Locke's philosophies, he shared the belief that senses and experience were important in learning and gaining knowledge. This empiricism led to the development of theories that focused on real, observable outcomes as a basis for morality, instead of inherent moral action.

Social Inequality: Just like many other materialists, Helvétius fundamentally believed that humans were naturally equal, and that only access to education and resources created social inequality.

As a pre-utilitarian thinker, Claude-Adrien Helvétius's ideas had some direct impacts and influences on the development of utilitarianism and future philosophers, some of whom would adopt or build these ideas into their own work. His theories on the role of social institutions and the importance of equality in society's happiness were especially impactful in inspiring utilitarian theory.

David Hume, the empirical sceptic
(1711-1776)

David Hume was born in Edinburgh in 1711, during a period where the Scots were adjusting to their involvement in the new United Kingdom – Great Britain. Hume was one of the central figures of the Scottish Enlightenment and one of the most influential philosophical figures of the 1700s. He was raised in a religious household, and his father died when he was just an infant, leaving his mother to care for the children alone.

When he was just 12 years old, Hume was accepted into the University of Edinburgh. There he learned a wide range of subjects, including the classics, philosophy, science, and mathematics. Even though his family expected him to study law, Hume became interested in philosophy and literature as he was exposed to the writings of Enlightenment thinkers like John Locke.

In 1729, Hume left the University of Edinburgh early, choosing to learn on his own instead of completing his degree. He began to study the ideas of scepticism and empiricism. After a series of health issues, Hume moved to France in 1734 where he began to rub shoulders with French Enlightenment thinkers, writing his first work *A Treatise of Human Na-*

ture. When the work was eventually published in 1740, it received a disappointing reception. This book was where Hume first presented the "is-ought problem," now known as Hume's Law, a logical argument against assuming moral judgement from the state of nature.

Over the next decade, Hume continued to publish philosophical writings that contained many of the building blocks that would directly influence utilitarians. These building blocks included an initial concept of utility, as well as early forms of consequentialism, which were further developed in *An Enquiry Concerning the Principles of Morals* in 1751.

Over the later part of his life, he spent time with several of the popular thinkers from the French Enlightenment, before eventually returning home to Scotland – finally passing away just a month after the signing of the Declaration of Independence in 1776.

—

While David Hume's philosophical work pre-dated the development of a formal theory of utilitarianism by almost 50 years, some of the concepts he developed directly laid the foundation for Bentham and future utilitarian thinkers. These influential concepts include the following.

> **The Is-Ought Problem**: Now more commonly known as Hume's Law, Hume highlighted the problem with using descriptive statements (what is) as a basis for deriving prescriptive statements (what ought to be). For example, an observation that aggressive behaviour can be linked to certain genetic markers doesn't itself justify differential treatment for people in whom these genes are present. This presented a challenge to many ethical theories and directly influenced the development of the utilitarian principle of "maximizing utility" in order to bridge the gap between the two.

Empiricism: Hume was an empiricist, a prominent advocate for the idea that humans understand the world through experience instead of through the pure application of reason. Hume's empiricism even led to scepticism of *all* concepts that didn't originate in empirical observation, including religion.

Moral Sentiments: Laying the foundation for classical utilitarianism's focus on happiness and suffering as the basis for morality, Hume argued that morality is a result of the emotional responses that come from pleasure and pain, not rationality.

Common Good: Hume's theories often focused on the common good and the public interest, including the role and importance of justice, and the moral foundations of
actions that benefit every member of society.

Utility: One of Hume's major impacts on utilitarian theory was his principle of utility. Although it was different from Bentham's later attempt to create a measurable metric, Hume argued that actions were moral according to their usefulness, which was based on the social benefit gained, and more directly on our emotional responses to the action.

Consequentialism: Although Hume did not develop a full consequentialist theory himself, his version of utility did relate the morality of actions to their outcomes, focusing on social benefits and the effects of actions on the public. His unique approach can be considered a mix of both virtue ethics with consequentialism.

Overall, many of the principles outlined in Hume's work would go on to heavily influence Bentham's views on utility, happiness, and pain as the source of morality, and the focus on common good as the goal of moral action.

Cesare Beccaria, the justice reformer
(1738-1794)

Eighteenth-century Italian Cesare Beccaria is another philosopher whose work had a major impact, not only on utilitarianism, but on Western civilization and justice overall. Born in Milan in 1738, Beccaria was the oldest son of an aristocratic family. His father, Marchese Gian Beccaria Bonesana, was a member of the Austrian Habsburg Empire, and his mother, Maria Visconti, also belonged to an influential and well-connected family.

During his early years, he attended the Jesuit school *Collegio dei Nobili*, where he was exposed to classical literature, philosophy, and theology. In 1758, Beccaria enrolled in law at the University of Pavia, where he developed an interest in Enlightenment philosophy, specifically the value of reason, liberty, and scientific inquiry. These ideas would go on to become the founding values behind most of his work in criminal justice reform.

At the age of 23, Beccaria joined a group of young intellectuals from Milan named the "Academy of Fists" (*Accademia dei Pugni*), who, despite their fiery-sounding name, were focused on intellectual, not physical, attacks against traditional ideas and norms of the era. As a part of this group, he read and debated the works of philosophers like Montesquieu, Voltaire, Hume, and Helvétius, discussing and promoting Enlightenment ideas across politics, economics, and criminal law.

At the same time as the Industrial Revolution was getting started in Great Britain in 1764, Beccaria published his greatest work, the groundbreaking *On Crimes and Punishments* (*Dei delitti e delle pene*). This treatise not only inspired Jeremy Bentham but was instrumental in shaping America's foundational legal documents—the Declaration of Independence, the U.S. Constitution, and the U.S. Bill of Rights. Heavily influenced by Helvétius, Beccaria argued that the punishment of criminals should be evaluated based on the amount of damage done to "social welfare," which he measured through the very utilitarian concept: the "greatest happiness for the greatest number."

—

Beccaria's unique approach to criminal law and punishment had a major impact on utilitarianism in the following areas.

> **Emphasis on Consequences**: Beccaria's work stressed the importance of considering consequences of laws and punishments for society. This increased focus on consequences laid the foundation for utilitarianism and became one of the central principles of the theory, judging morality by looking at the outcomes of actions and policies.
>
> **Proportionality in Punishment**: One of the major themes in Beccaria's work was that punishment should be proportional to the severity of the crime committed. In *On Crimes and Punishments*, he made the case that greater punishment is not only unjust, but also counterproductive to maximizing social welfare.
>
> **The Deterrence Principle**: Beccaria was a strong believer that the primary goal of punishment should be to deter crime in order to protect society. This influenced both Bentham and Mill, who later wrote about the importance of deterrence in their own theories on punishment and aligned the idea with utilitarianism's focus on maximizing social well-being.

Influence on Bentham: A sneak peek at our next thinker; Jeremy Bentham is widely known as the father of utilitarianism, and much of the initial theory was directly influenced by Beccaria's work. Bentham cited *On Crimes and Punishments* as an inspiration in his own writing on criminal law, where he incorporated Beccaria's ideas on proportionality, deterrence, and the focus on consequences.

Cesare Beccaria is most certainly one of the philosophers who has had the largest impact on the development of both utilitarianism and Western legal principles. Many of the ideas in Beccaria's work led directly to the ethical theory laid out by Bentham and helped influence the founding legal documents of the United States.

Jeremy Bentham, the father of utilitarianism
(1748-1832)

In 1748, while the European powers were wrapping up the Austrian War of Succession, the father of utilitarianism came into the world. Jeremy Bentham was born into a middle-class family and was recognized as a child prodigy from a very young age. Bentham is said to have been learning Latin by the age of four and at age 12 he was admitted into Queen's College in Oxford. Here he completed his bachelor's degree in law by the age of 15 and a master's degree by 18.

After finishing his master's degree, he went to Lincoln's Inn to continue his legal education, while also taking a seat as a student in the King's Bench division of the High Court. While listening to a lecture by one of the leading legal authorities of the day, Sir William Blackstone, Bentham was disillusioned, finding it filled with logical fallacies. After the experience, Bentham decided not to practise law, instead becoming a fierce critic of the legal system.

Over the next 20 years, Bentham would write about law, politics, and economics, before eventually publishing his book *An Introduction to the Principles of Morals and Legislation* in 1789. In this writing he reinterpreted Hume's principle of utility, combined and reimagined concepts by Beccaria and others, and laid the foundations of his monumental ethical theory – utilitarianism. As a key concept in his theory, he argued that all legislation should try to promote the "greatest happiness of the greatest number," and that since pain is evil, punishment should only be used to prevent greater evil.

Bentham's concept of utility was very different from Hume's original concept, and he tried to create a version that could be measured and then used to calculate the morality of actions. Bentham's utility was a guiding force behind most of his ideas and continues to be one of the foundational concepts in modern utilitarian thought.

When his father passed away in 1792, it left him with enough money to spend the rest of his life writing, and over the next four decades he is said to have written between ten and twenty pages every single day. Today, thousands of these pages are still in collections at the UCL and British libraries, along with a "scientific" display containing his mummified body – a final request that sat somewhere between altruism and narcissism.

–

Some of the specific influences that helped shape Bentham's philosophies included the following:

> **Classical philosophy**: Bentham was familiar with the works of ancient hedonist Greek and Roman philosophers, such as Epicurus. Their ideas on the pursuit of pleasure as the highest good laid the

groundwork for his development of the "greatest happiness principle," the core of his utilitarian philosophy.

David Hume: Bentham's theories were deeply influenced by David Hume, who believed in the empirical approach to knowledge, focusing on the senses, observation, and experience. This empiricism, as well as Hume's work on the original version of utility and the importance of consequences, all contributed to Bentham's focus on outcomes, using an action's results to determine its moral value.

Claude-Adrien Helvétius: Helvétius was an important influence on Bentham. His ideas on materialism, human motivation, pleasure and the role of education and social institutions in promoting the greater good are central to Bentham's theories of utility and the purpose of legislation.

Cesare Beccaria: Beccaria's groundbreaking work *On Crimes and Punishments* also had a major influence on Bentham, with its focus on rationality, utility, and humanity in the criminal justice system. Beccaria's ideas on proportionality and the social value of punishment directly inspired Bentham's own views on legal and penal reform.

—

When writing his formal theory of utilitarianism, Bentham assembled and developed a variety of different concepts that were unique compared to earlier philosophers whose works helped guide his ideas. A summary of these ideas is as follows.

The Greatest Happiness Principle: This principle is the foundational concept of utilitarianism and is what makes it unique compared to other ethical theories. It states that the morally right action is the one that promotes the greatest happiness for the greatest number of people.

Hedonic Calculus: Bentham created the idea of "hedonic calculus," an attempt to quantify happiness and suffering in order to determine an action's net utility. By trying to accurately measure the morality of an action's consequences, Bentham tried to create a more precise and objective system of making ethical decisions.

Real-world Application: Using his utilitarian principles, Bentham was an avid proponent of legal and social reform, advocating for equal rights, democracy, and the separation of church and state, among other issues. The application of his theories to real political and social issues set him apart from many other philosophers – utilitarian and otherwise.

Panopticon: One of Bentham's most famous ideas was the "panopticon," a design for a prison that would allow a single guard to observe multiple prisoners without them knowing they were being watched. The concept was an example of how utilitarian ideas could be applied to architecture and social control, a demonstration of Bentham's desire to use utilitarianism as a tool for social reform.

Bentham's initial version of utilitarianism was unique mostly as a result of his development of the greatest happiness principle and hedonic calculus, as well as his focus on practical applications and real social issues, bridging the gap between theory and practice.

John Stuart Mill, the pragmatic utilitarian
(1806-1873)

In 1806, when Lewis and Clark were completing the last few months of their famous expedition across the United States, John Stuart Mill was born in London, England. His father was Scottish philosopher, historian, and economist James Mill, who was a close associate of Jeremy Bentham. His father's membership in the "Philosophical Radicals," alongside Bentham and other utilitarians, influenced a lot of Mill's childhood and education.

Mill's father believed that education was of the highest importance and took personal responsibility for his son's learning. Said to be a child prodigy, by the age of three, Mill was already learning Greek, and by the age of eight, he reportedly had read several works of classical literature, history, and philosophy. It is estimated that Mill had an IQ over 200 by today's standards, and his father made sure that Latin, mathematics, logic, politics, and economics were all a big part of his education from a very young age. Even though his father encouraged him to read different perspectives, the high exposure to utilitarian ideas and the close guidance of his education resulted in John adopting many of his father's mannerisms, attitudes, and beliefs.

This education continued through his childhood, and when he was a teenager, he began to publish his writings in *The Traveller* and *The Morning Chronicle*, two newspapers published by friends of his father and Bentham. After his father and Bentham founded the *Westminster Review* in 1827, he began to publish there as well, continuing to improve his skills as a writer and public thinker. Over the next 15 years, while the first Industrial Revolution was coming to a close, Mill published a large array of different works and essays on topics ranging from analysis of other authors and poetry to history, economics, and more.

After a long and scandalous relationship with Harriet Taylor, the two were married in 1851 a short while after her husband passed away.

Harriet Taylor had a profound impact on the development of his personal beliefs, including views on women's rights, gender equality, and personal liberty. Many of Mill's famous works contain evidence of their collaboration, including *On Liberty* and *The Subjection of Women*.

Mill's marriage only lasted for seven years before the death of Harriet, and during this period he spent most of his time working at the British East India Company, while the amount of work he published declined significantly. Almost immediately after the company was dissolved in 1858, Harriet died, and Mill returned to his villa in Saint-Véran, France, where he began writing and publishing again.

In 1859, Mill published *On Liberty*, where he introduced the utilitarian requirement to act, raising the idea that we are responsible for harm that results from choosing not to act, in his following quote:

> *A person may cause evil to others not only by his actions but by his inaction, and in either case, he is justly accountable to them for the injury.*

In 1861, Mill published *Utilitarianism* in *Fraser's Magazine*, where he defended his ethical theory and hoped to clear up objections and misconceptions about his views on utilitarianism. This was the work where he wrote his arguments that not all pleasures were the same, and where he introduced rule utilitarianism, the idea that following consistent rules based on utilitarian ideas was in the interests of the greater good.

After spending a couple of years in parliament, in 1868 he retired after losing in a general election, and he returned to Avignon, France where he lived until his death in 1873.

Other than Bentham, John Stuart Mill's contributions to utilitarianism have had the largest impact on the theory, including the introduction of several new concepts that have since been adopted by modern governments. Some of the more notable ideas that were introduced by Mill include the following.

> **Rule Utilitarianism**: In a departure from Bentham's ideas, Mill's version of utilitarianism focused heavily on the consequences of following general moral rules instead of evaluating individual actions – hence the name "rule utilitarianism." He argued that following rules would lead to better outcomes than determining the consequences of every single action.
>
> **Distinction of Pleasures**: Similar to Epicurus's claims that not all pleasures are equal, Mill believed that some pleasures are qualitatively better than others. He distinguished between "higher" and "lower" pleasures, believing that intellectual pursuits like learning or creating art were more fulfilling than physical pleasures like eating or relaxation.
>
> **Harm Principle**: Introduced in *On Liberty*, Mill's harm principle declared that the only reason to limit an individual's freedom is to prevent harm to others. This principle has had a lasting impact on Western culture and discussions about individual liberty, rights, and the role of government in society.
>
> **Utilitarian Rights**: Mill argued that utilitarianism should provide the foundation for individual rights, since actions that protect and respect rights tend to promote overall happiness. This approach was different from other ethical theories like natural law that treated rights as inherently valuable, regardless of consequence.

Rights are reimagined in this argument as a tool for increasing social well-being, an idea that has steadily increased in popularity ever since.

Feminism and Equality: Influenced by his wife Harriet, Mill was an early advocate for gender equality and women's rights. His work *The Subjection of Women* is considered a classic feminist text and has had a lasting impact on feminist philosophy. In the book he argued for equal opportunity and fair treatment of women, which are reflections of utilitarian principles.

Built on Bentham's ideas, John Stuart Mill's rule utilitarianism, utilitarian rights, and the harm principle are evident throughout Western ethical and political systems today.

Henry Sidgwick, the systematic moralizer
(1838-1900)

In 1838, a year after Samuel Morse invented the telegraph and Morse code, Henry Sidgwick was born in Yorkshire, England to a deeply religious upper-middle class family. His father was Reverend William Sidgwick, a priest and the headmaster of a local grammar school.

Throughout his childhood, Sidgwick was taught at home by both his father and other private tutors. At the age of 17, he went to study at a boarding school in Warwickshire, where he won a scholarship to continue his studies at Trinity College in Cambridge.

While studying mathematics at Cambridge, Sidgwick was exposed to a range of philosophical ideas, including those of Kant, as well as early utilitarians like Bentham and Mill. Their theories about maximizing happiness and minimizing pain as the basis for ethical behaviour influenced him to develop his own brand of utilitarian thought.

One of the groups that Henry was involved with during his time at university was the secret intellectual society known as the "Cambridge Apostles." The group included many high-profile thinkers of the time such as poet Alfred Tennyson and philosophers F.H. Bradley and G.E. Moore. The influences of these individuals can be seen in Sidgwick's writings on the connection between utilitarianism and other moral theories.

After he completed his studies, he stayed at Cambridge as a lecturer and eventually became a professor of moral philosophy. In 1874, Sidgwick published *The Methods of Ethics*, a book that is often considered to be one of the greatest contributions to ethical theory in the 19th century. Shaped by his time in the Cambridge Apostles, the work integrates concepts from utilitarianism, Kantian ethics, and moral intuitionism – the idea that people instinctively know right from wrong.

—

Sidgwick's theories built on the earlier utilitarian ideas of Bentham and Mill, including some unique additions that can be summarized as follows.

> **Intuition vs. Utilitarianism:** Sidgwick is known for identifying the tug-of-war between utilitarianism and moral intuition. He raised the concern that decisions that come from utilitarian calculations and the ones that come from intuition – or gut instinct – don't always align. Sidgwick called this tension the "dualism of practical reason," and it is still a major challenge to moral philosophy even today.
>
> **Refined Utilitarianism:** Sidgwick's *The Methods of Ethics* was a systematic examination and comparison of multiple theories, including intuitionism, Kantian ethics, egoism, and utilitarianism. As a part of this analysis, he helped refine many of the ideas behind

utilitarianism, making it more robust and adding new principles that have become central to the theory, including the role of impartiality and the belief that "ought" implies "can" – in others words, you can't be obligated to do something that is impossible.

Act vs. Rule Utilitarianism: Sidgwick identified the distinction between Bentham's act utilitarianism – evaluating every action – and Mill's rule utilitarianism – following moral rules. Even though Sidgwick himself leaned more towards act utilitarianism, he mentioned the appeal of rules, and he contributed to the overall conversation between the two different approaches.

Henry Sidgwick's exploration of utilitarianism, alongside other popular ethical theories, and his overall contributions to utilitarianism helped shape and improve the theory.

J.J.C. Smart, the classic utilitarian
(1920-2012)

John Jamieson Carswell Smart – known as J.J.C. Smart – was born in Cambridge in 1920, the son of a Scottish astronomer and professor at the University of Cambridge. Just like many of the other philosophers covered, Smart was raised with a considerable focus on intellectual development and education, and throughout his childhood he went to school at a number of prestigious institutions, including The Leys School in Cambridge.

Although he started studying philosophy and mathematics at the University of Glasgow in 1938, the outbreak of World War II put a pause on his studies. During the war Smart served in the British Army as a meteorological officer, where he was stationed in India and Burma – discovering Indian philosophy in the process. After the war, Smart returned to his studies, eventually receiving a Bachelor of Arts in moral sciences from the University of Cambridge at the age of 28.

In 1949, Smart was offered the Hughes chair of philosophy at Adelaide University, where he worked for the next 23 years. Over this period, he made many of his contributions to moral philosophy and utilitarian theory, including his 1956 essay *Extreme and Restricted Utilitarianism*. In this essay, Smart argued for a completely unrestricted version of utilitarianism that would focus on maximizing overall happiness without paying attention to specific moral rules. Unlike many of the other utilitarians of the modern era who advocated for more restricted or rule-based forms of utilitarianism, Smart advocated for a return to more traditional act utilitarian ideas.

Over the course of his career in academia, Smart held positions at several different prestigious institutions, including universities in Australia, Oxford and Reading in the United Kingdom, as well as visiting professorships at Princeton, Harvard, and Yale.

—

J.J.C. Smart's contributions to utilitarianism mainly involved engaging in debates defending the theory, addressing criticisms of utilitarianism's core concepts, and helping to popularize a variant known as 'negative utilitarianism.'

Moral Dilemmas: Smart defended utilitarianism against a variety of moral dilemmas and arguments raised by critics, including concerns with how demanding it appears and the potential for validating horrible actions. He also acknowledged that the theory wasn't always intuitive but claimed that this was the case with all consequentialist ethical theories, and that utilitarianism should be more of a guide instead of a strict moral code.

Negative Utilitarianism: Although he disagreed with the concept, Smart played an important role in popularizing and discussing the idea of negative utilitarianism. This utilitarian variation ignores the happiness and well-being side of the utility calculation, focusing instead on exclusively reducing suffering.

Smart was influential in academic circles during the 20th century, known for popular debates about ethical theories as well as his attempts to address flaws and criticism of utilitarianism.

Peter Singer, the modern activist
(1946-)

One of the most controversial philosophers of the modern age, Peter Singer was born in 1946 in Australia to Jewish parents who had fled Austria to escape the Holocaust. Many of his family members, including his grandparents, were unable to escape and ended up being deported to concentration camps in Poland and what is now the Czech Republic.

Singer started his undergraduate studies at the University of Melbourne, where he studied history, philosophy, and law, receiving a Bachelor of Arts after graduating with honours in 1967. It was during this time at university that Singer was introduced to many philosophical ideas and traditions that would shape his later work, including utilitarianism, existentialism, and the works of philosophers such as Immanuel Kant and John Stuart Mill.

After graduating with a Master of Arts degree in 1969 from the University of Melbourne, Singer went on to the University of Oxford where he earned a Bachelor of Philosophy, under the guidance of earlier philosopher – and founder of preference utilitarianism – R.M. Hare. The topic of his dissertation was on civil disobedience, work that would be republished in 1973 under the title *Democracy and Disobedience*.

Most of Singer's work is related to topics that are considered social activism, including civil disobedience, animal rights, vegetarianism and veganism, and global poverty. Published in 1975, his book *Animal Liberation* was a driving force behind modern animal rights movements, with arguments that centred around the idea that utilitarian principles should apply equally to all beings that feel pleasure and suffering – animals included.

In 1979, Peter released *Practical Ethics*, a controversial book that was translated into over ten languages and sold more than 500,000 copies over the next 20 years. In the book, Singer attempted to challenge many deeply held beliefs. This included making arguments that the lives of animals could be worth more than a person's, that there are situations where it may be moral to kill infants, and others.

Since then, Singer has remained a polarizing public figure, the subject of many furious articles, and even the subject of public demonstrations on his first day as a lecturer in 1999. He currently spends his time between Melbourne, Australia and the US, where he remains active in the academic community.

–

Peter Singer, more than any other modern utilitarian, has brought conversations around utilitarianism and overall ethics to the general public. His approach has been unique and has focused heavily on issues that have inspired many forms of activism in the 20th and 21st century. Highlights of Singer's utilitarian approach include:

> **Preference Utilitarianism:** Singer built on R.M. Hare's preference utilitarianism, greatly popularizing some of the concepts and applying it to practical ethical issues like poverty, animal rights, and concerns about the environment.

Animal Rights: *Animal Liberation* (1975), one of Singer's groundbreaking books, laid much of the foundation for the modern animal rights movements. He argues that the interests of nonhuman animals should be taken into account along with human interests in utilitarian calculations. He is an advocate for vegetarianism and veganism as a consequence.

Effective Altruism: Singer has been one of the leading advocates for the effective altruism movement, which applies utilitarian principles to philanthropy and charity. He argues that people have a moral obligation to maximize the positive impact of their resources. An example of this movement is "The Giving Pledge," a movement that started with 40 wealthy American families who pledged to dedicate the majority of their fortunes to charitable causes and has since expanded.

Poverty and Inequality: Singer wrote extensively on the moral obligations of individuals in wealthy societies to address global poverty and wealth inequality. In his influential essay *Famine, Affluence, and Morality* (1972), Singer argued that we have a duty to prevent suffering when we can. His arguments challenged traditional ideas of charity and have been a part of debates and discussions of moral philosophy ever since.

Practical Application: A large portion of Singer's works have focused on applying utilitarian principles to real-world situations and dilemmas, including euthanasia, abortion, and environmental ethics. His book *Practical Ethics* (1979) helped to popularize ideas on ethics and morality across a general audience and has been influential in academic and activist circles.

Peter Singer's work in applying moral philosophy and utilitarian ideas to real-world applications has continued to have a major impact on popular culture, modern activism, and academic theory. One of the few living philosophers covered in this book, he continues to publish and contribute to the field today (2024).

3

Ideas Aligned with Utilitarianism

It is important to keep in mind that every one of the following social, political, and moral systems has its own unique properties and context that cannot be reduced to a simple comparison with utilitarian ideas. That being said, for the sake of this discussion it will be helpful to examine how some of the core principles of utilitarianism have been reflected outside of Western philosophy throughout history.

It is also worth noting that many of the beliefs held by these cultures and philosophies directly contradict utilitarian ideas. However, since our current focus is on utilitarian and natural law theories, we are only going to take a look at the ways in which these theories share common concepts.

Even though utilitarianism is often associated with Enlightenment-era moral philosophy, similar ideas have appeared in a variety of forms and philosophies over the millennia. Principles related to consequentialism, the greatest good, and maximizing happiness have appeared in schools of thought around the world for thousands of years. In order to get a better sense of how widespread some of these concepts are, we will look at a few instances, including examples from ancient China, India, and the Americas.

Confucianism
(551 BCE)

Our first example from outside the Western tradition reaches back to ancient China, where we see similarities with some of the ideas of Confucius, a philosopher whose followers still number in the millions.

While the world of the ancient Greeks was forming into city-states like Athens and Sparta, Confucianism originated in ancient China in between the Spring and Autumn Period (~770-476 BCE), and the Warring States Period (475-221 BCE) that came afterwards. It was founded by the philosopher Confucius – also known as Kongzi – who wanted to restore social values and harmony in a time filled with political chaos, and what he viewed as moral decline.

All of Confucius's teachings are secondhand, recorded by his disciples across a handful of surviving texts, which make up the basis of the Confucian tradition. After Confucius's death in 479 BCE, his ideas continued to evolve and were developed through the works of later philosophers, such as Mencius (Mengzi) and Xunzi.

During the Han Dynasty between 206 BCE and 220 CE, Confucianism became the state ideology, where it exerted influence over Chinese culture, politics, and social life for centuries. The ethical system of Confucianism has since spread beyond China, shaping the values and beliefs of East Asian societies, such as Korea, Japan, and Vietnam.

Even though there was a decline in many of these areas during a rise in Buddhism and Taoism during the Song Dynasty (960–1279 CE), China saw a return of Confucian ideas during the 1600s, and it still remains popular in many areas of the world.

–

Although Confucianism and utilitarianism are independent systems with different origins and foundations, they share some similarities. These shared ideas include the following:

Social Harmony: Similar to many of the goals of utilitarianism, Confucianism stresses the importance of promoting social harmony and welfare through one's actions.

Altruism: The Confucian principle of "ren" or "benevolence" is central to its theory of ethics, promoting altruistic behaviour and empathy, and encouraging individuals to act in ways that benefit society as a whole.

Practicality: Both Confucianism and utilitarianism stress the importance of practical action and real-world consequences in moral decision-making. Confucianism promotes the cultivation of inner virtues and moral character through everyday actions, while utilitarianism focuses on the outcomes of actions themselves, and the effects of ethical decisions on overall happiness or utility.

Role of the State: Confucius and utilitarian philosophers both offer moral guidance for rulers and government officials. Confucius believed that rulers should act virtuously, benevolently, and with wisdom to ensure the welfare of their people, and utilitarian actions, while they equally apply to individual action, are most commonly seen in governance and policymaking.

Even though there are similarities with some utilitarian concepts, Confucianism also contains elements of many different types of ethical theories, including virtue ethics and deontological ethics.

Mohism
(470 BCE)

Like Confucianism, Mohism was an early Chinese philosophical school that emerged during the Warring States Period (475-221 BCE), founded by Mo Tzu. Mohists were the first group in ancient China to engage in what could be called systematic reasoning – the use of logical premises and the application of reason – an attempt to reach objective moral standards.

Not only were the Mohists responsible for some of China's first ethical and political theories, but the first version of consequentialism in known history. Because of these contributions, the movement played a monumental role in defining many aspects of Chinese philosophy and its concepts.

Several concepts developed by the Mohists were unique to Chinese philosophy, including "impartial caring," an idea similar to the impartiality principle in utilitarianism, as well as opposition to violence, a devotion to usefulness, and the reduction of both waste and luxury.

Near the end of Mo Tzu's life, on the other side of the ancient world in Greece, Plato was preparing to open his Academy in Athens. And similar to Plato's argument for a philosopher king, Mohists believed that people should be ruled by a centralized, authoritarian state, with a virtuous and kind leader. But, unlike Plato's desired outcomes of justice, order, and moral virtue, Mo Tzu's goals were focused on practical outcomes, social harmony, and universal love.

—

Mohism is widely accepted as the world's first consequentialist ethical theory, even though it represented a wholly unique system in several key ways.

Impartiality: Similar to utilitarian ideas, Mo Tzu emphasized the importance of impartiality through his concept of "universal love" – *jian ai* –, a core tenet of his philosophy. He argued that people should care for each other equally regardless of social status or personal relationships.

Consequentialism: Mohists believed in a results-based approach to governance. Mo Tzu argued that rulers' primary focus should be the welfare of their people, promoting policies and actions that resulted in increased overall happiness.

Meritocracy: Like some of Plato's ideas for his philosopher-king, Mo Tzu believed that leaders should be chosen based on their abilities and their virtues instead of social status or personal ties. He argued that this would result in more competent leaders who were more likely to make decisions that benefit the greatest number of people.

Frugality and Waste: One of Mo Tzu's criticisms of Confucianism was that its rituals and ceremonies were wasteful. He believed that it was a waste of resources that would be better spent on helping people – a utilitarian criticism that good wasn't being maximized.

Mo Tzu's beliefs share quite a lot of similarities with later utilitarian thinkers, and many of his core philosophies are mirrored in utilitarianism, even though he didn't directly influence these Western ideas.

The Iroquois Confederacy
(~1142 CE)

The Iroquois Confederacy, also known as the Haudenosaunee (People of the Longhouse), was an alliance made up of the Mohawk, Oneida, Onondaga, Cayuga, Seneca, and later Tuscarora nations in early North America. It is unknown when exactly the Confederacy was founded, but estimates range from between 1142 and 1600.

Somewhat consequentialist in nature, the Iroquois Great Law of Peace, which governed the Confederacy, contained rules for many different social situations. These included the settling of disputes between tribes, rules for collective decision-making, the rights and responsibilities of clans, chiefs, and individuals within each nation. Even though their system of governance was very different from Western versions at the time, some of the ways that the law had similarities to utilitarian ideas include the following.

> **Consequentialist**: The Seventh Generation Principle, one of the tenets of the Great Law of Peace, requires that your actions should have a positive impact for the next seven generations. Among others, this requirement looked at the morality of action in terms of its consequences, a core component of utilitarian thought.
>
> **Collective Decision-making**: The democratic system of governance in the Iroquois Confederacy involved decision-making through consensus. This allowed each of the tribes to have a hand in making decisions that benefited the majority of member nations and people.
>
> **Rule Based**: With similarities to rule utilitarianism, the Iroquois Confederacy set out many rules which they believed would bring greater peace among the allied tribes. These rules included checks

and balances to avoid the concentration of power, outlines of both the rights and responsibilities of individuals, leaders, and tribes, as well as other principles meant to bring lasting harmony.

The primary aim of the Great Law of Peace was to promote the collective well-being of the disparate tribes and overall society, enacted through a series of laws and principles aimed at bringing peace, order, and harmony to tribes that had traditionally been at war.

The Incan Empire
(1400-1533)

The Incan Empire was a civilization that spanned across the western part of South America during the 15th and 16th centuries, the largest empire of its kind in the Americas. With systems of governance that were highly complex – including a mixture of monarchy, theocracy, and agricultural collectivism – the Inca civilization was like no other socio-political system in recorded history.

The land was divided into three parts, the king's land, the priest's land, and the lands of the subjects. The Incas took tribute from the subjects in the form of both mandatory work, as well as goods, and redistributed it towards the interests of the people, funding the state and keeping some in case of shortages and emergencies.

Though it is difficult to compare the complex social values in the Incan Empire with utilitarian ideals, many of the themes of individual sacrifice for the greater benefit of society can be drawn in parallel between the two. The Incan state redistributed resources to meet the people's basic needs, completed major public works projects, including food storage facilities, agricultural terraces, and roads, at the cost of both direct forced labour and the taxation of their output.

4

A Brief History of Western Natural Law

From its first glimpses in ancient Mesopotamia, natural law theory has a rich history that has echoed through Athens, Rome, and Byzantium to the modern day. Over thousands of years, great thinkers like Aristotle, Aquinas, and John Locke have helped shape and develop theories that combine nature and human morality. The history of natural law in Western thought starts with Aristotle, the ancient Greek philosopher, who laid the foundations of what would eventually be natural law theory in his work *Nicomachean Ethics*.

The ideas were carried forward by Cicero, the Roman philosopher, lawyer, and politician, who used Aristotle's work as a stepping stone to incorporate concepts of natural law as a reflection of a higher, divine law. Many thinkers – both Christian and Islamic – were later influenced by Cicero's work and weaved his ideas into their own theological frameworks. Throughout much of the Middle Ages all the way up to the Enlightenment, the religious schools of natural law fused the ancient Greek and Roman ideas together with their own faiths, developing variations of natural law theories based on both reason and faith.

During the Middle Ages, St. Thomas Aquinas took these ideas and developed them even further in his crowning achievement, a work that has served as a cornerstone of Christian thought for over 750 years, the *Summa Theologica*. Aquinas argued that God was the source of nature – and by extension natural law, but that through reason we can discover both its moral principles and even our true purpose.

Centuries after Aquinas, philosophers during the Enlightenment argued that the principles of natural law were at the core of protecting human rights, and that the primary purpose of government was to protect human rights in the form of a social contract. According to Locke in particular, if the government failed to protect the natural rights of the people, the social contract was violated, and the people could dissolve and reform the government to regain their rights.

With thousands of years of human philosophy behind natural law, it was difficult to choose only a handful of people whose ideas had unique or sizeable impacts. The thinkers in this section have been selected because of their unique insights or contributions to the theory, even though countless others throughout history helped influence the development of these ideas.

Aristotle, the natural scientist
(384-322 BCE)

In the year 384 BCE, almost 100 years before the birth of Epicurus, Aristotle was born in northern Greece in a small village called Stagira. He was the son of Nicomachus, the personal physician to King Amyntas III of Macedonia, and Phaestis, although we don't know a lot about his mother. Details of his childhood are scarce, but it is likely he was well-educated because of his family's connection to the court. When he was just a boy his parents died, and he was raised by Proxenus of Atarneus, who took over his education, teaching him Greek, rhetoric, and poetry.

When Aristotle was 17, he moved to Athens to study at Plato's Academy, where he stayed for twenty years, first studying philosophy, mathematics, astronomy, and rhetoric, before eventually becoming a teacher himself. While he was at the Academy, Plato was the most significant influence on Aristotle's beliefs and ideas, first as a teacher, and then later as a peer. Even though many of Aristotle's writings from this period have been lost to time, some of his surviving works include *Topics* as well as *Sophistical Refutations*, which is one of the first texts on the discipline of logic ever recorded.

After Plato's death, Aristotle left the Academy to travel and research, making several contributions to zoology – including two treatises, *On the Parts of Animals*, and *On the Generation of Animals*. In these works, Aristotle classified more than 500 animals into genus and species, while also recording anatomy, diet, habitats, and much more. Aristotle's work on biology was unprecedented at the time, and in addition to influencing his later writing on ethics and metaphysics, he is often credited with being the father of both zoology and biology.

Around 343 BCE, Aristotle was invited by King Philip II to the Macedonian capital to tutor his son – a boy who is now known as Alexander the Great. After about eight years teaching Alexander, Aristotle returned to Athens where he founded his own school and one of the world's first great libraries – the Lyceum – where he spent the rest of his life teaching, researching, and writing about ethics, politics, metaphysics, and biology.

–

Like Epicurus's influence on utilitarianism, Aristotle didn't explicitly develop a theory of natural law as we understand it today. However, his ideas on "nature" in ethics and politics, as well as his work on human purpose, set up quite a bit of the groundwork for natural law as an ethical theory. Highlights of some of the concepts related to natural law theory include:

> **Natural Purpose (Teleology):** Aristotle's philosophy is based on the idea that everything in the natural world, including human beings, has an inherent purpose – or *telos*. This is a key concept in his ethical theory, which proposes that living according to your natural purpose leads to a good life.

Rationality: Aristotle believed that a distinctive feature of human beings is their capacity for rational thought. He believed that practical wisdom – *phronesis* – could be achieved by understanding the moral principles that can be discovered through rationality.

Virtue Ethics: Aristotle's virtue ethics stressed the importance of developing personal moral virtues as an essential step towards human flourishing. Even though it is a different branch of ethics, the concepts of human virtue influenced several natural law theorists like Aquinas, who integrated some of the ideas into his natural law theory.

Unlike natural law philosophers, Aristotle was more focused on the individuals' purpose and virtue. However, his beliefs about the natural origins of morality have had a lasting impact on both natural law thinkers and on ethics as a whole.

Cicero, the Roman statesman
(106-43 BCE)

Marcus Tullius Cicero was a statesman, philosopher, author, and lawyer, and is known today as the greatest orator in ancient Rome. He was born in 106 BCE in what is now present-day Italy to an influential family. He was educated in both Rome and Athens, where he studied philosophy, law, and rhetoric from several well-known teachers of the era, including Philo of Larissa, and Antiochus of Ascalon. During his studies he was exposed to and influenced by the works of Epicurus, Plato, Aristotle, and most importantly, the Stoics. His own version of natural law was developed while trying to integrate many of these ideas with Roman legal and political thought of the time.

Cicero began his legal and political career in 75 BCE where he served as quaestor – a financial administrator – in western Sicily for almost nine years, a period that included the Roman suppression of Spartacus's slave rebellion in the Third Servile War. In 66 BCE he became a praetor – a judicial officer – a role that allowed him to make an impact with his first speech in support of Pompey the Great, a general of the Roman empire. In an ambitious and meteoric rise through the ranks, by 63 BCE he became consul, the highest political office in the Roman Republic. While he was acting as consul, he prevented a conspiracy to overthrow the republic, an event that cemented his reputation as both a speaker and as a defender of Rome.

Over the course of his political career, Cicero experienced quite a few successes and setbacks, including being exiled in 58 BCE because of his political stances. He was allowed to return to Rome a year later. After returning to Rome, Cicero wrote two books in the style of Plato's dialogues, *De Legibus* (The Laws) and *De Re Publica* (The Republic). These books contained his theory and arguments for natural law, including his belief that natural law is universal, unchanging, and eternal, grounded in both reason and *logos* – the divine order of the cosmos. He argued that this law was accessible to all people, no matter their culture or status, and that it was the basis for a just and well-ordered society.

At the end of his life, Cicero was caught in the power struggles between Julius Caesar, Pompey, and later Mark Antony, which eventually led to his execution in 43 BCE, but not before publishing his final work in 44 BCE, *De Officiis* (On Duties).

—

Cicero developed one of the earliest versions of natural law, influenced by the Greek philosophers including Aristotle, Epicurus, and the Stoics. Some of the unique aspects of his theories on natural law are listed here:

Divine Order: An important distinction is that unlike religious natural law theorists' beliefs in a divine deity as the source of nature, the Stoics believed in "logos," the idea that the universe itself was rational, ordered, and had a purpose. Cicero's ideas on natural law were influenced heavily by the Stoic beliefs in this divine force that governed the universe, and he suggested that it was the source of nature and morality. This belief was also different from previous theorists like Aristotle, who focused on human purpose.

Universality: One of Cicero's core ideas was that natural law is a universal moral law that applies to every human being, regardless of their circumstance or origin. This idea provided an objective and unchanging standard for moral behaviour, a core concept that would become the basis for later theories on natural law and the development of natural rights.

Human Reason: The human capacity of reason was a determining factor in Cicero's belief that natural law is universal and accessible to everyone. He believed that through reason, every person could discover the moral principles embedded in the natural order of the universe.

Law & Politics: Cicero was not only a philosopher but also a politician and a lawyer. His ethical theories strongly influenced his views on law, where he believed that human laws should be based on the principles of natural law.

Influenced heavily by the Stoics, Cicero's ideas focused on universal moral law and the connection between natural law and human reason. Not only did these ideas influence future natural law theorists, but they have had a lasting impact on Western society in their own right.

St. Augustine, the doctor of grace
(354-430 CE)

St. Augustine of Hippo was a Christian theologian and philosopher who influenced both modern theology and the development of natural law. He was born in 354 CE in Thagaste – present-day Algeria – to a Christian mother and a pagan father. Throughout the first parts of his life, Augustine was taught rhetoric, Latin, and literature in both Carthage and Madauros.

During this period of his life, Augustine was heavily influenced by several different philosophies and religious views, including Manichaeism, a religion that combined elements from many of the other religions of the era. After almost ten years as a follower, he became disillusioned with his beliefs and turned initially to scepticism, and then later to a sect of philosophy called Neoplatonism. In 383 Augustine moved to Rome, and then later to Milan where he met Bishop Ambrose, whose teachings – combined with his mother's Christian influence – led to his conversion to Christianity a few years later. After being baptized by Ambrose, Augustine returned home to Africa where he founded a monastic community in order to spread Christian doctrine.

In 396 Augustine became the bishop of Hippo, a position he held for more than three decades until his death. Over the final decades of his life, Augustine was active in many theological debates and wrote a number of influential works, including *Confessions*, *City of God*, and *On Christian Doctrine*. Most of Augustine's contributions to natural law were found in his work *City of God*, where he explored ideas inspired by Cicero – the relationship between divine law, human law, and the moral order of the universe.

Shortly after his death in 430 CE, Augustine was recognized as a saint by the Christian community, long before a formal canonization process was established by the Roman Catholic Church in the 12th century.

—

St. Augustine's work made some contributions to the development of natural law theory, primarily from the perspective of Christian theology. Some of the unique aspects of St. Augustine's approach to natural law include the following.

> **Christianity**: Augustine was among the first to integrate the concepts of natural law with Christian theology. Unlike Cicero's belief in a rational order and Aristotle's belief in human purpose, Augustine asserted the divine law of God was the foundation for human law and morality. He believed that natural law was an expression of God's eternal law, which is imprinted on the human heart.
>
> **Rationality and Revelation**: St. Augustine believed that even though human reason was necessary to discover natural law, humans required divine revelation to properly understand the moral principles that they discovered. He argued that to be able to fully comprehend the divine law, people needed scripture and the teachings of the Church in order to interpret and apply it.
>
> **Original Sin**: The doctrine of original sin played a large part in Augustine's views of human nature, believing that humans were inherently flawed. Because of this, he believed that people's effort was insufficient, and that they needed God's help to overcome their flaws and truly follow the divine law.

Religious Intolerance: As a result of his view that God was required to interpret a universal natural law, over the course of his life he became less tolerant of religious differences. Eventually, his arguments became utilitarian in nature, justifying the use of coercion and authority in order to bring people "salvation" – arguments that were later quoted during the Inquisitions.

St. Augustine inherited some of the views of earlier thinkers, merging the concepts with Christian theology. His theories emphasized divine revelation and the importance of divine grace in understanding and helping humans to properly interpret natural law. Perhaps St. Augustine's greatest impact on the theory was the groundwork he laid for the thinkers that would come after him, most notably St. Thomas Aquinas over 800 years later.

St. Thomas Aquinas, the prince of scholastics
(1225-1274)

Of all the thinkers covered in this book, St. Thomas Aquinas is the one whose ideas have had the greatest lasting impact on Western religion. He not only developed ideas that would shape Christian doctrine for almost a millennium, but his ideas spawned a school of thought – Thomism – that remains popular to this day.

In 1225, at the height of Genghis Khan's conquests to expand the Mongol Empire, far away in Italy, Aquinas was born to a noble and influential family. His father Landulph was the count of Aquino, and his mother Theodora was the countess of Teano – a member of the Hohenstaufen dynasty of Holy Roman emperors. Ever since he was born his parents had held high expectations for his future, preparing him to become the abbot of Monte Cassino – a life that would come with prominence and luxury for him and prestige for them. At the age of five they sent him to the Benedictine monastery of Monte Cassino to study, where he was taught for almost a decade until political conflict caused him to return to Naples at the age of 13.

After coming back to Naples, he continued his learning at a Benedictine house, where he studied the works of Aristotle and Dominican philosophy, both of which had a powerful impact on his own beliefs. The Dominicans encouraged the use of both faith and reason together in order to reveal truth, a view that Aquinas adopted and would later apply to his theory of natural law.

In 1244, Aquinas decided against becoming a Benedictine monk, instead joining the Dominican Order and committing to a life of poverty and service, a decision that enraged his family. After they found out his plans, they kidnapped him and imprisoned him in his family home for almost a year. Eventually, after realizing Aquinas was not going to change his mind, his mother allowed him to sneak out a window, a move that enabled him to become a Dominican and her to save face.

After he escaped and returned to the Dominican order, Aquinas was assigned to study and serve in Paris, where he became a student of the renowned philosopher and theologian Albertus Magnus, also known as Saint Albert the Great. At the time, Albert was without a doubt one of the greatest intellectuals in Europe, knowledgeable in a wide range of subjects including natural science, history, astronomy, music, philosophy, and theology. Albert's teaching had a major impact on his philosophy, and after following Albert to Cologne, Germany, Thomas became a professor of Sacred Scripture, before eventually returning to Paris in 1252 to complete a master's degree in theology. Over the next couple of years he produced several works, including his famous philosophical work *De ente et essentia* (On Being and Essence) where he explored the nature of existence, arguing that all beings apart from God have both an essence (what it is) and an existence (that it is).

Over the next decade Aquinas spent time teaching and writing in both Paris and Italy, including his first contributions to the *Summa Theologica* in 1265, his magnum opus and one of the most influential theological works ever written. It was here that Thomas developed the concepts of natural law, integrating the works of Aristotle and Christian theology together to form the foundation of his theories. Aquinas would continue working on his masterpiece until shortly before his death in 1274, ultimately leaving it unfinished – at more than 3,000 pages.

–

Aquinas's theories reflected his religious and educational background, synthesising Christianity with Aristotle's ideas on human purpose and the role of reason in moral behaviour. Some of the primary aspects of Aquinas's natural law are as follows.

> **Christian Theology**: Aquinas's theories were based on the belief that God is the source of nature – and by extension natural law. He believed that the order and rules embedded in nature reflect these eternal laws, which is God's rational plan for the universe.
>
> **Greek Influence**: Aquinas was heavily influenced by Aristotle's ideas on human purpose (telos), the importance of reason in ethical decision-making, the role of developing personal virtues, and the relationship between nature and ethics.
>
> **Hierarchy of Law**: Aquinas developed an order of laws, breaking it down into four levels: eternal law (God's rational plan for the universe), natural law (accessible to human reason), divine law (revealed through scripture), and finally human law (created by human societies). He argues that while these levels are connected,

human law is invalid when it comes into conflict with either natural or divine law.

Practical Reason: Even though earlier philosophers had raised the role of reason in discovering the laws of nature, Aquinas made a unique argument that we will explore in more detail later in the book, claiming that God wouldn't have embedded laws in nature if he didn't also give us a way to discover them independently. This leads to his conclusion that humans were given the ability to use reason to discover these laws.

Primary and Secondary Precepts: Aquinas divided the rules of natural law into two categories, *primary precepts* and *secondary precepts*. The first group were universal and self-evident principles that guide human action, like the preservation of life and the pursuit of knowledge. The second group were specific moral rules that could be derived from the first ones through reason.

Synderesis: Aquinas introduced the concept of *synderesis*, which refers to people's innate ability to grasp basic moral principles. In some ways this was almost an early form of moral intuitionism, and he believed that combined with the use of reason, humans could intuitively understand and apply natural law to different situations.

Moral Intentions: Another principle in Aquinas's natural law theory was called the *Doctrine of Double Effect,* aimed to give moral guidance on making complex decisions that could result in good or bad outcomes. Aligning with beliefs on inherent morality of actions, it proposes that an action is moral if the good effect is intended, the bad effect is not intended but can be tolerated, and the good effect is not achieved through the bad effect. This idea provided a crucial foundation for arguments against the ends justifying the means.

Aquinas's theories on natural law were more comprehensive, more clearly defined, and more influential than any other form of natural ethics that had come before. Many of the unique aspects of his work continued through to later versions of the theory, including the idea that human laws are invalid or unjust if they conflict with natural law.

Hugo Grotius, the father of international law
(1583-1645)

Hugo Grotius, also known as Huig de Groot, was born in 1583 in the Dutch Republic to Jan de Groot and Alida van Overschie. Hugo's father Jan was a public official who bounced around across several jobs, including alderman, mayor, and the curator of the University of Leiden. Like many of the great thinkers in this book, Grotius was considered a child prodigy, entering the University of Leiden at the age of 11 to study law and philosophy – publishing his first book at 16.

In 1599, at only 16, Grotius began to practise law in The Hague where he earned renown, before being appointed as the official historian for the Dutch Republic in 1607. Over the next decade, while Galileo was revolutionising astronomy in Italy, Grotius wrote and published several influential legal works, including *De Jure Praedae* (On the Law of Prize and Booty), and *Mare Liberum* (The Free Sea), laying the groundwork for his ideas on natural law and his future international law theories.

Around this time, a schism that occurred within the Dutch Church – part of the larger Protestant Reformation – led to Grotius being imprisoned when Prince Maurice of Nassau seized power. As a supporter of the opposing hardline faction, the prince cracked down on the Arminian faction who believed in a more moderate, tolerant, and inclusive interpretation of Calvinist doctrine, arresting Grotius and charging him with treason and undermining unity.

After three years in prison, Grotius made a dramatic escape from the fortress of Loevestein by hiding in a chest of books – a scene straight out of an adventure story. He first fled to Antwerp, and then on to Paris, where he stayed in exile for several years. It was during this time in Paris that Grotius wrote his most important work, *De Jure Belli ac Pacis* (On the Law of War and Peace), which he published in 1625. The book combined classical Roman law, medieval scholasticism, and works from earlier natural law theorists, establishing the foundations of international law, as well as his own systematic approach to natural law.

The last decades of Grotius's life included a failed attempt to return to Holland, a move to Germany, and finally a period as the Swedish Ambassador to France from 1634 until his death almost eleven years later.

–

Hugo Grotius is often called the "father of international law," developing theories of natural law both on an individual and international scale that considered actions between sovereign states. Some of the highlights of his ideas are as follows.

> **Secular Approach:** Despite being religious himself, Grotius was one of the first thinkers to develop a secular natural law theory, claiming that as a universal law it could be understood by people from different religious backgrounds. In his famous assertion *"etiamsi daremus non esse Deum"* (even if we were to assume that God does not exist), he declared that the principles of natural law would still hold true because of their rational foundation. As a result, he was an advocate for peaceful coexistence between different religions and religious tolerance.

International Law: A pioneer in the field of international law, Grotius applied the principles of natural law to relationships between sovereign states, arguing that these principles provide the basis for international order and justice. The idea of natural laws that transcended national borders and governed international relations was unprecedented before Grotius's work.

Rights of Nations: Expanding on the concept of natural rights, Grotius developed a system of rights and obligations that applied to states and international relations. Similar to those of individuals, he argued that states had rights and duties under natural law, such as the right to self-defence and the duty to respect the sovereignty of other states.

Individual Rights: Grotius asserted that individuals have certain natural rights by virtue of their humanity, including the right to life, liberty, and property. These ideas have since had an incredible influence, legally, culturally, and philosophically.

Just War Theory: Hugo made important contributions to the just war theory, a branch of natural law that deals with the ethics of warfare. He outlined conditions that he believed would contribute to a war being considered just, as well as principles to govern conduct in war.

Hugo Grotius's secular version of natural law was unique in many ways from those of earlier natural law theorists, especially those whose ideas combined divine origins with rational thought. His contributions to secular ethics, international law, and individual rights were instrumental in guiding Enlightenment thinkers like Kant and Locke.

John Locke, the father of liberalism
(1632-1704)

Also known as the "Father of the Enlightenment," John Locke was born in 1632 in Somerset, England at the height of the scientific revolution. He grew up in a rural area, the son of John Locke Sr, a lawyer and a captain in the parliamentary forces during the English Civil War. Many of his early ideas were influenced by the parliamentarian arguments against a king's divine right to rule, a result of his father's role in opposing the Royalists.

From the age of 14 he went to school at the very prestigious Westminster School in London, before eventually attending the University of Oxford in 1652. When he was at Oxford he learned philosophy, and medicine, including classical works by Aristotle and Cicero.

Locke found it to be dull and unstimulating, focusing too much on Aristotle and logic while ignoring lots of newer topics like epistemology by more recent philosophers such as Francis Bacon and René Descartes. As a result, he spent a lot of time engaging with these thinkers' writings on his own. Completing a bachelor's degree in 1656 and a master's degree two years later, Locke went on to work as a physician, a tutor, and an advisor to a variety of nobles, including the influential Earl of Shaftesbury. After joining the English Royal Society in 1668, Locke learned from – and even befriended – many famous scientists, mathematicians, and thinkers of the era, including Isaac Newton, the chemist Robert Boyle, and the physician Thomas Sydenham.

Throughout the 1670s, Locke lived in Paris – the home of the Enlightenment – where he was exposed to the writings of the Jansenists, followers of St. Augustine, and other thinkers who shaped his views on toleration, government, and natural law. Following the Earl of Shaftesbury – his patron, in 1683 Locke went to Holland, where he encountered Hugo Grotius's ideas, influencing his views on the role of governments and natural law.

Locke returned to England after the restoration of the monarchy, when William and Mary retook the throne of England in what historians call The Glorious Revolution. In 1689 he published his two most impressive works *An Essay Concerning Human Understanding*, a text that became a core piece of empirical philosophy, and *Two Treatises of Government*, an essay that combined his political philosophies and natural law.

In the second treatise of *Two Treatises of Government*, Locke introduced the concept of the social contract, that – unlike Hobbes's or Rousseau's versions – makes the now famous claim that political authority is derived from the consent of the governed. It also contained his ideas on the natural rights of individuals and the rights of society to form and even overturn government under certain conditions.

Locke died in 1704, leaving behind a legacy of political ideas that would shape both the American and French revolutions. Locke's contributions to natural law and social contract theory have gone on to influence many different aspects of Western political and legal theory, including the separation of powers in government, the enshrining of individual rights, and even views on religious tolerance.

–

John Locke's interpretation of natural law theory, particularly in the context of political philosophy, included some of the following unique aspects.

State of Nature: Unlike Thomas Hobbes's pessimistic view of nature, which he saw as being in a constant state of chaos and war, Locke – echoing Aristotle – believed that individuals had a natural tendency towards peace and cooperation. For Locke, people in nature had perfect freedom and equality unless it was explicitly violated.

Natural Rights: Though some earlier natural law theorists like Thomas Aquinas focused on moral duties derived from nature, Locke was influenced by Grotius, focusing on individual rights. He believed that these rights are inherent to all beings and exist independently of government or society.

Social Contract Theory: Locke's version of the social contract was in sharp contrast to Hobbes's views on the social contract. Hobbes saw the social contract as a binding agreement where individuals gave up all of their rights to a central authority with absolute power. Locke, on the other hand, saw it as a temporary agreement between people and authority where they would give up some of their personal freedom in exchange for – and conditional on – the greater protection of their rights.

Limited Government: In addition to defining the government's primary responsibility as the protection of the individual's natural rights, Locke stressed the need for a limited government with checks and balances to prevent the abuse of power. He advocated for the separation of power between executive, legislative, and judicial branches of government, an idea that has since been adopted in many modern political systems.

Consent of the Governed: Unlike earlier thinkers who viewed political authority as a result of divine right or tradition, Locke argued that political legitimacy comes exclusively from the consent of the governed, an idea that has been essential to the modern concept of liberal democracy.

Right of Revolution: As an extension of his view that the social contract was only there to protect people's rights, Locke argued that all people have the right to revolution. If a government failed to protect natural rights, or if they acted against people's interests, the people had the right to resist, overthrow, and replace the government. This idea was a major force behind both the American and French Revolutions.

Religious Tolerance: Locke argued that religious beliefs should be a personal issue that the government had no authority over, advocating for religious freedom, tolerance, and the separation of church and state.

Locke's work on natural law, specifically the ideas of individual rights, limited government, and religious tolerance had a sizeable impact on both the American and French Revolutions. His ideas shaped the core principles of early American political thought, including the United States' founding documents – the Declaration of Independence, the U.S. Constitution, and the Bill of Rights.

Immanuel Kant, the father of modern ethics
(1724-1804)

Though he is not a natural law theorist, there is some significant overlap between some of Kant's ideas and natural law, particularly the role of reason in guiding moral behaviour, the absolute nature of morality, and an incompatibility with consequentialism. For this reason, Kant has been included in this list, as his ideas have impacted many of the other thinkers in this book.

Born to devout Protestants in East Prussia – now Kaliningrad, Russia – in 1724, from an early age Immanuel Kant was educated at a religious school where he learned Latin, Greek, and Hebrew, as well as the natural sciences and philosophy.

At the age of 16, Kant was enrolled at the University of Königsberg, where he studied a wide range of different subjects, including mathematics, physics, and philosophy. He was particularly impressed with the writings of Christian Wolff, a German philosopher and mathematician whose work centred around attempting to combine rationalism with the empirical approaches of John Locke and David Hume.

In 1746, Kant's father passed away, and he was forced to leave university and work as a private tutor for several families until he could eventually afford to return to his studies in 1755. After completing his master's degree he began lecturing on both natural science and physics, during which time he was further exposed to natural law, and the works of Jean-Jacques Rousseau and David Hume. The ideas would deeply influence his thinking on the role of reason, rationalism, and metaphysics. Hume's work *Enquiry Concerning Human Understanding* is responsible for Kant's famous "awakening from his dogmatic slumber," motivating him to develop his own critical philosophy referred to as deontological ethics – or the ethics of duty.

Kant's moral philosophy was captured in several works, including *Groundwork of the Metaphysics of Morals* in 1785, *Critique of Practical Reason* in 1788, and *Metaphysics of Morals* in 1797. Kant's ethical system emphasized the importance of rationality, autonomy, and his famous "categorical imperative" as the foundations of ethical behaviour.

At the age of 73, Kant retired from teaching at the University of Königsberg, and in 1804 he died, leaving behind ideas that have shaped debates on the nature of morality, human rights, and the foundations of society for the past 200 years.

–

Even though there are many differences between his theories and more traditional ideas on natural law, some of his views were influenced by philosophers like Aristotle, John Locke, and Jean-Jacques Rousseau. With that in mind, let's look at some of his primary ideas and their relation to natural law.

> **Deontology:** In complete opposition to consequentialist systems, Kant, like natural law ethicists, believed that the ends do not justify the means, and that the autonomy and rights of individuals are sacrosanct.
>
> **Pure Reason:** Kant believed that ethics and moral action were grounded in rational thought, much like natural law theorists. Unlike Locke and others who believed that reason needed to be applied in order to extract morality from the state of nature, Kant believed that pure reason alone should be used to define moral behaviour.
>
> **Secular Approach:** Kant, like Grotius, and to an extent Locke, believed that morality could be explored independently and was separate from religious beliefs. Kant argued that religion should be grounded in moral principles, rather than the other way around.
>
> **Categorical Imperative:** The core concept in Kant's system of ethics is the *categorical imperative*, a principle that asserts that an ethical rule can only be considered moral if it can be turned into a universal rule and still doesn't contain contradictions.

In his writings on natural law, Kant believed natural law was flawed because it was empirical instead of purely rational, and because it relied on the assumption that the natural order is inherently moral. Even so, his ethical philosophy shared many common threads with natural law theorists. His focus on rationality, the belief that morality is separate from religious belief, the discovery of universal principles, and the rejection of consequentialism are all principles that are shared between them.

Lysander Spooner, the voluntaryist
(1808-1887)

Jumping ahead to the 19th century, Lysander Spooner was an early American lawyer, philosopher, and political theorist whose work played a role in both the abolition of slavery and the origins of American anarchist movements. A direct descendent of the Mayflower pilgrims, Spooner was born in 1808 Massachusetts to a family of farmers. During his early years, Spooner developed an interest in law and political philosophy, and after apprenticing with a lawyer, Spooner passed the bar in 1831. During his time studying and practising law, he was heavily influenced by many natural law theorists like John Locke, Hugo Grotius, and Thomas Hobbes, as well as many of the legal texts and founding documents of the United States.

Bucking authority from the start, Spooner set up his own practice after only three years, ignoring the law requiring lawyers without college to study for five years alongside an attorney, challenging laws that he viewed as discriminatory and monopolist. In 1836, Spooner's petition to overturn the law was successful, his first win in what would be a lifetime commitment towards individual rights, self-determination, and standing up to authority.

After giving up his legal career in 1844, Spooner started the American Letter Mail Company in order to compete with the government's monopoly through the U.S. Post Office. At the time, Congress had prohibited the private delivery of mail, and Lysander wanted to challenge the ruling in the same way he had with Massachusetts's legal requirements.

In 1845, Spooner became heavily involved in the anti-slavery movement, publishing *The Unconstitutionality of Slavery*, containing his arguments that the institution of slavery was incompatible with both natural law and the U.S. Constitution that was based on it. This was followed by *Trial by Jury* in 1851, where he argued for jury nullification cases involving fugitive slaves – a practice where a jury returns a "Not Guilty" verdict on moral grounds.

While his mail company took off, opening offices in Baltimore, Philadelphia, and New York, it quickly became the target of legal challenges by the government, forcing it to close its doors in 1851, before Spooner had even gotten a chance to litigate his constitutional claims.

Just before the beginning of the Civil War, Spooner published *A Plan for the Abolition of Slavery*, an essay that outlined his ideas for a strategy to peacefully end slavery in the United States. Consistent with his natural law beliefs, even though he was fiercely opposed to slavery, Spooner was against the Civil War and the North's use of force to preserve the Union. Echoing Locke's arguments for the natural right to rebellion, he argued that the southern states had a right to leave a Union that no longer represented them.

Spooner's position against slavery made him very unpopular in the south, and his arguments against the Civil War made him very unpopular in the north, beliefs that conflicted with popular opinions and the official positions of both governments.

Shortly after the end of the Civil War, Spooner wrote and published *No Treason*, several essays that argued against the legitimacy of the United States government. In these essays, Spooner makes the case against the claim that people's agreement to the social contract could be implied, arguing that individuals have the right to consent or withhold consent to be governed, and – building on Locke's ideas – that consent had to be explicit. He also criticized the idea that voting implies consent to be governed, the use of taxation to fund overt force, and ultimately rejected the foundations of government authority – arguments that were picked up by later anarchist thinkers.

In the decades that followed the Civil War, Spooner continued to write, publishing *Natural Law; or The Science of Justice* in 1882. Echoing previous natural law theorists, Spooner argued that natural law is a set of universal principles discovered through reason, but expanded on these claims to make the case that natural law is the basis for justice itself.

Much of Spooner's work took previous natural law principles to their most extreme conclusions. He argued that because existing legal systems often let governments act against the interests of their own citizens and violate their natural rights, a truly just society could ultimately only be achieved through complete voluntary cooperation of individuals, removing the coercive state entirely.

–

Lysander Spooner – political philosopher, lawyer, abolitionist, and anarchist – made quite a few contributions to the development of anarchist flavours of natural law theory. A highlight of some of the unique aspects of his approach include:

Self-ownership: Spooner argued strongly for the natural right to self-ownership, arguing that people have an inherent right to control their own bodies and lives. His belief that any infringement on this right constituted a violation of natural law was a driving force behind his anti-slavery activism.

Social Contract: Unlike Locke and Hobbes's arguments for the social contract as an implied agreement between individuals in a society, Spooner argued that unless individuals explicitly consented to be governed, the contract and the government that resulted was not legitimate.

Anarchism: Unlike many natural law theorists who accepted various forms of government authority as necessary, Spooner was an individualist anarchist. He was an advocate of individual freedom, self-ownership, and voluntary associations, believing that any form of government, even a democratic one, violated the natural rights of individuals and was therefore unjust and coercive.

Abolitionism: Spooner was an avid abolitionist and activist, basing his opposition on natural law arguments. Unlike other philosophers who simply debated the morality of slavery, Spooner was an activist and unwavering in his arguments that slavery was a violation of the natural right to self-ownership.

Spooner's ideas have had a major and lasting impact on both individual anarchist and libertarian movements, inspiring later thinkers like Benjamin Tucker, Murray Rothbard, and Noam Chomsky.

5

Ideas Aligned with Natural Law

Much like utilitarianism, ideas that are usually associated with Western natural law theory can be found in many different cultures, theories, and belief systems around the world. This overlap between philosophies generally revolves around accepting that there are moral principles or laws that can be found in nature, and that they universally apply to all human beings.

In ancient China for example, Confucianism and Daoism both introduced concepts that had similarities to natural law, like the Confucian belief in customs and rituals that were thought to align with the natural order of the universe. In Indian philosophy the concept of *Dharma* can be found in Hinduism, Buddhism, and Jainism, an idea that there is a cosmic law that governs both the natural world and human behaviour. Some variations of Islamic law and theology also contain versions of natural law that fuse together nature and divine will.

Many indigenous cultures like that of the Maori people of New Zealand, the Inca civilization, the North American Navajo and Lakota Sioux, and the Sami people in Northern Europe have also incorporated ideas about harmony with nature, natural order and the significance of individual rights and responsibilities into their worldviews and belief systems.

While many of these belief systems share ideas with natural law, they also often contain significant differences, conclusions, and principles that conflict with the building blocks of Western thought. In order to fully understand the breadth of different views that attribute morality to some form of natural order, we will cover some of the key concepts and notable thinkers from other traditions.

The Buddha
(~6th Century BCE)

Siddhartha Gautama – also known as the Buddha – was a spiritual leader and the founder of Buddhism, one of the major world religions that currently boasts over 400 million followers. There is some debate about the date that he was born, with the year estimated to be between 623 BCE and 560 BCE.

Born into a life of privilege and luxury, it is said that he embarked on a spiritual journey of enlightenment after he witnessed the suffering that existed as part of the human condition. Through meditation and self-discipline over a period of seven years, he is said to have reached enlightenment, becoming the Buddha or "Enlightened One."

He spent the rest of his life travelling, teaching, and establishing a monastic community to preserve and spread his teachings. Several of these teachings share similar concepts to natural law, including the following.

> **Universal Morality:** In Buddhism, the concept of *Dharma* refers to the idea that there are universal truths and ethical principles that govern human behaviour, derived from the natural order of the universe. This idea of a naturally derived universal morality is a major similarity between natural law and Buddhist beliefs.

> **Moral Reasoning:** Similar to natural law's emphasis on the use of reason to discover morality, Buddha's teachings encourage individuals to question the nature of their own reality, leading to a deeper understanding of nature and its ethics.

Personal responsibility and virtue: Several early natural law theorists from Aristotle to St. Thomas Aquinas shared Buddha's belief in the importance of personal responsibility and development of a moral character through virtues like compassion, wisdom, and truthfulness.

Although the two belief systems have many differences, they share a powerful connection in the idea that morality is discovered through reason from the natural order of the universe.

Mencius
(372-289 BCE)

Earlier on, we looked at some Confucian ideas that aligned with utilitarianism. However, some of the later philosophers also incorporated concepts that were closer to natural law. One of these thinkers is Mencius – also known as Mengzi or Meng Ke – who is considered the second-most important figure in Confucian thought.

Mencius was a Chinese philosopher during the Warring States period in ancient China, around 300 BCE. Born in the present-day Shandong Province of China, we don't know much about his early life before he became a disciple of Confucius's grandson, Zisi. We do know that afterwards Mencius devoted his life to promoting the teachings of Confucius, becoming a travelling advisor who encouraged leaders to adopt principles of benevolent governance based on Confucian principles. His own ideas expanded on Confucius's teachings – beliefs that human nature is fundamentally good, and that ethical behaviour can be nurtured through education and self-focus on virtues.

Mencius suggested that rulers have a natural moral duty to govern with benevolence, harmony, and justice. Similar to future natural law advocates like Locke, he also claimed that rulers who failed to uphold these principles could be justly overthrown by the people.

Though details of Mencius's life are scarce, his additions to moral and political philosophy during the Warring States period had a lasting impact on Chinese thought and culture for more than 2,200 years. A highlight of his ideas related to natural law include:

Innate Moral Goodness: Comparable to the views of some natural law theorists like Aquinas and Locke, Mencius argued that people are born with a tendency for good, or innate moral goodness. He defined these natural tendencies as compassion, a sense of shame, a sense of propriety, and intuitive ideas on right and wrong.

Universal Morality: Mencius argued that there is a moral order to the universe that is expressed through human nature, also a core belief of natural law theory. Additionally, similar to Cicero and Aquinas, Mencius believed that this universal order was governed by a divine force – *Tian*.

Moral Virtues: Like Aristotle, St. Augustine, and Aquinas, Mencius expressed the importance of practising virtuous behaviour, believing that education, self-reflection, adherence to ritual, and moral guidance were necessary for people to reach their full moral potential.

Role of Government: Mencius believed that the purpose of government was to create a fair and harmonious society in accordance with the natural order. He argued that the legitimacy of the ruler depended on their ability to provide and maintain moral order, and that illegitimate rulers could be overthrown, ideas that were paralleled by John Locke's political theories.

Even though natural law wouldn't be formally developed for at least another 1,000 years, Mencius's ideas about human nature, virtue, morality, and the role of government were similar to later ideas by natural law thinkers like Aristotle, St. Thomas Aquinas, and Locke. Currently (2024), there are an estimated six million people who identify as Confucianists. However, another 400 million people practise other Chinese traditional religions, many of which have been heavily influenced by Confucian thinkers over time.

Al-Farabi
(870-950 CE)

Al-Farabi – also known as Abu Nasr – was one of the most influential philosophers of the Islamic Golden Age, a period of scientific, mathematical, and cultural flourishing in the Islamic world between the 8th and 13th centuries. Covering philosophy, political theory, metaphysics, ethics, and logic, Al-Farabi's writing explored a range of ideas, including his own version of natural law based heavily on the works of Greek philosophers Plato and Aristotle.

Born in the city of Farab (in present-day Kazakhstan) in 870 CE, at the age of 30 he moved to the centre of intellectual and cultural life in the Islamic world – Baghdad. Here he studied under different prominent Islamic scholars while becoming proficient in several languages, including Arabic, Greek, and Syriac. These languages gave him the opportunity to study and translate the writings of the ancient Greek philosophers, works that would end up guiding many of his own beliefs.

Similar to some of our Western theorists, Al-Farabi developed his ideas on natural law under the influence of Plato and Aristotle, arguing for the existence of an ultimate, unchangeable reality that governs the natural order of the universe. He believed that this natural order provided the foundation for both moral and political principles. Continuing to borrow heavily from the Greeks, Al-Farabi also believed that people should aim to be virtuous and supported Plato's idea of a philosopher king – particularly one who ruled based on natural law.

Over the course of his life, Al-Farabi produced a number of written works on different subjects, many of which have since been translated into Latin, Hebrew, and other languages. His contributions to natural law, ethics, and political philosophy not only had an impact on Islamic philosophy but the other Abrahamic religions throughout the Middle Ages as well. Many of the concepts and themes were later shared by Christian thinkers like St. Thomas Aquinas. Highlights of his approach to natural law include:

> **Islamic and Greek Fusion**: Al-Farabi was one of the first Muslim philosophers to combine the ideas of the ancient Greeks with Islamic theology. He applied Aristotle's ideas on teleology and virtue ethics to Islamic beliefs on divine revelation, Islamic justice, and faith.
>
> **Human Reason**: A common vein between natural law philosophers, Al-Farabi placed a strong emphasis on the role of intellect and reason in discovering the principles of natural law. He also believed that humans could use reason to understand the rational natural order of the universe and the moral principles that govern human action.
>
> **Philosopher King**: Al-Farabi also extended Plato's idea of the philosopher king, believing that the ideal ruler should be a religious prophet who not only rules according to natural law but also Islamic teachings. He viewed this ruler as someone responsible for guiding the citizens towards moral and intellectual virtues.

Similar to St. Augustine in the Christian tradition, Al-Farabi built on the work of the Greek philosophers in order to develop his own version of natural law that integrated both theology and reason together. His work had a significant impact on later Islamic philosophy and theology, especially the development of ethical theories. Over a 1,000 years after his death, Al-Farabi's ideas are still studied and debated in Islamic philosophy.

Qadi Abd al-Jabbar
(935-1025)

Qadi Abd al-Jabbar – also known as Abu al-Hasan – was another influential Islamic theologian, philosopher, and jurist who lived during the Islamic Golden Age. Even though both thinkers contributed to Islamic natural law, and both were alive during the same period, Al-Farabi's and Al-Jabbar's influences, contributions, and approaches to natural law were completely different.

Born in an area of present-day Iran in 935 at a time when Western Europe was under constant threat from Viking raids, Qadi Abd al-Jabbar spent much of his childhood receiving a more Islamic education. After studying in both Nishapur and then later Baghdad under Mu'tazilite scholars, he quickly gained a reputation for his analytical abilities and intellectual aptitude.

The Mu'tazilite school of Islamic theology was a group whose ideas were based on the use of reason and rationality to interpret and understand religious concepts. Many of these Mu'tazilite ideas provided the basis for his theory of natural law, including the importance of reason, the beliefs in divine law, and the universality of ethics.

Over the course of his life, Abd al-Jabbar held positions in religious and legal institutions, eventually being appointed as the chief judge of Rayy, a position that allowed him to directly influence Islamic law and theology during a pivotal time in the development of Islam. His extensive writings included essays on history, political philosophy, Islamic law, defences of the Quran, as well as a comprehensive work on theology and ethics. His writings on ethics and natural law involved some of the following aspects.

> **Mu'tazilite School**: Qadi Abd al-Jabbar's theories on natural law were deeply influenced by the Mu'tazilite school of rational Islamic thought.

> **Secular Natural Law**: Abd al-Jabbar believed that the moral and ethical principles of nature could be discovered exclusively through reason and human intellect. His view was that natural law was separate from religion, and that although divine revelation was essential for religious guidance, it was not the only source of morality.

> **Moral Intuition**: Similar to Mencius's philosophy and the future ideas of Locke, Abd al-Jabbar believed that people are naturally inclined to want justice and fairness, allowing them to intuitively recognize moral principles from nature. According to Abd al-Jabbar, humans have an inherent moral sense of right and wrong, which is essential for understanding and following natural law.

> **Free Will**: Abd al-Jabbar believed that humans have free will, a concept that is a core part of his natural law views, stressing that people are morally accountable for their own actions. He argued that evil is a result of people choosing not to follow the obligations of natural law.

> **God and Nature**: In another similarity with Aquinas, Abd al-Jabbar argued that natural law is a reflection of God's law, and that the rational order of nature demonstrates the rationality of

God's divine commands. This combination of divinity and rationality allowed him to develop a theory that balanced both faith and reason.

Qadi Abd al-Jabbar's work had a direct impact on Islamic thought, particularly within the Mu'tazila tradition, and is still studied and debated by scholars of Islamic theology and philosophy to this day.

6

Anarchism and Natural Law

Anarchism – although there are different varieties – is a political philosophy that is traditionally centred on the idea that involuntary authority should be opposed, and that society should be based on voluntary cooperation, mutual aid, and individual autonomy. The viewpoints are typically grounded in the belief that power structures and hierarchies are inherently coercive and oppressive, instead advocating for freedom of association and self-governance.

Throughout history, the ideas of many anarchist philosophers like Lysander Spooner, Mikhail Bakunin, Peter Kropotkin, and Emma Goldman have been grounded – often indirectly – in the concepts of natural law. Even though anarchists commonly reject the idea of being subjected to moral authority, many anarchists also believe that all humans have inherent dignity and rights as a result of natural or social order. Quite a bit of both classical and modern anarchist theory has used these views of inherent human value to shape arguments for a just, equitable, and stateless society.

With many philosophers like Locke and Mencius using the principles of natural law to challenge the legitimacy of authority under certain conditions, anarchists like Spooner took these arguments further, challenging the legitimacy of authority itself and advocating for a completely voluntary and free society.

During the classical period of anarchism – spanning from the mid-19th to the early 20th century – anarchists like Pierre-Joseph Proudhon, Peter Kropotkin, Mikhail Bakunin, and Benjamin Tucker emerged, looking to expose state authority as unjust. They argued that both authority and hierarchy violated the natural principles of freedom, autonomy, and mutual aid that are embedded in human nature, laying the foundation for future generations of anarchists of all social and political stripes.

Within a short period of time, many of these anarchists influenced each other's work, leading to a rapid evolution of ideas over several decades. Since quite a few anarchists had similar views, we will discuss a few notable examples whose ideas related more closely to natural law. For example, Proudhon, Bakunin, and Kropotkin all acknowledged the individual's natural rights to life, freedom, autonomy, association, self-governance, and the fruits of one's labour. Bakunin and Kropotkin, however, believed that these rights were less important than the collective well-being of society, a more utilitarian approach.

Over the past century anarchism has continued to evolve and diversify, with new variations based on both natural law and on alternative ethical views. Let's take a look at some of these founding anarchists, their ideas of anarchism, and the connections to classical ideas of natural law.

Pierre-Joseph Proudhon
(1809-1865)

Considered by many to be the "father of anarchism," Pierre-Joseph Proudhon was a French political theorist and philosopher born in 1809, a decade after the end of the French Revolution, and shortly after the start of Napoleonic France.

Proudhon was raised in a poor working-class family, and like many peasants of the time, he didn't have the opportunity to get a formal education. Instead, he worked from a young age, holding several jobs before eventually becoming an apprentice printer. His role at the printer gave him the opportunity to read a wide variety of writing, teaching himself Latin, Greek, and Hebrew in the process. He was particularly influenced by the works of socialist Charles Fourier and Enlightenment thinkers like Jean-Jacques Rousseau.

Proudhon might be best known for his provocative statement, "Property is theft!", which was published in his most famous work *What is Property?* in 1840. In the book he argued against the type of private property that leads to the exploitation of labour and perpetuates social inequality – specifically *rent-seeking*, a term used to describe the ownership of land without contributing to its productivity. Instead, he proposed a system that was based on cooperation and voluntary exchange rather than competition and hierarchy.

It is worth noting that Proudhon was not completely against ownership of land, and he believed that it was essential for farmers (for example) to have the right to own the land that they worked in order to preserve liberty.

Over the course of his life, Proudhon was involved in different political movements and wrote extensively on topics like property, labour, and social reform. Some highlights of the common threads between his views and natural law include the following.

Inherent Dignity: Proudhon was sceptical of abstract natural rights, believing that they were a construct that could be used to justify inequality and oppression. However, he did believe that all humans have a natural inherent dignity and that the nature of human interaction implies certain moral ideas, concepts that are foundational in natural law.

Moral Order: Unlike abstract or theological ideas on natural law, Proudhon believed that moral order could emerge from the natural tendencies of individuals to work together for collective benefit. He argued that this order was based on mutual respect, voluntary cooperation, and mutual aid.

Property Rights: Proudhon's famous declaration "Property is theft!" demonstrated his views that exclusive ownership without contributing labour – especially of land and resources – was a violation of the moral order. He believed that property rights should be based on the principle of mutualism, where individuals have the right to use and occupy resources but cannot hold absolute ownership over them.

Opposition to Centralized Authority: Proudhon – like Spooner – believed that society should be decentralized, with decision-making being carried out at a local level. He argued that centralized authority, like that of the state, was inherently coercive and violated the "natural" moral order.

Social Contract: Similar to natural law theorists like Locke and Rousseau, Proudhon believed in the idea of a social contract. Unlike the others, he argued that this contract should be a direct agreement between individuals and their community, not managed through a centralized authority.

Many of Proudhon's ideas drew different conclusions from natural law theorists based on his perspective of society, but some of his underlying beliefs were very similar, such as inherent natural dignity and rights stemming from human interaction. Proudhon's work was instrumental in the development of anarchism as a unique political philosophy and theory.

Benjamin Tucker
(1854-1939)

Born in Massachusetts in 1854, Benjamin Tucker was an American individualist anarchist who played a major role in promoting anarchism in the United States during the "classical age of anarchism." At the age of 16, Tucker got a job as a journalist, where he was quickly exposed to a large variety of both political and social issues.

After reading the works of Josiah Warren and French anarchist Proudhon in the 1870s, Tucker was immediately captivated by Warren's ideas on individualism and Proudhon's ideas on property rights, both of which he incorporated into his own flavour of anarchist philosophy.

In 1881, Tucker founded *Liberty*, a journal that promoted individualist anarchism and similar ideas in the United States for more than 25 years. Shortly after he began publishing, he was introduced to Lysander Spooner's writing, and he began blending the ideas of natural law and individual rights into his own philosophy, which he published in the book *State Socialism and Anarchism* in 1887.

Throughout the 1880s, Tucker translated and republished writings by European socialists, anarchists, and philosophers, including works by Proudhon, Bakunin, and Max Stirner. His work translating these authors was crucial to the introduction of European anarchist thought into the United States during the late 19th century.

In 1908, Tucker's Unique Book Shop in New York City was destroyed in a fire, along with his entire publishing operation, his inventory of written works, and his printing plates. This effectively ended the publication of his journal and resulted in Tucker's decision to leave the United States for France, where he spent the remainder of his life.

Similar to Spooner, Benjamin Tucker viewed individual rights as sacred and inviolable, and believed that all authority was by default a violation of natural law. His focus on the individual was opposite from collectivist branches of anarchism that take more utilitarian approaches – like the socialist ideas of the time. Some of the unique aspects of Tucker's approach to anarchism and natural law are as follows:

Individual Sovereignty: Tucker argued that each person has inherent natural rights that cannot be justly violated by any external authority, including the state. He believed that people should be free to associate voluntarily and create their own social and economic relationships without any coercion or interference.

Egoism: Tucker was influenced by German philosopher Max Stirner who advocated for egoism, a philosophy that rejects all external influences over the individual, suggesting that the only source of value and meaning comes from within yourself.

Property Rights: Similar to Proudhon's views on property, Tucker believed that individuals have a right to own and control property as long as it is being occupied and actively used. This contrasted views by collectivist anarchists like Bakunin who were opposed to private ownership and believed that land should be managed by the community.

Free-market anarchism: What would later be coined "anarcho-capitalism" by Murray Rothbard, Tucker was a proponent of all forms of voluntary interactions, including voluntary exchange and free markets without the intervention of authority.

Four Monopolies: Tucker identified four institutional barriers to economic freedom and equality for individuals, specifically the money monopoly, the land monopoly, the tariff monopoly, and the patent monopoly. He believed that these monopolies were responsible for all of the systemic injustice and inequality in society.

Like Spooner, Benjamin Tucker's views on anarchism were different from the more collectivist and socialist versions of anarchism that were developed by thinkers like Proudhon and Bakunin. Tucker's views on the primacy of the individual had a major impact on other American anarchists like Emma Goldman, as well as future anarcho-capitalists like Murray Rothbard.

7

On the Shoulders of Giants

From the ancient thinkers like Buddha and Confucius in the 6th century BCE through to the modern era, concepts aligning with natural law and utilitarian thought have been a core part of world philosophy for millennia.

Like many of the great ideas that have influenced Western society and philosophy, the roots of both theories can be traced back to ancient Greece. Epicurus's thoughts on hedonism were a direct inspiration for Bentham's work, and Aristotle's beliefs in rationality and nature inspired many others like Cicero, Aquinas, Locke, and Kant in their own views.

During the Roman era, Cicero took the principles of rationality and nature, and incorporated ideas on divine order and the universal aspects of morality from nature. These ideas were a direct influence on the religious scholars who developed theories of natural law by weaving together ideas of natural order and divinity. For most of the Middle Ages, philosophy was driven by religious scholars across both Europe and the rising Islamic caliphates of the time, and ethical theories in the natural law tradition were developed by thinkers like Aquinas, Al-Farabi, and Qadi Abd al-Jabbar.

With the Age of Reason came a flood of new ideas, based on both new and historical theories. During this period, Jeremy Bentham drew inspiration from Epicurus's and Helvétius's ideas on hedonism and social well-being, Hume's ideas on consequences and utility, and Beccaria's work on crime and punishment. All of these ideas were merged, reshaped, and refined into the formal theory that we now call *utilitarianism*. Over the next few centuries, many different thinkers like John Stuart Mill, J.J.C. Smart, and Peter Singer would develop the concepts in their own ways, inspiring variations like "rule," "negative," and "preference" utilitarianism.

Natural law also saw a philosophical boom during the Enlightenment, with the introduction of formal natural rights – applying to individuals and nations – and a wealth of new theories on political autonomy and the legitimacy of authority. In particular, the work of John Locke was a driving force in the application of natural law theory to both legal and political philosophy, ideas that would directly inspire both the French and American Revolutions in the late 18th century.

After the end of the Enlightenment era, natural law saw a decline in popularity in contrast to the rise of utilitarian ideas. During this time, new variations of natural law began to emerge, centred on the rising anarchist movements and the conclusions that most – if not all – authority was illegitimate. These movements were inspired by the works of Proudhon, Lysander Spooner, and Benjamin Tucker, each with their own takes on the implications of natural human dignity and self-ownership.

In the end, the sum total of ideas presented by the thinkers covered here – and others – have laid the foundations for so much of modern society, law, and politics. Over the last millennia these great philosophers have developed ideas that are so ingrained in our cultural fabric that it can sometimes be hard to separate the ideas, both from each other and from our active decision-making processes.

In the next section we will dive deeper into the concepts themselves, viewing the theories' building blocks, variations, and misconceptions in more detail, allowing us to truly stand on the shoulders of these intellectual giants.

PART II

THEORIES

1

Overview

A train is barrelling down the tracks, and in its path are five people. You can pull a lever to switch the train onto a new track, where only one person is tied. If you don't act, five people will die. If you do act, then one will die – what do *you* do? This classic trolley problem gives us an effective way to visualize and understand moral decisions and trade-offs, an opportunity to put our theories to the test.

Over the past section we saw the evolution of theory across thousands of years. During this journey we also met the people who developed and assembled the ideas, building comprehensive moral frameworks that have since changed modern society. So far, our look at these concepts has been in the context of the individuals who helped define them, and now, it is time to put them all together.

As we saw, ethical systems based on utilitarianism are centred around the idea of maximizing utility – whether utility takes the form of happiness, preferences, or harm reduction. In this way, utilitarianism aims to achieve the goal of the *greatest happiness for the greatest number* of people – often measured through social well-being. Looking back at our trolley problem above, the answer is immediately clear, pull the lever and save five people at the cost of one.

On the other hand, the natural law schools of ethics are based on the core principle that morality can be identified through the observation and rational analysis of human nature. These theories declare that being based in the natural order, these moral rules supersede human laws, and that natural rights are absolute and inviolable. In this case, the trolley problem above is also clear; you do not have the right to take a life, regardless of the circumstance.

As we can see in the example above, these two theories have a fundamental disagreement. Utilitarianism claims that only moral outcomes matter, not the actions taken to get there; in essence – the ends justify the means. Natural law is the opposite, declaring that moral action is the only thing that matters – that the ends *are* the means.
Over the next chapters, we will dig deeper into these belief systems, breaking down their most fundamental assumptions, concepts, and applications. With a fuller understanding of the concepts covered here, we will be prepared with the tools to identify and evaluate examples of these theories later in the book, a way to measure how effective these moral goals are in practice.

2

Core Concepts of Utilitarianism

Even though there are several major variations that have been popularized over recent centuries, many of the underlying ideas of utilitarianism have stayed the same since they were originally developed by Jeremy Bentham. Some of these variations include rule-based utilitarianism, which offers general guidelines – or rules – for the best ways to maximize utility, as well as preference and negative utilitarianism, which propose specific ways of determining how utility should be conceptualized and/or calculated.

Over this next chapter, we will examine in more depth the various ideas behind these different types of utilitarianism, as well as the foundational concepts that they are built on. The first aspect of the theory we are going to explore is the basic argument that underlies utilitarianism as a whole.

Basic Argument

A logical argument that we can look at to better understand the essence of utilitarianism can be presented in the following way:

1. Happiness is good, suffering and pain are bad.

2. Actions can have consequences that result in happiness or suffering.

3. The morality of an action is tied to the total good or bad (utility) that results.

4. If an action produces both good and bad, the difference of the two is considered (net utility).

5. If two choices lead to different outcomes, the one that produces the greatest "net utility" is the moral choice.

Highlight of Core Concepts

Although there are many different forms and twists on utilitarian ideas, some basic concepts are central to defining the ethical theory. These concepts include:

Hedonism: Classical utilitarianism is rooted in hedonism, the idea that pleasure is the ultimate good, and that pain and suffering are the ultimate evil.

Greatest Happiness Principle: The core principle of utilitarianism is the idea that an action is morally right if it results in the greatest overall happiness or pleasure for the greatest number of people. This is also known as the "Greatest Happiness Principle," or the "Principle of Utility."

Consequentialism: Utilitarianism is a consequentialist ethical theory. This means that the morality of an action is determined exclusively by its consequences or outcomes. "The ends justify the means" is a common way of capturing this idea, as utilitarians believe that as long as the end result is the greatest overall happiness or well-being, the action itself is moral.

Impartiality: Impartiality is a key principle of utilitarianism, requiring that every person's happiness or well-being should be considered equally when making decisions. This principle aims to prevent people from weighing the needs or impacts of personal relationships differently than others.

Quantitative Approach: A common thread in all utilitarian theories is the idea that happiness or well-being can be quantified and measured across different actions in order to determine what is moral. This is represented by Bentham's concept of "hedonic calculus."

Requirement to Act: A central tenet of utilitarianism – since introduced by John Stuart Mill – is the idea that inaction and action are morally equivalent, highlighting the belief that you are morally obligated to help others if you are able.

These are the core concepts that make up the foundation of utilitarian theory.

Flavours of Utilitarianism

With concepts that can be traced back as far as Epicurus in the 3rd century BCE, there have been many different perspectives on and varieties of utilitarian theory over time. Most of these variations build on the principles of calculating and weighing moral action, and the evaluation and judgement of moral outcomes. The primary variations of utilitarianism we've already seen attempt to present different ways of applying these core principles to moral decisions and dilemmas, usually by modifying the utility calculation itself – including people's desires, or even excluding happiness. Each of these types has its own goals, strengths, and weaknesses, from the original theory to the offshoots that attempt to solve the challenges or weaknesses of the classical theory. Let's recap the popular variants we talked about earlier.

Classical Utilitarianism

Classical utilitarianism is the name of the original form of utilitarianism developed by Jeremy Bentham. It emphasizes hedonism, the idea that pleasure is the ultimate good, and pain is the ultimate evil. This original version tries to calculate "net utility," and suggests that the morally right action is the one that maximizes pleasure and minimizes pain for the greatest number of people.

Act Utilitarianism

Act utilitarianism is more of a subset of classical utilitarianism, one that suggests that the best method for moral action is to calculate the best choice available for every single action. It specifies that each action should be judged by its outcome, according to the principle of utility. In theory, this means that every single decision should undergo a series of moral calculations, and that the option with the greatest utility should be chosen every time.

Act utilitarians argue that this approach has several distinct benefits compared to other approaches including the following:

Flexibility: Making decisions on individual actions allows a person to take the context of the situation into account. This makes act utilitarianism adaptable to any situation.

Moral Awareness: By focusing on the utility of each action independently, this approach encourages decision-makers to consider the actual consequences of their choices, making them more aware of the impacts of their choices and the morality of their actions.

Minimizes Bias: Assessing each situation objectively and impartially can help to reduce the systemic biases that might exist under forms of decision-making that are based on rules.

Proponents argue that the benefits of this moral system – listed above – give us the tools to be able to make decisions in any environment, and to be able to choose actions based on the information and context of the present situation.

As with any other ethical theory, there are also plenty of critics of using act utilitarianism as a moral decision-making tool. A few of the high-level concerns against this variation raised by critics include:

Demanding: Judging the morality of every single action and its alternative choices is very demanding, requiring constant calculation of possible outcomes, impacts, and morality. This has the potential to make even insignificant interactions into very time-consuming, mentally exhausting, and highly impractical exchanges.

Counter-Intuitive: Actions that are justified by calculations of potential outcomes can result in "moral" suggestions that violate widely accepted moral intuition, as long as they lead to a greater overall utility. Just like we will see later on, this can lead to counter-intuitive moral judgements that might be difficult to reconcile.

Subjectivity: It is incredibly difficult (if not impossible) for people to fully separate their own personal biases, judgements, and preferences from calculations of utility. This is often seen when people place different values on the same outcome in the same situations.

Relationship Compatibility: The principle of impartiality and the focus on maximizing utility for every action can lead to conflict with close relationships, like friends or family.

Some critics argue that many of the benefits and challenges of act utilitarianism are a result of human nature. People tend to find it difficult to remain neutral and unbiased, so applying moral judgements is often quite difficult to begin with. However, using utilitarian moral judgement for every action can also give us the flexibility to maximize overall well-being in every unique situation, something that is probably not possible using rule-based utilitarianism. The following examples demonstrate real-world situations where moral judgements are applied on individual actions.

Example – Emergency Triage

In emergency situations – like a hospital ER – when medical resources are scarce, healthcare professionals will often prioritize treating patients based on the severity of their condition. This generally results in less attention or care for patients with less serious conditions or injuries but is accepted as a process that results in the greatest benefit overall.

Example – Organ Transplants

Similar to emergency triage, recipients of organ transplants are typically prioritized not only on medical urgency but based on a number of factors, including likelihood of a successful transplant, life expectancy after the transplant, and even personal choices like alcohol and cigarette consumption. This can result in two similar recipients having very different outcomes due to one being considered a benefit to society and the other not meeting selection criteria.

Rule Utilitarianism

Mill's rule utilitarianism focuses on the importance of following general rules that are considered moral. It suggests that when consistently followed, the rules will result in greater outcomes over the long term. Rule utilitarianism tries to overcome some of the potential issues of evaluating every action, such as the high degree of effort required to evaluate individual actions, the focus on short-term outcomes and the potential to justify morally questionable decisions.

In theory, rule utilitarians could look at historical precedents, consult with experts in various fields, and even examine the outcomes of different social or moral systems when considering which rules have the greatest overall impact on happiness. As you can imagine, this process could be complicated and different people will often disagree on which rules will be the most effective. Utilitarians who advocate for using rules as moral guides suggest that this variation offers some of the following benefits over classical or act utilitarianism.

> **Social Stability:** Rules help to provide clear and consistent moral guidelines, which make decisions more predictable, help create shared expectations, and result in more social stability overall.

> **Simplicity:** By following established rules, decision-making in complex or morally challenging situations becomes simpler, removing the need to constantly calculate utility.

> **More Intuitive:** By focusing on moral rules instead of individual actions, rule utilitarianism can avoid counter-intuitive conclusions that conflict with widely accepted moral beliefs.

Long-term Thinking: By focusing on the adoption of moral rules that maximize happiness over time, decision-makers are able to calculate results of policies or rules over a longer period.

Rule utilitarians believe that predictable and stable rules, along with the simpler and more intuitive utility calculations, result in significant benefits over the long term, even if it results in short-term losses in utility that could be gained by breaking the moral rules. However, the idea of mixing utilitarianism – a system based on maximizing utility – with rules that have the potential to reduce short-term utility has plenty of critics. Here are a few of the more popular criticisms of rule utilitarianism.

Rule-Worship: One of the concerns about rule utilitarianism is that the focus on following rules can lead to situations where the rules themselves are seen as the goal, instead of a tool to achieve the goal, which is maximizing happiness or well-being.

Rule Selection: Choosing which rules have the most utility in the long term can be very difficult, especially since different rules can lead to different outcomes depending on the situation or context. This makes it challenging to establish a universal set of rules that everyone agrees with.

Rigidity: Even when not following the rules could lead to obvious greater overall happiness in a particular situation, it can be incredibly difficult to break the rules when that is the foundation of your moral system.

Indirectness: Some critics argue that rule utilitarianism still tries to maximize overall utility, so using rules can just lead to a more convoluted and less effective way of achieving the same goal.

Many of the laws and government policies that have been put in place can be described as inherently rule utilitarian. A couple of the more obvious examples we can use to highlight the concept are laid out here.

Example – Traffic Laws

Governments establish traffic laws such as speed limits, traffic signals, and driver licensing with the purpose of increasing the safety and efficiency of road transportation. By following these rules, drivers prevent or reduce accidents, and traffic flows more smoothly, even if occasionally breaking the rules might seem like a better option in specific instances.

Example – Environmental Regulations

Most governments implement environmental regulations, like limits on pollution emissions, guidelines for disposing of waste, and protection of endangered species, in order to protect both ecosystems and the health of the general public. Even though following environmental rules can inflate the operational costs for many businesses, the rules aim to contribute to overall well-being in the long run by reducing pollution, conserving natural resources and more.

Example – Anti-Discrimination Laws

Anti-discrimination laws are an example of rules that have been put in place in order to protect individuals against unfair treatment based on their race, religion, sexual orientation, and other characteristics. These laws contribute to the greater good by promoting fairness and equal opportunities, even though they can be viewed as a violation of people's freedom of association – namely the right for people to enter into agreements with whomever they choose.

Preference Utilitarianism

Several utilitarians, such as R.M. Hare and Peter Singer, advocated for a version of utilitarianism that focused on people's individual preferences or desires. This was an attempt to incorporate people's different values and the types of pleasures that are important to them into the utilitarian calculation. This variation tries to address the criticism that people prefer different things, so finding actions that result in the greatest happiness requires knowing what people want, and what makes them happy.

Supporters of preference utilitarianism suggest that it offers the following benefits over other forms of utilitarianism.

Respects Individual Values: With a strong focus on satisfying individual preferences and desires, supporters suggest that it is more respectful of individual's values and autonomy, since each person is in the best position to determine what will improve their own well-being.

Objectivity: By trying to measure and include every individual's preferences, advocates suggest that we avoid the challenge of making decisions for others using our subjective experiences and values. This lets us be more objective in our approach to making decisions that maximize utility for everyone.

Democratic: Some people suggest that democracy is inherently compatible with this utilitarian variation, since voters are able to express their preferences directly through voting for their ideal policies and candidates that share their values. This can make moral decisions even easier to adopt and apply.

With a major shift away from classical utilitarianism's hedonism, preference utilitarians also face quite a lot of criticism. Some of the common arguments against this form of utilitarian calculation are summarized below.

Harm Enabling: Some people's personal preferences could be considered harmful or morally questionable, leading to concerns about the ethical implications of satisfying those preferences.

Conflicting Preferences: Different people can have preferences that are incompatible or even contradict each other, leading to situations where it can be very difficult to identify which preferences should be prioritized in order to maximize utility.

Instability: People's preferences very often change over time, and their short-term preferences might not line up with their long-term preferences. This raises the question of which preferences are more important, and which ones should be taken into account when making decisions.

While many of our existing laws or policies may align more closely with other types of utilitarianism, preferences are still often taken into account in our society. Some examples of policies that follow preferential models are as follows.

Example – Assisted Dying Laws

Some governments have put in place assisted dying laws. These laws will often allow terminally ill patients who meet certain criteria to request medical assistance in dying. This type of policy aims to respect the preferences of individuals who would like to end their own lives, while also providing safeguards to protect vulnerable members of the population.

Example – Flexible working arrangements

In some countries, government policies mandate that employers provide the option for flexible working arrangements to their employees, including remote work, adjustable schedules, and other preference-oriented options. These policies have been developed to satisfy the needs or desires of employees by promoting work-life balance and flexibility.

Example – Public consultations

Despite increasing the cost and time of implementing policies or projects, many levels of government from municipalities to federal policymakers will attempt to take public preferences into account through public consultation processes. This allows for people to raise objections or advocate for projects that may affect them.

Negative Utilitarianism

With the root concepts originally introduced by Karl Popper in 1946, and then later formalized in 1958 by R.N. Smart, the theory gained significant prominence through the works of J.J.C. Smart. In essence, negative utilitarianism focuses on reducing suffering instead of maximizing happiness. According to supporters, the morally right action is the one that results in the least amount of suffering for the greatest number of people. The goal of this variation aimed to make utility easier to calculate, as well as restricting otherwise moral utilitarian choices that still include sizable negative trade-offs. These benefits of negative utilitarianism suggested by proponents can be summed up as follows.

> **Reduces Suffering**: Negative utilitarianism focuses on the importance of minimizing pain and suffering. This results in fewer trade-offs and sacrifices for the greater good and is viewed by some

as a more compassionate and morally empathetic way to make decisions than simply maximizing happiness.

Worst-case Mitigation: By prioritizing the reduction of suffering instead of maximizing happiness, this approach tries to prevent the worst-case trade-offs of utility, where huge amounts of suffering are caused for an even greater potential good.

Simplifies Decision-making: According to advocates, ethical decision-making can be simplified a great deal by removing the need to calculate both positive and negative outcomes and weigh them against each other. By focusing on the negative effects, it can become much simpler to identify morally desirable actions in very complex situations.

Risk Averse: Negative utilitarianism focuses on minimizing harm, which aligns with the general tendency for humans to be risk-averse, making this approach a more intuitive and relatable ethical framework for a lot of people.

Even though negative utilitarians argue that harm reduction is more empathetic and compassionate than other hedonist approaches, there are also plenty of critics of these modifications to utilitarian theory. Some of these concerns can be summarized in the following ways.

Overemphasizes Suffering: By ignoring everything except pain and suffering, our decisions are likely to lead to neglecting other important values like happiness, pleasure, and general well-being, creating an ethical framework that doesn't do good, just minimizes bad.

Extreme Conclusions: Similar to many other forms of utilitarianism, this variation can still result in extreme conclusions that it considers to be completely moral. For example, it could judge that in order to eliminate centuries of humanity's natural suffering, a quick extinction of sentient life would be the best possible outcome.

Short-Term Focus: The emphasis on avoiding harm could result in situations where it can be difficult or impossible to choose short-term negative consequences in order to gain significant longer-term benefits.

Critics of negative utilitarianism often argue that though it uses some of the concepts of utility and moral calculation, it ignores the parts that make utilitarianism impactful and moral. By trying to minimize suffering, negative utilitarian examples in the real world usually focus on helping vulnerable members of society and reducing inequality. Let's take a look at some examples of this type of policy.

Example – Social Welfare Programs

Most governments implement social welfare programs, like food assistance, housing support, and unemployment benefits, the majority of which are solely focused on reducing negative outcomes among potentially vulnerable groups. These policies usually prioritize the reduction of suffering, even though they don't lead to direct promotion of happiness for all members of society.

Example – Disaster Relief

Governments often allocate resources for emergency relief in order to minimize the suffering caused by natural disasters or other events. By providing first aid, food, water, shelter, and more to affected people, these policies focus on minimizing or dealing with the negative impacts of these situations, not explicitly on generating happiness.

Example – Mental Health Initiatives

By investing in mental health programs and initiatives like awareness campaigns, accessible treatment, and addiction counselling, governments often try to alleviate distress and suffering for people in difficult situations, even if it isn't directly promoting happiness for the wider society.

Utilitarianism and Collectivism

With our goal of exploring both theoretical concepts and practical applications over the course of this book, it would be difficult to evaluate the theory without discussing the relationship between utilitarianism and collectivism. In many ways, collectivist movements in recent history can be seen as political manifestations of utilitarian ideas, especially the prioritization and measurement of group impacts instead of single individuals. Even though both mainstream collectivist and utilitarian decisions do consider individual treatment and rights, they generally view these interactions within the context of an individual's value as a part of the "net utility" – in other words, as the means to an end.

In addition to sharing some of utilitarianism's foundational approaches towards group – or collective – utility, collectivist political ideologies sometimes contain elements of both rule and preference utilitarianism, attempting to account for both preferences and general rules that protect the wider population. However, just like other types of utilitarianism, collectivist respect for individuals and their preferences is still just a part of the larger calculation, since the ultimate goal is still achieving what is best for the group.

Even though rule utilitarianism was developed as a way to protect individuals, it also falls victim to the same issues for the following similar reasons. The rules are chosen and put in place in order to maximize group well-being, with respect for individuals being seen as a means to achieve that end. In both systems – utilitarianism and collectivism – when the rules that protect individuals conflict with group benefits, they ultimately face a choice: They can maximize collective happiness at the expense of individuals, or they can choose *not* to pursue maximum utility and well-being, resulting in a violation of core utilitarian and collectivist principles. The treatment of members of society as a piece of the larger whole is an inherent part of both utilitarian and collectivist systems, both of which aim to optimize group outcomes. As a result, the two are often similar in terms of intent and implementation – moral and political twins in real-world policy.

3

Core Concepts of Natural Law

Since theories based on human nature and natural order have been around for thousands of years, there is an incredibly diverse range of views that fit under the "natural law" umbrella. Many of the thinkers from different eras, religious persuasions, and cultural backgrounds that we covered took similar ideas and concepts of natural order in entirely different directions, focusing on legal, political, ethical, social, religious, and rational implications of natural law theory. Even though there is a large variety of arguments and conclusions that were reached by different theorists over time, some of these views can be grouped together and their common concepts and approaches can be compared.

In this chapter, we will dig into some of the basic arguments, common and unique concepts, and the major categories and varieties of natural law.

Basic Argument

A logical argument for the core principles of natural law is as follows:

1. The universe, and by extension humans, exhibit regular patterns, relationships, and principles demonstrating a natural order.

2. Human beings possess the ability to observe, reason, and discover the underlying principles and laws that govern this order.

3. The state of nature is objective, so the application of objective reason results in objective principles.

4. Human interactions and behaviour are a part of the natural order and are therefore governed by objective principles.

5. By following these objective principles – moral behaviour – we can maximize respect for human dignity, justice, and cooperation.

Highlight of Core Concepts

Even with the many different interpretations and theories under the umbrella of natural law, there are some concepts that apply to each of them – namely that there are principles inherent in nature, particularly in human nature, that define what is morally permissible. The several basic concepts that define natural law as an ethical theory, include the following:

Universal: A core concept of natural law is the idea of universality. Since natural law is derived from human nature, it applies universally to all human beings, regardless of their ethnicity, culture, religion, or politics.

Reason & Rationality: Another of the basic concepts present across natural law theories is the idea that reason is required to discover the moral principles embedded in nature.

Individual Rights: A key principle in natural law is the idea that every person has fundamental rights that cannot be taken away by any legitimate authority. While the specific rights vary a bit across different theories and philosophers, the idea of inalienable rights is a cornerstone of natural law.

Absolute: Natural law can be described as a morally absolute theory. Because of the universality of natural law, the moral principles and individual rights that are discovered through reason are seen as objective truths that do not change based on context or circumstance.

Governing Law: A common thread across these theories is the belief that natural law transcends human laws. This means that if a human law or authority conflicts with a principle of natural law, it is considered to be unjust and illegitimate.

These core concepts make up the underlying theory of natural law. From here, different philosophers and thinkers developed their own variations and added their own concepts, as we discovered in previous chapters.

Flavours of Natural Law

As we saw when looking at our different thinkers and their flavours of natural law, there is a large variety of types, focuses, and concepts in the different philosophers' approaches. Some of these theories took a religious perspective, looking at nature through the lens of Islamic or Christian theology, and others believed that natural law was independent of religious customs and doctrine.

Others considered the personal implications of the natural order on individual behaviour and action, while still others looked at hierarchies, authority, and the morality of group dynamics. Finally, some thinkers looked at law and justice, building theories that evaluated these themes on both local and international scales.

Even though there is a huge range of thoughts, ideas, and contributions in these different theories, we will look at some of these rough categories and both their unique and common concepts.

Divine Natural Law

In many of the earliest versions of natural law, philosophers such as St. Augustine, St. Thomas Aquinas, Al-Farabi, and Qadi Abd al-Jabbar all believed that natural law was a reflection of a greater divine law. These types of thinkers we looked at in earlier chapters often combined their personal theological beliefs with their perspectives on nature and moral behaviour. Some of the aspects and concepts typically associated with their viewpoints are as follows:

> **Divine Source:** Theologians who advocate for natural law generally believe that natural law is an expression of God's will – reflected in nature. Even when their specific beliefs and arguments are different, they share a belief that we (humans) need to use reason in order to identify and understand this divine law.

> **Revelation & Scripture:** Some of the religious theorists – though not all – believe that religious teachings and sacred texts are either required or can at least provide guidance in understanding and applying these principles of natural law.

Secular Natural Law

Many other natural law theorists believed that natural law was independent of religion, instead focusing on the reason-based or the rational aspects of discovering natural law. These thinkers typically talked about the discovery of laws based on human nature, without examining it in the context of religion. This category includes some of the philosophers we covered earlier like Aristotle, Hugo Grotius, and John Locke. It is worth noting that some of the individuals who believed in natural law's divine origins – like Aquinas and Qadi Abd al-Jabbar – stressed that religion could provide context but ultimately isn't required to interpret the principles of natural law. Some of the concepts that help define the secular school of natural law include:

> **Reason**: Secular natural law theorists highlight the role of observation, reason, and rational thought in the process of discovering natural moral principles. They normally maintain that these tools are enough to discover natural law, not requiring any external direction – like religion.

> **Religious Compatibility**: Thinkers like Grotius and Locke believed that since it is completely independent from divine guidance, natural law is compatible with different religious belief systems. Consequently, they advocated for religious tolerance and impartial treatment under natural law.

Personal Natural Law

Some philosophers like Aristotle, St. Thomas Aquinas, and Immanuel Kant looked at morality from the perspective of how it guides individual action, instead of mainly exploring religious, legal, or political authority. These thinkers often incorporated ideas on virtue, duty, or purpose into their theories as a guide for how individuals should act. Highlights of some of these concepts are as follows:

> **Virtue**: Both Aristotle and St. Thomas Aquinas believed that individuals should try to live virtuous and fulfilling lives. They posited that by aligning your actions with natural and divine law, you can achieve fulfilment.

> **Duty and Obligation**: Although not a natural law thinker, Kant's views on personal moral action influenced many others and were

shared by some natural law theorists. His ethical theory highlights the importance of personal duty and obligation in moral behaviour. He believed that people have a responsibility to act according to moral law, no matter the outcome.

Legal Natural Law

Many philosophers like Cicero, Grotius, Locke, and Lysander Spooner developed their theories from the perspective of the application of law and justice, instead of the context of personal morality. The building blocks of this approach to natural law include some of these concepts:

> **Natural Equality:** Even though it is a core component across all variations of natural law, the idea of the equality of all individuals was most pronounced in the context of law and justice. This principle reinforces the belief that everyone should be treated equally and fairly, no matter their social status, background, religion, or other properties.
>
> **Social Contract:** Locke in particular developed the idea of a social contract, a concept that considered the relationship of individuals and legitimate authority under natural law. An example of this is John Locke's famous claim that a government's legal authority comes from the consent of the governed and how well it aligns with the principles of natural law.
>
> **Justice:** Legal natural law theorists shared a concern for justice, believing that the primary purpose of laws – and the legal system itself – was to enforce natural law through the respect and protection of individual rights. In Grotius's case, he extended his theory to cover both individual justice and justice between sovereign nations.

Political Natural Law

Very similar in many ways to the legal perspective, many natural law philosophers approached the theory through the lens of political implications, both in terms of social and political organization. Some of these concepts from theorists like Cicero, John Locke, Lysander Spooner, as well as most thinkers in the anarchist tradition, include aspects of the following:

> **Consent of the Governed**: Locke and later Spooner both argued that legitimate political authority is only justified and lawful with the consent of the people. This idea sets up the barometer for judging which political actions and systems are considered valid. Locke's ideas on the people's right of revolution or to reform the government whenever they wish are an extension of this principle.
>
> **Limited Government**: Most political natural law theorists advocate for limited government power, believing that the government's primary – or sometimes only – responsibility is to protect the natural rights of its people. An example of this principle is the Tenth Amendment of the U.S. Constitution, an attempt to restrict government power from growing unchecked.
>
> **Separation of Powers**: Some theorists argued for the separation of powers within the government as a way to prevent the concentration of power and the potential for tyranny. Originally proposed by Locke at a time when many people still believed in the divine right of kings, it was considered radical at the time. However, centuries later it has been incorporated into most Western systems of government.

Anarchist Natural Law

The incorporation of natural law into anarchist ideas was often indirect, adopting ideas that include inherent human value and dignity and moral order that come from natural cooperation between individuals. However, many of these basic principles of anarchist thought are based on, or related to, similar concepts that originated or were popularized in natural law theory. Some of these are as follows:

Individual Sovereignty: Anarchists in the natural law tradition believe that individuals have inherent rights and liberties that should not be violated by any authority.

Voluntary Cooperation: Mutual aid and voluntary cooperation are argued to be the only legitimate foundations for the organization of society, rather than coercive and illegitimate state authority.

4

Natural Rights

The most common way that natural law theory is applied is through the recognition and protection of *natural rights*. In essence, these natural rights identify the activities or properties inherent in human nature which individuals cannot legitimately be prevented from exercising. Since these rights are derived from human nature, they exist independently of man-made laws, social customs, and religious beliefs, and therefore, natural law theorists argue that they cannot rightfully be taken away or granted by either individuals or authorities. This idea is reflected in the following quote from French economist and writer Frédéric Bastiat's *The Law*, published in the mid-19th century.

> *Life, liberty, and property do not exist because men have made laws. On the contrary, it was the fact that life, liberty, and property existed beforehand that caused men to make laws in the first place.*

Historically, there have been a variety of individual rights that were identified during the development of different theories, including the right to life, liberty, property, and the pursuit of happiness. Even though philosophers sometimes had different interpretations of what those natural rights include, the idea that rights are the most fundamental aspect of a just and moral society is a core belief that is shared by all. Let's take a look at some of the most common natural rights that have been identified over the history and development of natural law.

Right to Life

The right to life is the most fundamental natural right, and one of the core principles of natural law theory itself. At its core, it asserts that:

- Every individual has an inherent right to their own life and has the right to protect themselves from harm or actions that threaten their existence.

The right to life is based on a couple of arguments. The first is that for natural and social cooperation between individuals to flourish, there has to be acknowledgement and respect for the intrinsic value of other people's lives. The second argument is the belief that the natural instinct for self-preservation is an essential aspect of not only human nature but the nature of all living organisms.

From these two arguments, we can conclude that for any lasting social cooperation to occur, each individual must respect each other's right to life. The right to life is often seen as self-evident and is one of the simplest and most straightforward examples of a natural right that has been derived from human nature. The most important fundamental right, it also serves as a basis for all other rights since life is one of the necessary preconditions for exercising all other rights and freedoms. Without the right to life, the other rights become meaningless.

Right to Self-Defence

The right to self-defence, even though it is commonly discussed and referenced as its own right, can really be viewed as an extension of the natural right to life. After all, once you accept that a person has a right to their own life, it would be a contradiction to suggest that they don't have the right to protect their life from harm or aggression.

Another argument that often goes hand in hand with the right to self-defence is the right to own and use "arms" – or weapons – for the purpose of protection. In essence, if you are being prevented from accessing the tools needed to protect yourself effectively, your ability to defend yourself – and by extension your right to life – is being compromised.

Right to Liberty

The right to liberty is another essential natural right that stems from the right to life. Also sometimes described as the right to self-determination, this natural right can be presented in the following way:

- Every individual has an inherent right to make their own choices, free from the arbitrary and coercive interference of other people or authority.

This argument for this natural right is based on the recognition of people's natural capacity for independent thought, personal judgement, and the ability to form and pursue their own personal preferences. In essence, the right to liberty ensures that individuals are able to exercise their natural abilities by making choices and taking responsibility for their actions – allowing for peaceful and prosperous cooperation.

It should be noted, however, that the right to liberty does not mean you can do whatever you want – there are inherent limitations when it comes to interactions with other people. A popular phrase that is used to present the idea is "your rights end where mine begin," which stresses that everyone's rights must be respected – not just your own.

The requirement to respect the rights of others can also be examined through the lens of Kant's work on the categorical imperative. Basically, if there is a universal principle that every person has the right to liberty, infringing on the liberty of others presents a contradiction of the principle, leading to the violation being judged immoral.

Right to Property

One of the more complex natural rights that is widely accepted by theorists is the individual right to property. Even though property ownership is a key part of almost every variation of natural law, there are some important differences in the approaches of different theorists. The general argument for the right to property that is accepted by natural law theories can be defined as follows:

- Every individual has the right of self-ownership, and as an extension, has a right to their own bodies and the product of their labour.
- Labour that has been applied to resources to produce goods or cultivate resources, results in ownership of those resources (known as Locke's *labour theory of property*).
- Since ownership is predicated on the application of labour and self-ownership, violations of property rights are equivalent to a violation of individual autonomy.

One of the major differences between the natural law theories of traditional thinkers compared to the anarchists is their approach to the topic of land ownership. Most natural law theorists hold the traditional beliefs that land can be bought, sold, used, and owned with very few limitations.

In contrast, many flavours of anarchism draw a distinction between personal property and private property, that is, property either for personal use or the result of direct labour versus property exclusively owned or controlled by someone for profit. An example of this can be seen in Proudhon's and Tucker's works, where they argued that people have a right to the results of their labour and to occupy the land that they are actively using, but not absolute ownership.

Freedom of Conscience and Expression

Another widely recognized natural right is the right to hold and express beliefs without interference or coercion – also referred to as freedom of conscience. On closer inspection this right is more extensive than it sounds and implies several other rights that are sometimes discussed independently, including freedom of speech, freedom of religion, freedom of politics, and the freedom to follow moral convictions. One of the most common arguments for freedom of conscience is as follows:

- Human beings possess the natural capacity for rational thought and moral reasoning, both of which are necessary for exercising personal liberty.
- The process of critical reasoning requires the freedom to consider, believe, and debate different ideas without coercion or persecution.
- Therefore, every person has the right to form, hold, and express their beliefs, as an extension of their right to self-determination.

This argument demonstrates the idea that human beings must be able to form and debate their own beliefs in order to fully realize their ability to determine the course of their own lives. In some ways this right can be considered an intellectual version of self-determination, where individuals can form and then make choices based on their own personal interpretations of the world.

When you break them down, the other rights we mentioned that arise from this principle – like freedom of speech and religion – are just different ways of saying the same thing. Ultimately, they all result in the tolerance of different opinions, religions, political ideas, cultural values, and personal moral codes.

Freedom of Association

Built on other rights, freedom of association refers to the natural right to associate with other people, including through forming or joining groups and communities. The argument for this natural freedom is as follows:

- A fundamental aspect of human interaction is the natural ability to form social bonds and relationships with others who share similar beliefs, interests, or values.
- By restricting people's ability to form associations with others of their choice, individuals are not able to reach their potential for peaceful and prosperous cooperation.
- Therefore, every individual has the right to form relationships with whomever they choose as an expression of their social human nature.

Even though the right to freedom of association is also covered – to some extent – by the right to liberty and the right to freedom of conscience, it also has a separate foundation in human nature and natural law. While some of the other rights serve to protect individuals from coercion and aggression within society, the right to freedom of association is crucial for the formation and maintenance of a natural peaceful society in the first place.

Right to Family and Procreation

One of the most straightforward natural rights is the right to family and procreation. This right is derived from the natural drive of all living mammals – including human beings – to reproduce and care for their young. An argument for this right is as follows:

- Reproductive instincts and the formation of personal relationships are an inherent part of human nature and are a fundamental aspect of human existence.
- The right to protect and raise one's children is a biological imperative, a natural instinct that ensures the child's protection, survival, development, and adoption of moral values.
- The formation of familial relationships and procreation as a result of these natural instincts are necessary for both social stability, personal fulfilment, and the continuation of the species.
- Therefore, individuals have a natural right to form families, procreate, and raise their children without interference.

By default, the right to protect family and children also extends to protecting their natural rights, not only physical safeguarding. These rights recognize the innate biological drives and behaviours that are a fundamental part of human nature and continued existence, actions that are often vital for personal fulfilment.

Right to Equal Treatment

The right to equal treatment is a natural right that identifies the need for equal and consistent application of laws and rules to all individuals. The right can be summarized in the following way.

- All individuals – regardless of their personal characteristics or circumstances – should be treated fairly and without discrimination, receiving the same rights and protections under the law.

This right is grounded in the idea that discrimination reduces social cohesion and stability, and that fair and equal treatment under the law is the basis for trust and cooperation between individuals in society. From the perspective of Locke's social contract, the legitimacy of authority depends on the protection of all rights, especially fair and just treatment. In effect, discrimination leads to the erosion of the natural social order and invalidates the legitimacy of the governing authority.

5

Notes on Natural Law

Like any other philosophy, the adoption of natural law views can result in expectations, implications, or relationships with other ideas that might not be immediately obvious or widely noticed. With natural law, several of these are worth looking at more closely to clarify some common misconceptions.

Many of these misconceptions are related to the modern blurring of lines between natural law theory and utilitarianism – particularly the work of John Stuart Mill. Alongside the shift towards popular acceptance of some concepts of natural law, arguments have begun to appear in society that are based on incomplete or mutated ideas of liberty, authority, and the sources of individual rights.

In addition, we will highlight natural law's unique compatibility with other belief systems, as well as the popular overlap between natural law theory and certain schools of economics. With that in mind, we can start by looking at how natural law can work together with other systems of moral guidance.

Supplementing Moral Beliefs

One of the unique aspects of natural law compared to other ethical theories is that it provides a baseline for moral action that can be combined with other cultural, religious, or personal values. Since natural law is primarily put into practice through the recognition and protection of natural rights, it is – in many ways – less prescriptive than ethical systems like utilitarianism which demand action. Instead, it simply focuses on preventing violations of individual rights.

For example, if you are considering which of several charities to donate money to, utilitarianism will provide active guidance by requiring that you evaluate potential outcomes and choose based on predictions of positive impact. Natural law, on the other hand, isn't as helpful at providing explicit guidance when making moral decisions that don't involve natural rights.

Although at first glance this seems to be a flaw in natural law as a practical moral framework, as both Locke and Grotius point out, this is actually a feature of the theory, not a bug. By providing a universal set of moral rules that govern human interaction, natural law can be combined with other prescriptive systems as long as they don't violate the basic principles of natural rights.

This method of combining moral systems was discussed by Aquinas in his argument for the hierarchy of law, where he argues that human laws can promote virtue and justice, as long as they don't conflict with natural law. In practice, these other types of moral guidance can take the form of religious, cultural, political, or personal moral frameworks. In fact, you could even use some utilitarian-type calculations as a secondary prescriptive moral system, as long as you first and foremost respect the natural rights of individuals.

Natural Law and Economics

As we've touched on already, the tug-of-war between utilitarianism and natural law often takes opposite approaches to moral judgement, not only theoretically but in practice. Natural law aims to pretty clearly define and protect individual rights from injustice and coercion but doesn't really concern itself with trying to calculate outcomes and proactively solve social problems. Utilitarianism, on the other hand, is proactive, and at its core contains the belief that inaction is immoral and that we all have a moral obligation to make decisions that improve society overall.

The result of these most basic concepts is that utilitarianism tends to trend towards larger forms of authority that have power and mandates to solve problems, balance social outcomes, and ultimately increase social utility. Even though there is a lot of complexity hidden behind this simplified statement, we can see the empirical result of this relationship every time a government expands its scope to try and solve problems in a new industry.

As a result of this continuous expansion, the primary method of implementing new utilitarian decisions is through new control, oversight, and economic intervention in markets. These techniques usually take the form of new regulations, requirements for businesses, or new forms of tax incentives designed to influence behaviour towards the desired outcomes. These market interventions and the incentives that they generate are one of the main reasons many economists from different schools of economics are often among the primary critics of large, centralized government decision-making, whether it is in the form of collectivist or utilitarian intentions. For that reason, some of the quotes in this book that have been used to convey ideas or principles of natural law are from economists like Milton Friedman, Frédéric Bastiat, Ludwig Von Mises, and more.

However, since the goal of this book is not economic analysis of policy but instead an exploration of moral philosophy, in further sections we are going to try to sidestep the economic analysis as best we can – leaving economic topics to the experts. That being said, many of the arguments we will look at later on are presented by these economists, and if you are interested in further reading, I highly recommend their respective works.

Natural Rights vs. Human Rights

Misconceptions about natural rights and modern concepts of human rights have grown dramatically in recent times. The concept of a "right" has shifted in the cultural sphere to capture two unique sets of ideas, *rights* based on natural law's idea of inherent human nature, and *rights* based on John Stuart Mill's utilitarian idea of optimal outcomes.

Although we will go into this in more detail later in the book, natural rights – sometimes referred to as *negative rights* – are centred around the idea that there are things that cannot be done legitimately to a person by virtue of their humanity. Examples of these that we covered above include infringements on life, liberty, property, family, and others.

Modern human rights, although they sometimes contain natural rights, are largely defined by ideas of what would make the human experience fair or would maximize social well-being. One of the most prominent areas of confusion is the modern human rights' inclusion of entitlements – sometimes known as *positive rights* – which effectively define an obligation for authority to ensure that individuals have access to certain goods or services. Through the mixed use of the term *right*, these concepts have become somewhat blurred – treating the right to life or the right to freedom of speech in the same way that one would treat a right to clean water or a right to access affordable housing.

Although utilitarianism may incorporate natural rights, these rights do not hold the same level of significance from a utilitarian perspective as they would under natural law. Natural law theory asserts that these rights are absolute and inviolable because they are derived from nature, whereas utilitarianism values these rights for their outcomes and the social benefits that they bring.

In other words, while natural rights' focus on *means* (action) instead of *ends* (outcomes), positive rights are the opposite, defining conditions that are believed to result in the best *ends* for society to achieve successful outcomes and to live secure and fulfilling lives. Since these utilitarian "rights" are subject to context and situation like any other utilitarian calculation, they have continued to grow and change over time, including the right to access healthcare, adequate food, free education, protection from unemployment, clothing, housing, protection from disability, access to cultural goods, paid leave, clean water, and others.

In the end, when considering an idea such as "freedom of speech" as a right, even though both natural law and utilitarianism each consider it to be a right, the implications are vastly different. Natural law believes it to be uncompromisable and absolute, whereas the utilitarian perspective is that the right is valuable for its outcomes, and the "right" may be modified as needed, depending on context and expected outcomes.

Rights vs. Privileges

Another misconception that is likely tied to the migration from natural rights to modern mixed rights is the belief that all rights – just like entitlements – are privileges to be granted by authority. With the rise of government services under the banner of human rights, it has become a popular belief that these natural rights and entitlements are equivalent in all respects, and that they may be granted, modified, or removed depending on context.

The principles of natural law define individual rights to be a reflection of the state of human nature, and as such are not subject to the moods of authority. While governments can choose not to respect individual rights, as is common in many countries around the world, the existence of these inherent rights does not change. This distinction is reflected in the following quote by Thomas Jefferson from 1774.

> *A free people [claim] their rights, as derived from the laws of nature, and not as a gift of their chief magistrate.*

Individuals vs. Authority

Largely related to the same shift between natural rights and modern human rights that include entitlements, there is often a misconception between interactions involving authority and private individuals, and their respective roles in respecting or providing these rights.

Over the past decade, an increasingly common example can be seen in discussions involving freedom of expression and online censorship, as well as the role of private institutions in controlling speech. The natural right to freedom of speech was identified and recognized in order to prevent authority from suppressing individual's rights to hold beliefs and to advocate for those beliefs, no matter how unpopular.

In contrast with this natural right, one of the modern rights defined in the Universal Declaration of Human Rights states that "Everyone has the right freely to participate in the cultural life of the community" (Article 27 (1)). With the rise and prevalence of private online platforms on which to share thoughts and engage with other members of the public, the crossover between freedom of expression and the right to participate in cultural life has been interpreted as a right to access private forums without restriction.

This is especially true from the utilitarian perspective, where the right is defined by the desired goal – in this case, access to cultural participation. So if an individual must be able to participate in "cultural life," then by not providing access to a private platform where cultural discussion takes place, their rights can be said to be violated.

From the perspective of natural law, this utilitarian right conflicts with natural law rights. By being legally required to provide access to everyone, the property – or online forum in this case – owner is being stripped of their rights of both freedom of association and their right to manage their property as they wish. The same conflict extends to other entitlements, where being *required* to provide goods or services may satisfy utilitarian rights but would violate the right to property, liberty, et cetera.

That being said, even though proponents of natural law would generally argue that these services are outside the scope of authority in the first place, once they are enacted, natural law applies differently to the government than it would to individuals. For example, the right to equal treatment under the law, freedom of conscience, and other rights would necessitate that an online forum provided by the government – which is a body that does not have individual rights – could not discriminate against individuals.

Although in the example of a government provided forum both natural law and utilitarianism would lead to required access for every individual, the reasons for doing so would be different. Utilitarianism would be unable to restrict people's access to the services because it views the service as a right for all people, and natural law would be unable to restrict people's access because that would violate their right to equal treatment by authority.

Expansion of "Harm"

Both natural law and utilitarianism have at times shared similar approaches to reconciling conflicts at the intersection of different rights. An example of this can be seen with the right to liberty and the implications of effects on others. Although you cannot be legitimately prevented from exercising your liberty to live your life as you wish, that does not extend to freedom to violate the natural rights of others. This idea, as we touched on in the earlier chapter on natural rights, is often expressed in the following form:

> *Your rights end where mine begin.*

This neatly sums up the principle of how universal respect for your rights requires the respect of natural rights for others. A similar idea was also developed in parallel by utilitarian John Stuart Mill with his *harm principle*.

In effect, Mill declared that the only reason to limit rights is to prevent harm to others.

In modern contexts, this idea of "harm" has begun to expand in several ways, incorporating types of distress that are not based on natural rights. A modern example of this is visible in utilitarian restrictions on the natural right to freedom of expression. In essence, proponents of these restrictions often argue that it is not the explicit action of speech, but instead the consequences of the words that should be evaluated. With strong parallels to blasphemy laws throughout history, these beliefs claim that the expression of certain views has the potential to cause both non-physical and indirect harm – like influencing others to violence – and should be restricted.

It is worth highlighting the distinction between action and consequence in terms of speech because the action of offensive speech itself is not a violation of natural rights. Speech itself is offensive in its receipt, and its consequence is an entirely subjective experience, as two people can hear the same words and be affected differently. Because of this, through the lens of natural law speech itself is inherently inert, contrasted with the consequentialist focus on the result, which includes the offence taken.

Once it has been argued that speech results in harm, it is a simple jump to declare that restrictions of rights to speech are acceptable, or even necessary, in order to reduce the harm done to recipients. The widespread acceptance of this expanded principle of harm has led to limitations on the natural right to freedom of expression in most Western nations, including Canada, the United Kingdom, Germany, France, Sweden, Australia, and many more. Although these countries often focus on speech that incites hatred or violence towards specific minority groups, some countries – like the UK – have greatly expanded laws restricting speech even further.

In the Public Order Act of 1986, general language that can be considered abusive or threatening, as well as speech likely to cause "harassment, alarm, or distress" became a crime. A further law passed in the UK in 2003, the Communications Act, made it an offence to use the internet in order to send a message considered "grossly offensive or of an indecent, obscene or menacing character."

In the modern age, discussions around freedom of speech and its restrictions are common, and as natural rights are blended with more utilitarian forms of rights, concepts around how to deal with these conflicts have blurred. Although from the utilitarian point of view these laws are coherent, they directly violate the natural rights to freedom of expression, liberty, and others, in order to protect people from versions of harm that include subjective reactions and their consequences.

Action vs. Inaction

Another one of the major points of contention between utilitarianism and natural law is John Stuart Mill's utilitarian belief that inaction is equivalent to action. In other words, if you do *not* act to help someone, that is no different from you actively hurting them. This view has grown in popularity alongside the rise of utilitarian thinking in progressive movements and can be seen expressed through slogans such as "Silence is Violence" and "Silence equals Genocide."

From a certain perspective, namely looking at the world through the lens of outcomes, a utilitarian argument begins to arise. Out of the full array of potential decisions, choosing to do nothing may have a greater likelihood of negative outcomes. For example, if you see a robber who is about to assault an innocent person, you have the choice to either intervene or not. If you choose to intervene, it may result in an outcome where the robber is scared away. However, if you do not act, the violent act is sure to happen, and the outcome will be negative.

Since utilitarianism is entirely focused on outcomes, the claim that doing nothing guarantees a negative outcome in that situation is true. However, the claims that inaction is equivalent to direct participation confounds the responsibility for the negative outcome, unreasonably transferring culpability to observers instead of the actor themselves. This line of reasoning also implies an unsustainable level of responsibility for all members of society to solve every potential issue that could arise.

    For example, does every person share responsibility for every negative action that is done by another person if there is the smallest potential it could have been prevented? Should we each become a Batman-esque vigilante in order to prevent as much crime as possible? How much am I morally required to sacrifice to prevent – or even reduce – negative outcomes? My health, my financial security, my personal safety, my life? And finally, if I am responsible for outcomes within my control, am I morally required to interfere with the self-destructive activities of others, such as gambling, smoking, or potentially even alcohol consumption?

    From the natural law standpoint, each of these questions makes demands that directly contradict both human nature and the ideas of self-preservation and self-determination. For that reason, among others, no such requirement for action or responsibility for inaction exists. The theory leans heavily on the belief that we are each responsible for our own decisions, and that in the situation presented above, the robber is the only one culpable.

That being said, some natural law thinkers – especially anarchists like Spooner– believed that individuals have a duty to protect the natural rights of others, or at least ensure that justice is upheld. This anarchist view still doesn't apply requirements or assign equivalent blame to both action and inaction but asserts that we *should* intervene in the situation above to prevent a violation of rights.

6

Ethics & Justice

Another significant difference between the two theories is their approaches to legal justice. This idea of ethical justice outlines how the systems direct society in responding to violations of the law, which in the case of natural law is rights violations, and in the case of utilitarianism is rules determined to maximize well-being.

As you can imagine, given the concepts we looked at above, utilitarianism and natural law both share some common ideas of justice and have some radical differences. For example, both systems stress the importance of impartiality and proportionality, although the idea of proportional justice is less absolute under utilitarian principles. Even though concepts of justice under natural law are more clearly defined and reactions to specific situations are more straightforward, utilitarian justice is heavily dependent on both the current context and the expected outcome of legal action.

Over this next chapter, we will touch on some of the core components of justice under both systems, as well as examples of these ideas in practice. With that, let's begin with a look into utilitarianism and justice.

Utilitarian Justice

Given utilitarianism's core focus on maximizing positive outcomes, the implementation of law and justice under a utilitarian moral framework depends a lot more on the specific situation than other moral systems. With many different thinkers like Beccaria and Bentham contributing ideas on justice to the theory, there is no "one-size-fits-all" approach, as long as each response is believed to lead to the best result.

For the most part, in order to gain consistency and social stability, utilitarian justice commonly follows the patterns of rule utilitarianism, however the use of situational judgements is still quite common. Judges, prosecutors, and other members of the justice system are able – and often expected – to diverge from the rules when it is believed it will result in positive outcomes in a particular circumstance. This could include flexibility in choosing punishments, allowing deals, or otherwise applying unequal judgement.

The utilitarian focus on consequences is also reflected in the utilitarian preference towards rehabilitation instead of restitution or punishment. The idea makes sense if you want to reduce recidivism and overall crime, a clear net benefit from a utilitarian social perspective. Successful rehabilitation without a doubt allows for reductions in the cost of the justice system and an increase in social harmony. That being said, utilitarian punishment has its place in some situations, especially as a deterrent, in order to reduce vigilantism, and even to bring closure to victims.

Restitution is also used in a utilitarian system of justice to provide compensation to victims, as a form of harm reduction, and a way to increase social stability. The balance between these methods of justice effectively boils down to utilitarian calculations, aiming to maximize social well-being through the careful and balanced application of these different tools.

Although Beccaria's work stressed the importance of proportionality, it is a principle that is of mixed value under utilitarian justice systems. While overall, "having the punishment fit the crime" is an important principle that brings benefits like social stability and predictability, there are strong utilitarian arguments for disproportionate punishments in some instances. These situations could include attempts to proactively deter certain behaviours or as a signal to the population highlighting the social priorities of the current authority. An example of common disproportionate punishment is the application of fines for violations of copyright law, where penalties can often be severe for downloading a song or a movie that would cost dollars to purchase legally.

Aside from variety in the severity of punishments, other forms of utilitarian justice are equally subject to situational judgements. These can include lighter sentences for people whose value to society is believed to be higher than others, or even stronger punishments for individuals who are prone to repeat offences – or whose motivations were decided to be less noble.

An example of preferential treatment based on perceived social value is the case of Dr. Amy Bishop, a neuroscientist and professor at the University of Alabama. In 2010, Bishop shot six colleagues during a faculty meeting, killing three people. After the shooting, it was revealed that earlier in 1986, Bishop had shot and killed her brother in what was – questionably – ruled an accident at their home. Although she had been briefly held by police, she was released without charges – a move attributed to her family's standing in the community and to her potential as a promising scientist.

Considerations of a crime's context is inherently more common in utilitarian judgements, since it has a greater impact on the outcomes that result from judgement. For example, unlike morally absolute judgements that would treat all murders the same way, the utilitarian evaluation of motivations or intent have led to distinctions between different "degrees" of murder. An individual whose actions accidentally result in the death of another person is treated differently than someone who commits a crime of passion, who is treated differently from the perpetrator of a premeditated murder. These considerations of context can also take into account the background of the offender, including criminal history, mental health issues, and histories of abuse, as well as potential for rehabilitation, and more.

In an attempt to keep judgements more consistent and reduce the subjectivity of the process, many Western systems of justice have implemented tools like mandatory minimum sentences. These guidelines define minimum sentences that should be applied to different types and categories of crimes, an attempt to prevent preferential justice towards different groups. Unfortunately, the complexity of the legal system and the flexibility of prosecution still allows the use of influence and wealth to circumvent mandatory minimums in other ways, such as plea deals, deferred prosecution agreements, and others.

All of these considerations ultimately result in a subjective system of justice when following utilitarian principles, where similar crimes can receive widely different punishments, sometimes biased towards individuals who are able to afford top-tier legal professionals. These differences can be seen when comparing the cases of Timothy Jackson and Jordan Belfort.

In 1996, an African-American man named Timothy Jackson walked out of a store without paying for a jacket worth $159. After realizing he was being followed by a security guard, he put down the jacket outside, but was eventually caught by police. Using a past crime from when he was 17 and two other previous non-violent criminal incidents, he was treated as a habitual criminal and sentenced to life in prison.

In contrast, in 2003 Jordan Belfort – founder of Stratton Oakmont – was sentenced to four years in prison for securities fraud and money laundering for defrauding investors out of more than $200 million. Despite the size of the theft and the number of people affected, Belfort only served 22 months in prison before his sentence was reduced via a plea agreement and he was released.

These two examples illustrate how difficult it can be to reconcile the maximization of social welfare with the consistent application of justice and equality under utilitarian systems, a balance between the greatest good in a particular circumstance and the greatest good of long-term social stability.

Natural Law Justice

While consistency was greater between natural law theorists when it came to the formulation and arguments for natural rights, approaches to handling violations of the rights weren't covered by every theorist. Many of the thinkers who approached natural law from the perspective of legality and justice, such as Aquinas, Locke, Grotius, and Spooner, developed ideas on how to manage violations, including thoughts on the use of both restitution and punishment.

Locke believed that even though individuals had the right to enforce the laws of nature on their own, it could lead to chaos and vigilantism. He advocated for the use of common laws and an impartial government formed by the people that would enforce those laws – the purpose of the social contract. Lysander Spooner, on the other hand, was sceptical about centralized authority's ability to effectively defend natural rights, instead believing that juries should have the final say in determining justice.

Unlike the utilitarian approach to justice where the actions are focused on maximizing potential outcomes, natural justice is entirely reactive, responding to violations of individual rights. In essence, this means that some methods of utilitarian justice, like pre-emptive punishments, are incompatible with natural law. Let's take a look at some of these core principles in more detail, including restitution, retribution, as well as other aspects associated with justice like proportional judgement and due process.

Restitution

Many natural law theorists, including Aquinas, Locke, and Spooner, argued that the most important goal when handling a violation of natural rights is to provide restitution to the victim. This means restoring the victim to as close to their original state – from before the violation occurred – as possible.

An example of restitution in action might be to return stolen or damaged property to the victim in order to make them whole, or possibly to seek repayment from the aggressor for the lost property or financial damage. Some of the debated implications of this principle include considerations about how to handle damage that cannot be restored, such as injuries that prevent someone from full-time employment, etc.

Retribution

Even though restitution is the primary goal of natural justice, many natural law thinkers also support the idea of retribution – or punishment – as a way of both deterring future offences and also as a way of restoring social and natural order. The importance of punishment as a tool of justice is especially common in situations where violations of rights can't be easily undone, or restitution is considered insufficient.

In these situations, punishment acts as a secondary objective, usually in order to provide closure and satisfaction to the victim. An example of the use of punishment instead of restitution would be as a response to murder, a situation where restitution is impossible. In these instances, while restitution could be paid to the victim's family, the victims themselves are beyond repair. While capital punishment is a highly contested idea by natural law theorists, there are arguments for the judgement in some extreme cases.

Proportionality

Proportional justice is one of the most important principles of natural law theory, suggesting that punishment for any violation of rights should be relative to the severity of the offence. The idea of a balanced response applies to both punishment and compensation; this was a key piece of the writings of many different theorists, including Aquinas, Locke, and others. The first instance of references to this concept in natural law can be traced back to Aristotle's *Nicomachean Ethics*, and it has since been expanded to focus on upholding fair and equal treatment under the law as the basis for social trust and stability.

For example, the principle of proportionality would mean that a minor offence like theft shouldn't earn a severe punishment like life in prison, and major crimes like murder shouldn't result in a small fine or slap on the wrist.

Due Process

The idea of due process is another fundamental principle of natural law theory. It refers to the legal requirement that every person is entitled to fair treatment and should have the opportunity for impartial judgement after they've been accused. Due process has its roots in natural rights, inherent human dignity, and the idea that an individual's rights cannot be arbitrarily taken away without some sort of fair evaluation.

Locke's work in his *Second Treatise of Government* covered the idea of due process in detail, arguing that no one could be deprived of their natural rights without due process of law, which he defined as a process that was fair, impartial, and properly administered. In his view this was one of the legitimate roles of the state and a driving force behind the social contract.

Protection of the Vulnerable

Another aspect of justice in the context of natural law is the existence of mechanisms that can protect vulnerable members of society and ensure their rights are also enforced. While there is some disagreement on the exact ways that society can or should protect these rights, the belief that they should be protected is widespread among natural law theorists.

One of the motivating factors behind John Locke's idea of the social contract is that by delegating the enforcement of natural rights to legitimate authority, the rights of every member of society can be protected. Spooner, on the other hand, believed that anyone who saw injustice had a duty to help correct it as part of ensuring natural justice – after all, if you don't protect the rights of others in society, your rights aren't protected either.

On a personal level, Locke also made the argument that parents have a natural duty to care for and protect their children, who are unable to protect their own rights. Some examples of this principle can be seen in society today, including child protection laws, as well as the U.N.'s Convention on the Rights of the Child, an international treaty that lays out a specific list of rights that children should have – an attempt to protect against abuse, neglect, and other types of harm.

7

Putting the Theories to the Test

One of the major differences between natural law and utilitarian systems is the requirement for action. As Mill pointed out, utilitarianism requires you to act in the way that has the greatest utility, whereas natural law doesn't require action, but instead restricts actions that violate the rights of others.

And although consequentialism and its variations are able to more flexibly choose solutions as long as they prioritize moral outcomes, we will see how natural law is morally absolute, preventing actions that violate the rights of others *no matter what*. Even though flexibility in potential decisions is reduced, in many ways this makes identifying moral decisions a lot easier. Since it doesn't require any calculations or estimation of possible outcomes, decisions can be made with the information available in the present situation, as well as by looking at the action's direct impacts on the natural rights of others.

Since both of our primary theories and each of the utilitarian variants often respond in different ways across a range of situations, let's start by going back to the trolley problem that we encountered at the beginning of the book, before moving on to new moral dilemmas.

Basic Trolley Problem

A runaway trolley is speeding towards five people who are tied to the track. You can pull a level to change the trolley to a different track, where one person is tied. How would you make a decision using the different flavours of utilitarianism?

Act Utilitarians: You would pull the lever, because saving five people outweighs the life of one when calculating "net utility."

Rule Utilitarians: It depends on the moral rules in place, but you would most likely choose to minimize the loss of life and pull the lever.

Preference Utilitarians: As a preference utilitarian, you would most likely assume that the preferences of the people are similar, and that the preferences of five people to live is stronger than that of one person, and therefore you would pull the lever.

Negative Utilitarians: You would pull the lever since the suffering of one person is less than the suffering of five.

As you would expect, in this straightforward example most utilitarians would choose to pull the lever and save the five people, each judging the decision as moral using different criteria. But what if you were subscribed to natural law?

Natural Law Theorists: Since natural law recognizes every person's right to life, you would choose not to take action, knowing that by flipping the level, it would directly result in the death of a person.

In this simple trolley problem example, the unfortunate outcome of your inaction would be the death of five people. However, natural law's absolute requirement to respect the one individual's right to life would prohibit any action that results in the death of an innocent person – no matter the cost.

Doctor Dilemma

Our next example is a darker twist on the trolley problem. You are a doctor with five patients who need organ transplants to survive. A healthy person comes in for a normal checkup. You can kill the healthy person and distribute their organs in order to save your other five patients. As our variation-shifting utilitarian, what would you do?

>**Act Utilitarians**: By most utility calculations, the death of the one healthy person would be outweighed by the five lives that you could save. As the act utilitarian doctor, you would choose to kill the healthy patient to save the others.
>
>**Rule Utilitarians**: As always, it depends on the rules in place. However, there would likely be moral rules in place against taking an innocent life or violating a patient's trust, so you would probably decide not to kill the healthy person, even though five others would die.
>
>**Preference Utilitarians**: As a preference utilitarian, you would likely calculate that the preferences of the five people still outweigh the preference of the one to live and would kill the healthy person to save the others. Alternatively, you may calculate the preferences of society to have trusted medical care and choose against the organ harvest.
>
>**Negative Utilitarians**: On one hand, the negative outcome of one death is less than the negative calculation of five deaths, but on the other hand, you might calculate that the loss of trust in the medical profession might result in a more negative outcome over the long term. Depending on your personal judgement, you might make either decision.

Even though the other forms of utilitarians would probably still calculate the utility of organ redistribution to be greater than not taking an action, the results would likely be split. Natural law, however, would be very similar to the previous example.

> **Natural Law Theorists:** Since natural law recognizes every person's right to life, you would not choose to violate the healthy patient's natural rights, even to save others.

Killing an individual in order to save others would be a direct violation of the natural rights of the healthy patient, and no action would be taken.

Martyr Dilemma

Our next example is one where theory and practice could be difficult to reconcile. Let's imagine that you and nine other people are crossing a suspension bridge across a deep canyon when the bridge begins to buckle. Someone suggests that one person will have to throw themselves off the bridge in order to lighten the load and save the other nine, but no one else will do it. How would your theoretical utilitarian counterpart proceed?

> **Act Utilitarians:** You would jump. The loss of your life would be outweighed by the saving of nine other lives in a truly impartial calculation.

> **Rule Utilitarians:** Like most modern societies, there might be rules against suicide, believing that suicides lead to worse outcomes for society. As a rule utilitarian, you might be morally obligated to watch everyone fall to their deaths, even though the greatest good would not be served.

Preference Utilitarians: The preferences of the other nine people wanting to live would outweigh your preference, leading you to jump off the bridge.

Negative Utilitarians: The negative outcome of your death is outweighed by the outcome of all ten dying, so you would jump off the bridge.

Just like the rules in many modern societies, rule utilitarians might choose rules that try to prevent suicide, believing it leads to less happiness or well-being over the long term. Other forms of utilitarians would likely calculate that the negative impacts of one death are far outweighed by the negative outcomes of all ten people dying. But what about natural law theory, what action would it direct you to take?

Natural Law Theorists: Unlike utilitarianism, there is no requirement to maximize outcomes for natural law theorists and neither jumping nor staying on the bridge would violate the rights of others. Depending on your personal cultural, religious, or other values, you could choose to either sacrifice yourself or not, without violating natural law.

As you will notice, this example highlights the difference between utilitarianism and natural law's contrasting beliefs concerning the morality of action compared with inaction.

Hostage Crisis

Our next example looks at indirect consequences, and in this example a terrorist group has taken over a building and is holding ten people hostage. They are demanding that one of their more violent members is released from prison in exchange for letting the hostages go. As the lead decision-maker and utilitarian with many hats, what would you do?

Act Utilitarians: You would consider the long-term consequences of releasing the terrorist and weigh the potential future harm against the immediate harm to the innocent hostages. Your decision would depend on the context, and which outcome you believe would maximize overall happiness in the current situation.

Rule Utilitarians: As a rule utilitarian, you would probably not complete the exchange, since there would presumably be a rule in place prohibiting negotiating with terrorists, or there might even be a rule against enabling harm to society.

Preference Utilitarians: It could be difficult to balance the preferences of the hostages, who want to be released, against the preferences of society, who might prioritize keeping the terrorist locked up. In the end you would probably not release the terrorist, choosing society's preferences against those of the hostages.

Negative Utilitarians: You would calculate that the potential damage done by the released terrorist would be greater than the ten lives being held hostage and choose not to release the prisoner in exchange.

Overall, the result of this decision for most utilitarians would likely be to weigh the potential for future terrorism against the lives of the ten hostages, resulting in a decision not to release the hostages. But what about the natural law perspective?

> **Natural Law Theorists:** The principles of justice under natural law are as absolute as the natural rights that they safeguard, and compromising the concept of justice in order to maximize social well-being would not be a consideration. Likely as a natural law theorist, you would refuse to release the prisoner, despite the outcomes.

Although this situation was contrived in order to demonstrate a rather extreme example, there may be other situations where principles of natural law justify suspending justice based on proportionality and context.

Mass Surveillance

The next dilemma explores a situation where lives are up against the erosion of civil liberties. A serial killer has been terrorizing a city, killing one person every week for the past year. Police are proposing a mass surveillance program that would record the whereabouts and movements of all citizens in order to catch the killer and prevent future attacks. How would you proceed using different utilitarian approaches?

> **Act Utilitarians:** You would support the mass surveillance program if you believed that the overall happiness gained by saving lives and reducing fear outweighed the unhappiness caused by sacrificing people's right to privacy.

> **Rule Utilitarians:** You might oppose the surveillance program because it would most likely violate general rules on infringing the privacy rights of individuals. You could argue that a rule protecting privacy will lead to greater utility in the long term. Alternatively, you might choose to implement rules around tracking individuals, specifically in times of crises, allowing the program.

> **Preference Utilitarians:** As a preference utilitarian, you could attempt to measure public opinion and believe that the overall preference would be the moral course of action.
>
> **Negative Utilitarians:** You would attempt to calculate the negative impacts of surveillance and measure that against the negative impacts of both the people being killed and the fear being created. If you believed that the surveillance would cause less harm over time due to the prevention of crime and murder, the surveillance program would go ahead.

In this scenario, there is no common approach to the utilitarian calculation across the various forms of utilitarianism. Depending on which utilitarian version you subscribe to, the moral action – and by extension your decision – could be different. But how would you proceed as a natural law theorist?

> **Natural Law Theorists:** Since privacy is generally considered under the right to liberty, this mass surveillance program would be considered a violation of individual rights. As a natural law theorist, you would not implement this program.

Yet again, you can see how the respect for natural rights would prevent the policy from going ahead, regardless of the proposed benefits that these violations would bring.

Trespassing Trolley Problem

A runaway trolley is speeding towards five people who are tied to the track. You can pull a lever to change the trolley to a different track with no people, but it would require breaking through a fence and trespassing on another person's property. From the straightforward utilitarian standpoint, what would be the moral action?

> **Act Utilitarians**: As an act utilitarian, you would determine that the lives of five people would outweigh the damage to the owner's property.
>
> **Rule Utilitarians**: Even with rules against respecting property, utilitarian calculations would weigh the lives of the five people much higher than respect for the rule.
>
> **Preference Utilitarians**: As a preference utilitarian, you would acknowledge the preferences of the five individuals to live would outweigh the preferences of the property owner.
>
> **Negative Utilitarians**: The negative impact of five deaths would be greater than the impact of the property violation, and you would save the people.

In this example the utilitarian outcomes are pretty clear: Saving lives has much higher utility than respecting the individual's property rights. But what about natural law? How do property rights stack up against the lives of others?

> **Natural Law Theorists**: Even though an individual's property rights would be violated, the recognition of the people's right to life could prompt you to break into the property in order to save their lives. However, as a consequence of violating the owner's property rights you would be required to restore the fence and/or compensate the owner for damages caused. Natural law theory

could allow you to pull the lever, or at least vindicate you for doing so.

Although natural law would suggest you cannot violate the rights of the property owner, you may choose to do so at the cost of facing natural justice, that is, being required to provide compensation or face proportional punishment.

Suicide Dilemma

In our final example we will look at a situation where social norms potentially conflict with personal preferences. While walking across a bridge you come across a person who is about to jump off and end their own life. You have a chance to pull them back and stop them from committing suicide. How would you react as a utilitarian in this situation?

Act Utilitarians: The calculation might be complex, you could weigh the happiness of the person, the effects on their family, the social impact of suicide rates, and other considerations. In the end, you would likely choose to save them and provide them with mental health or other forms of assistance.

Rule Utilitarians: As with most societies, there would likely be rules against suicide that you would follow. You would probably choose to save their life.

Preference Utilitarians: You would attempt to account for the jumper's preferences. If you believed that the action was a cry for help, you could save them and provide further assistance. If you believed they truly wanted to jump, you would let them.

> **Negative Utilitarians:** You would calculate the negative impacts of the person's death against the negative impacts of violating their decision and would choose to save them.

Outside of preference utilitarianism, the calculations of utility would lead you to save the jumper, even against their wishes. But what would natural law suggest that you do in this situation?

> **Natural Law Theorists:** In this instance, you would recognize the individual's right to self-determination and self-ownership. Pulling them back would be in violation of both. You would let them jump.

The recognition of the bridge jumper's autonomy and right to control their own life would take precedence over your wishes to save them. While natural law would not prevent you from speaking with them and trying to convince them not to jump, you would be prohibited from physically restraining them from living – or dying – as they choose.

Different Approaches

Through this array of elaborate situations and trolley problems, we can begin to see how all of the concepts that we've been looking at start to fall into place. In these examples, we also gave each of the theories the benefit of the doubt – applying the theories according to their principles with the most complete information available. Of course, if we had access to more comprehensive information such as statistics, polling data, and historical examples, we may have chosen different outcomes on the utilitarian side, but otherwise these choices were accurate.

We can see that although each of the different systems and variations have their own unique ways of making decisions based on the situation at hand, general themes emerge. Utilitarianism and its variants examine the situation and attempt to evaluate which potential outcome would lead to the best results – whether they aim to maximize happiness, preferences, or harm reduction.

Natural law, on the other hand, effectively acts as a gatekeeper for validating moral decisions. When potential actions are available, instead of prescribing which option to take, it asks the question: *Does this action violate natural rights?* If the answer is yes, the actions are considered immoral and should not be taken, but otherwise the choice is yours.

8

Unravelling the Ideas

As we've seen so far, at its core, classical utilitarianism is centred around the idea of calculating the utility of decisions and actions, and trying to reach outcomes that generate the greatest happiness for the greatest number of people. Because utilitarianism is consequentialist in nature, it judges the morality of actions and decisions based on their outcomes, contrasting with other ethical systems that focus more on the morality of the actions themselves, or even the intentions behind the actions.

Criticisms and debate about the difficulty in consistently evaluating and choosing moral actions have led to variants of utilitarianism that try to resolve these challenges. As we explored earlier, both the act and rule variants of utilitarianism are focused on the method of choosing actions. The act variant carries with it the belief that each action should be judged for morality, while the rule variant offers the approach that actions should follow general rules that have been judged to be moral. The introduction of rule utilitarianism attempted to avoid challenges with counter-intuitive moral decisions, to reduce the difficulty of constant high-demand utility calculations, and to focus more on long-term outcomes through the promotion of consistent moral rules.

Preference and negative variants of utilitarianism were developed to change the way that utility itself is calculated. For example, the preference utilitarian argues that happiness is not the only thing that matters and that focusing on people's preferences allows utility to incorporate each person's diverse interests and values, making it inherently less subjective. The negative utilitarian believes that reduction of suffering is more important than maximizing happiness, in part because happiness is often harder to quantify, and suffering is easier to identify.

On the other hand, natural law is a restrictive system based on respecting the rights of people – rights believed to be an inherent part of human nature. Unlike the use of utility calculations in providing guidance in different circumstances, natural law simply requires that we avoid actions that violate these rights, whether that is the right to life, liberty, or freedom of conscience.

Many of these natural rights are also interconnected and related, or imply other protections – for example, the right to freedom of movement is generally accepted as an extension of the right to liberty. Many of these rights are still visible in modern contexts, whether through international treaties, founding documents, or the human rights charters of many nations.

A large portion of the rights that have been widely recognized over the past few centuries can be traced back to the ideas of John Locke during the Enlightenment. Even though we looked at these two theories in a series of hypothetical situations, there is a huge difference between theory and practice. In the next section of this book, we are going to explore the application of both systems in real-world situations, looking at how well the concepts translate to real decision-making.

PART III

ETHICS IN ACTION

1

Welcome to the Real World

Faced with a rising number of fatalities in traffic accidents linked to not wearing seat belts, dozens of U.S. states – beginning with New York – implemented mandatory seat belt laws in the 1980s. Adding to this, studies have shown that the chance of being fatally injured in a traffic accident is twice as likely when an individual is not wearing their seat belt. Considering the link between seatbelts and casualties, what effect would you expect these laws to have had on traffic deaths?

A) A decrease in fatalities
B) No change in fatalities
C) An increase in fatalities

In general, most of us would have said that A) seems obvious – if not wearing a seat belt leads to a higher risk of death in a collision, enforcing usage would reduce deaths. But in fact, we would have been wrong. Studies have shown that although enforcement increased seat belt adoption from around 14% in the 80s to over 90% in 2020, overall fatalities were unchanged. The legislation led to drivers feeling safer, resulting in an increase of reckless driving – balancing a slight decrease in motorist deaths with a slight increase in pedestrian and cyclist deaths.

The case of these seat belt laws gives us an interesting example of how difficult it can be to translate and apply theoretical principles to the real world. While the rationale behind the seat belt mandates made sense from utilitarianism's goal of decreasing harm, the surprising outcome left people scratching their heads and highlighted the unpredictable nature of action.

Over the first two parts of the book, we explored quite a bit about the history, the theory and the individuals who worked to help guide humans towards a more moral version of ourselves. Many of the basic ideas that make up both natural law and utilitarianism even showed up in different corners of the world, appearing in a diverse range of cultures, laws, and political structures from ancient Babylon to Mesoamerica.

Even though principles from both natural law and utilitarianism were often found together in these different cultures, at their core the theories are polar opposites. This conflict is based on the respective focuses of the two theories, with utilitarianism focusing purely on the ends – the consequences of the action, and natural law focusing completely on the means – the action itself.

We also looked at a few theoretical problems in order to help us understand the way that these two ethical theories guide decision-making. However, as the example above shows us, the bridge between theory and practice is not always simple to cross, especially when the utilitarian decisions depend so much on situational context. For these reasons, exploring the manifestation of theories in the real world can help us identify unexpected flaws and incorrect assumptions.

With that in mind, let's now take a look at a variety of real-world policies and laws inspired by each of the two theories, with a particular focus on how closely they align with their core principles. Our dive into utilitarian policies will explore how the intention of the policy lines up with the outcomes, the true test of any consequentialist system. In order to properly evaluate the policy's consequences in the context of their goals, we will break down our examples into four separate categories: policies with negative outcomes; policies with uncertain outcomes; policies with positive intended outcomes; and policies with positive unintended outcomes.

When reviewing the real-world impacts of natural law, we are going to take a slightly different approach. Since natural law mainly concerns itself with moral actions insofar as they align with respect for natural rights, looking at the consequences of policy doesn't make much sense. For this reason, we will explore natural law by looking at laws and civilizations throughout history that recognized – or at least aligned with – natural rights, effectively observing each moral framework on its own terms.

2

Utilitarianism in Practice

In practice, there is no shortage of policy examples that are based on utilitarian trade-offs and justifications. To balance out natural law's perspective that the government only exists to protect natural rights is the utilitarian argument that the government's sole purpose is to improve social well-being. In 1813, Robert Owen, the social reformer and founder of utopian socialism summed up this idea in the following statement, published in his work *A New View of Society*.

> The happiness of the human race in society is the end and object of all governments and legislation.

Aside from this aspirational view of government action, there are some other more grounded arguments that legislation is primarily a tool to achieve utilitarian outcomes.

One of the key arguments boils down to utilitarianism's proactive approach to solving problems, compared with natural law's main role of restricting action against individuals. Therefore, any policy aiming to increase the well-being of the population through the implementation of new rules, restrictions, fees and fines, or other interventions, can be considered inherently utilitarian – often conflicting with natural rights.

Even though this leads us to the conclusion that most policy is utilitarian and generally concerned with public outcomes, the checks and balances in the system, alongside the codification of these decisions, lean closer to "rule" utilitarianism than its "act" counterpart. This is especially true because of the rules that government action is bound to follow, including limitations on their power and reach in an effort to ensure long-term positive outcomes.

While the origins of these limitations in our modern society are definitively based on the principles and philosophies of natural law thinkers like Locke, they are certainly not absolute. Many countries have legal mechanisms in place that can be used to alter, remove, or bypass these restrictions under certain circumstances. In effect, these checks and balances are the realization of John Stuart Mill's belief that rights should be based on utilitarian calculations of what would achieve the greatest good instead of nature, and these rights should be the basis for rules in utilitarianism.

So if the vast majority of public policy can be considered utilitarian, where do we even start to look at policies that will illustrate the differences between theory and practice? What type of policy does it make sense to look at? Since utilitarianism evaluates morality based on the actual outcome of an action, this gives us three possible groups of policies that we can look at: positive outcomes, uncertain outcomes, and negative outcomes. However, since we can assume that policies are always intended to produce good results as Robert Owen suggested, we can break down the positive outcomes even further, into actions that had benefits that were intended and benefits that were unintended. Looking at these wide ranges of different intentions and outcomes will allow us to see the gaps in our theory and assess how consistent, effective, and reproducible the underlying ideas are.

Positive Intended Outcomes

As mentioned, most government policies that proactively aim to solve problems and improve well-being can be considered expressions of utilitarianism. With that in mind, the first group of policies that we are going to examine in this context are examples of actions that intended to improve outcomes or bring benefits to the wider population – and succeeded!

The other notable aspect of these real-world examples is that each of these policies involve trade-offs that can be considered significant – even a violation of natural rights. This context allows us to examine utilitarianism in its most effective form, a calculation that balances positive and negative outcomes in a way that intends to achieve the greatest possible end result. Keeping this context in mind, let's dive in!

The Cross Bronx Expressway

In the middle of the 20th century, New York City began development of the Cross Bronx Expressway, an eight-mile freeway that was designed to improve traffic flow and provide a critical traffic route across the Bronx, connecting the east of the city with the George Washington Bridge.

One of the major problems that the municipal government was faced with during planning was the large number of people living in the path of the proposed highway. In order to continue with the project, the state made the decision to invoke the power of eminent domain, allowing them to expropriate the private property they needed to complete the public infrastructure. Over the course of the project's development, more than 60,000 residents were displaced from homes and apartment buildings, which were then taken and demolished – decimating entire communities of people.

However, almost 70 years later the road is still proving invaluable, carrying more than 200,000 vehicles every single day and saving millions of hours of commute time every year[1]. These types of large infrastructure projects related to transportation, utilities, and even economic development around the world usually involve some level of eminent domain in their planning and execution.

The Cross Bronx Expressway and other large infrastructure projects that involve eminent domain are perfect examples of utilitarian ideals. The projects are based on the premise that the suffering and cost to people whose land is taken away is outweighed by the significant benefits the use of that land will bring to the public good. In the case of this project, even though the costs were high for the tens of thousands of people who were forced to relocate, by utilitarian standards the outcomes were unquestionably moral.

Australian Tobacco Tax of 2010

In 2010 the Australian Government established a 25% excise tax on all tobacco products, an attempt to tackle what they viewed as a public health crisis. The goal of the policy was simple: discourage smoking in order to combat lung cancer and heart disease, and to generate revenue to support the healthcare system.

Just like our other examples, this policy had some downsides. "Sin taxes" as they are often called, are well known to disproportionately impact low-income people, and this instance was no exception. According to a study conducted by Victoria University in Melbourne, people in the poorest parts of the country are seven times more likely to be smokers than people in high income areas[2].

Over the course of the next decade the tax had a major effect, leading to a decrease in the number of adults who smoked – from 18% of the population to under 13% – as well as contributing over $100 billion dollars in healthcare funding[3]. By utilitarian measurement, the tax was a resounding moral success, not to mention an incredibly effective policy. Even though the policy continues to be celebrated as a huge win by public health advocates, it does come at a cost to many members of society, particularly vulnerable communities who already struggle with addiction, poverty, and other social burdens.

National Minimum Wage Act

In 1998, the United Kingdom introduced the National Minimum Wage Act, providing for two different levels of minimum wages, one that applied to youth and trainees, another one for workers who were 22 years or older. In 2016 the law was further expanded, adding a new tier for those above the age of 23.

Minimum wage laws have been implemented in many different countries around the world and are often celebrated as successful examples of progressive policies. The laws are typically credited with a number of benefits, from helping to tackle income inequality by supplementing marginalized and low-income members of society, as well as driving economic growth as people have more disposable income.

Studies have shown that just as sin taxes affect low-income individuals more than others, minimum wage laws have the same effect. Every extra dollar earned in a low-income household has a greater economic impact than a dollar earned in a high-income household. Another common benefit attributed to minimum wage laws is that they aim to make sure that any individual engaged in full-time employment will be able to reach a decent standard of living.

However, in true utilitarian fashion, outside of natural law arguments related to authority and liberty, minimum wage laws also have some negative impacts that can be observed. Rising employee costs – just like any other form of cost increase – lead to increased prices for most goods and services that are affected, a phenomenon commonly labelled inflation. Since there is a wide range of costs that contribute to a price, the resulting increase from higher wages isn't one-to-one. For example, in the UK it was observed that a 10% increase in the minimum wage would result in a 1.1% increase in corresponding prices[4].

Aside from the direct cost and corresponding price increases, there are also secondary effects that impact consumers, employees, and businesses. Increases in staffing costs sometimes lead to employers trying to mitigate their costs in different ways, including limiting employee hours or benefits, or even – as studies showed after the implementation of the UK's laws – a reduction in the number of overall employees.

Just like a dollar taken from a low-income person hurts more than it would hurt a person who isn't as dependent on that dollar, small businesses are more impacted by price changes than bigger companies. Without being able to access the economies of scale that allow large corporations to reduce costs or increase margins, smaller companies are more likely to face negative consequences from any cost increases – including higher minimum wages. In some countries like the UK, these negative effects have led to the implementation of small business wage subsidy programs in order to prevent the disappearance of small businesses that cannot compete with rising costs.

Minimum wage policies have been – and continue to be – celebrated as successful policies, with supporters standing behind the utilitarian argument that the downsides of wage increases are far outweighed by the benefit they bring to vulnerable members of society.

Mandatory Smallpox Vaccination

At the dawn of the 20th century – between 1901 and 1903 – Massachusetts was faced with the outbreak of a major smallpox epidemic. In an attempt to combat the spread of the disease, the boards of health for both Boston and Cambridge ordered that every citizen was required to be vaccinated.

Understandably, the order faced quite a high level of resistance from some of the residents, most notably a man named Henning Jacobson. Jacobson fought against the mandate, eventually bringing his argument all the way to the Supreme Court in 1905, where the court finally ruled in a 7-2 decision that the state had the authority to require vaccinations during a public health crisis. This ruling set a precedent that is still being upheld and enforced over 100 years later.

Looking solely at outcomes, the policies were an incredible success, and as a result of vaccination campaigns and mandates across the U.S., the epidemic ended in 1903, and smallpox was ultimately declared eradicated by the World Health Assembly in 1980. In *Life and Death of Smallpox* published by Patrick Berche in *La Presse Médicale* in 2022, the death toll of smallpox during the 20th century alone was estimated to be between 300 and 500 million people[5]. In this situation, the good predicted by this utilitarian argument for eliminating smallpox is pretty self-evident.

However, just like the other utilitarian examples we've covered, vaccine mandates come with their own unique trade-offs. When he was a child, Henning Jacobson had been vaccinated against smallpox and had suffered an adverse reaction, one that – in his words – had caused "great and extreme suffering." Because of his own experience with the vaccine, he wasn't willing to risk his son having to go through the same experience. Even though vaccines are considered overwhelmingly safe, just like any other medical procedure there can be side-effects – like those experienced by Jacobson. In effect, this means that the use of mandates is likely to lead to a small number of people being forced to receive a vaccination that will result in physical harm, or even death.

From the perspective of natural rights, these mandates use coercion to remove a person's right not only to self-preservation but also to the individual right to self-ownership and autonomy. These policies effectively take away the individual's right to make their own medical decisions, in this case giving power to the same government that would go on to conduct the infamous Tuskegee Syphilis Experiment between 1932 and 1972. This was a study run by the U.S. Public Health Service and the CDC, which deceived, and even purposely withheld treatment from almost 400 African American men with the disease, a result which led to more than 125 deaths and numerous other infections[6].

From the utilitarian point of view, the case of mandatory smallpox vaccinations and the tangible benefits of eliminating the disease provide incredible utility, far outweighing the less tangible violations of natural rights.

Positive Unintended Outcomes

This second group of utilitarian policies focuses on a different type of results and outcomes. These examples look at policies that were – by utilitarian metrics – a resounding success, but for reasons that were different than predicted. These policies highlight the idea that by consequentialist standards, it really doesn't matter *why* you achieved your goal, what matters is the utility of the end result.

The other reason why the utilitarian moral judgement of these policies is interesting is that it demonstrates some of the concerns with the theory's core principles – namely the effect of luck on morality. It also allows us to consider how moral decision-making can be increasingly difficult when you are trying to predict consequences in complex situations. With that said, let's take a look at our first example.

The Clean Air Act of 1970

In 1970, President Richard Nixon signed the Clean Air Act (CAA) into law, a series of federal and state regulations that aimed to tackle the rapid rise in air pollution across the country. For years the quality of air in cities like Los Angeles had been getting worse and worse, and smog was becoming a common sight.

With a surge in environmental activism in the late 1960s, and more scientific research showing clear links between air pollution and health problems – including respiratory diseases and cancer – the government hoped to get pollution under control. One of the main impacts of the law was the creation of the Environmental Protection Agency – known as the EPA – that was empowered to enforce emissions standards.

In a nutshell, the policy achieved exactly what it was supposed to, with the EPA's *Report on the Environment* in 2020 showing that in the 50 years since implementation, emissions of the pollutants that were being tracked – namely lead, carbon monoxide, nitrogen dioxide, and sulphur dioxide – dropped by a staggering 77% overall[7]. In more practical terms, another EPA study in 2011 estimated that the legislation has prevented more than 230,000 deaths related to pollution over the same period[8].

Even though the Act's benefits were sizeable, there were also downsides. The regulatory and compliance costs of the CAA also had major cost impacts on utilities, refineries, and other businesses in the energy sector, most of which were passed on to consumers. An estimate from the EPA itself calculated that the direct costs of complying with the law would continue increasing, reaching at least $65 billion annually by 2020[9].

The negative economic consequences of the policy spread to other industries as well, primarily manufacturing. Many factories ended up moving their operations out of the country, effectively just shifting the negative environmental consequences to less fortunate countries, while eliminating a variety of high-paying jobs in the U.S.

Even though the legislation was effective, and the utilitarian calculations were already considered a success by policymakers, the Clean Air Act also resulted in other benefits that weren't originally anticipated. One of the specific pollutants that the Act was aiming to reduce was lead, which led to a drastic reduction in leaded fuel. This initiative led to a 98% reduction in lead concentration in the air between 1980 and 2014, which ultimately led to a reduction in levels of lead in the blood of children between one and five years of age[10]. Since then, lead exposure has been linked to direct impacts on academic performance, IQ levels, and even behaviour. A 2007 study by economist Jessica Wolpaw Reyes also suggested that the elimination of leaded gasoline was directly responsible for a 56% drop in violent crime in the United States across the 1990s[11].

As if these additional benefits weren't enough, the impact of reduced air pollution had a huge impact on the wider ecosystem, including crops and agriculture. Studies in different publications have shown that declines in sulphur dioxide and nitrogen oxides directly resulted in less acid rain and improved forest ecosystem recovery. One study from 2021 published by David B Lobell in *IOPscience* estimated that yields of corn and soybeans have increased up to 20% due to improvements in ozone levels[12], and that the extra yields o are valued at over $5 billion annually[13].

Even though both the expected benefits and downsides materialized, in the end, it was the unanticipated benefits of the Clean Air Act that truly dramatically changed the calculation of utility, some of which are still being identified today.

Legalization of Medical Marijuana

In 1996, California became the first U.S. state to legalize medical marijuana with the passage of Proposition 215. Also known as the Compassionate Use Act, the purpose of the legislation was first and foremost to make sure that Californians who were seriously ill had the right to buy, possess, and consume marijuana for medical reasons – verified by a doctor.

The law acknowledged marijuana's potential for therapeutic and medical treatments, including pain relief, the suppression of nausea, and its role in providing treatment for conditions like muscle contractions, glaucoma, and arthritis. It also intended to make sure that patients and doctors who were involved with the prescription of marijuana for medical reasons were not the subject of criminal action or prosecution, creating a safe and affordable supply for patients.

In the end, California's legalization of medical marijuana was successful in achieving its purpose, providing alternate methods of pain relief. According to a study in the *Journal of Pain*, the use of cannabis has been associated with a 64% reduction in opioid use for patients with chronic pain[14], and another small-scale 2000 study in the *Journal of Psychoactive Drugs* found that medical marijuana was often being used to treat symptoms for a variety of conditions including chronic pain, depression, migraines, and HIV/AIDS-related problems[15].

But as you can imagine, there were a variety of issues that appeared because of its implementation. The difference in marijuana's legal status in state and federal laws led to conflict and some pretty major complications for patients, businesses, and even investors. Even regionally within California, the fact that context of use implied different legal statuses led to increased costs and inconsistent policing from law enforcement, sometimes leading to harassment of individuals who were following the law.

The expected results of the policy were generally positive, but many of the most significant benefits were unintended by the original policymakers. For example, as a result of the effectiveness of pain relief from marijuana, a study published in 2018 in *JAMA Internal Medicine* found that states that had legalized usage for medical users saw a 5.88% reduction in opioid prescriptions[16]. These findings reinforced an earlier 2014 study in the same publication that showed a relation between the use of legalized marijuana and a reduction in opioid overdose deaths of 24.8% in the period between 1999 and 2010[17].

California's legislation also helped boost medical research in a wide range of fields, and recently cannabis – and its derivatives – have been found to treat rare forms of epilepsy, PTSD, anxiety, as well as neurodegenerative diseases like Parkinson's and Alzheimer's, Crohn's disease, and more.

This first step towards legalization in California set the stage for the eventual decriminalization of the drug on a recreational level, not only in the state but across many U.S. states. The policy also helped shift public opinion by reducing stigma and demonstrating medical benefits, setting legal precedents that would be used by other regions.

With decriminalization and legalization spreading to more states, law enforcement resources and priorities were shifted back to more serious offences, reducing imprisonment and costs on the justice system for non-violent crimes. California alone saw a 74% decrease in felony arrests for cannabis between 2016 and 2018, freeing up court, prison, and law enforcement resources, and saving many young people from prison sentences that would destroy their lives[18]. Not only that, but by providing legal ways for people to buy marijuana, illegal demand declined, reducing revenues and the influence of both national and foreign criminal organizations.

But the secondary benefits didn't stop there. Tax revenues from legal sales in California alone were reported at over $800 Million in just 2020, contributing new funding to social programs and health care across the state[19]. By 2021, it was estimated that over 300,000 full-time jobs had been created in the bustling legal cannabis industry.

In retrospect, the legalization of medical marijuana is a perfect example of a utilitarian policy that had unintended consequences that were much greater than the original goals of the legislation. From the initial goal of providing relief for patients with pain and treatment of some medical conditions, Proposition 215 has been an enormous success, creating an entirely new industry in the United States, alongside a wide range of other benefits – legal, medical, and economic.

Uncertain Outcomes

Our next group of policies are centred around outcomes that aren't immediately and obviously positive or negative. Sometimes even years later, the calculation of utility for these decisions doesn't produce simple or observable outcomes, often because of the wide range of different positive, negative, and mixed results – or even because of future uncertainty.

Like the previous category that looked at unintentional benefits, this group of policies also demonstrates the difficulty involved with both predicting and quantifying an action's wide-ranging effects and outcomes. Overall, the potential for ambiguous results highlights that there is often a wide gap between intentions, expectations, and consequences, a fact that we will see play out over these next few examples.

Food Safety Modernization Act

The Food Safety Modernization Act (FSMA) was a piece of federal legislation enacted in January of 2011 that focused on substantially expanding food safety regulations in the U.S. The primary goal of the legislation was controlling incidents of *E.coli* and *Salmonella* outbreaks that had been making thousands of people sick every year. This policy was presented as a new way to increase food safety, moving towards a more preventative approach instead of simply responding to contamination.

The regulations included many new standards that food processing facilities were required to comply with, as well as new rules for growing, harvesting, and distributing produce. These comprehensive and strict new rules also extended past food production, including certifications for consumable goods that were produced outside the U.S. and imported there. Policymakers were convinced that by enforcing a high level of care across the industry, illnesses caused by commercial foods would drop dramatically – or even be eliminated entirely. But these benefits never seemed to materialize.

Even 12 years after being signed into law, there has been very little data to support the regulation's effectiveness and quantifying the benefits of FSMA has been difficult. Since then, the expectations for compliance have been clarified and more thoroughly defined by regulators, and the policy did result in an increased ability to identify and trace pathogens through the supply chain. But ultimately, even though these improvements gave regulators more power to quickly enforce and respond to food concerns, the benefits have stayed mostly theoretical.

Statistics have shown that even with producers and facilities being required to implement a much higher standard when dealing with food production, cases of foodborne illness from *Shigella* and *Listeria* have only slightly declined – or remained stable – and cases of *E. coli* and *Salmonella* have been unaffected or have even increased. Like many of the other policies we've looked at, the cost of complying with the regulation has been criticized for its massively disproportionate effect on smaller producers, while the impact on large producers has been minimal[20]. The policy also had impacts on international trade – especially during and after COVID – including situations where shortages of a product in the U.S. couldn't be supplemented by foreign imports because of compliance issues.

In the end, many of FSMA's benefits have stayed purely theoretical, and the few that have materialized are centred around observability in the industry – a far cry from balancing the costs and negative effects on both small producers and consumers. Even more than a decade later, the evidence hasn't shown the legislation's effectiveness in either preventing or reducing cases of foodborne illnesses. The FSMA has continued to change and adapt as new issues and concerns arise, including new exemptions that try to offset the higher cost of the regulation on smaller producers, hoping to tip the scales more clearly towards an effective and undeniably positive utilitarian outcome.

NAFTA (North American Free Trade Agreement)

In 1994, the North American Free Trade Agreement – better known as NAFTA – was implemented. This agreement between Canada, Mexico, and the United States had the goal of removing trade barriers between the countries. Policymakers hoped to increase trade, investment, and economic growth across the continent in order to create more of a balance in trade between the three countries.

As expected by the respective governments, some of the predicted benefits came to fruition, with trade between the three countries more than tripling over the next twenty years. Consumers from across North America had access to lower prices on goods as import fees were reduced. Foreign investment also grew dramatically, particularly in Mexico, as new industries and jobs were created, and American and Canadian agricultural exports also increased, with brand new access to Mexican food markets.

However, not every effect of NAFTA was positive. Manufacturing industries in Canada and the U.S. faced massive job losses as factories relocated to Mexico, and the influx of the new agricultural goods from the U.S and Canada – many of which were subsidized – hurt small Mexican farmers who just couldn't compete. With Mexico's more lenient environmental regulations, industrial pollution and toxic emissions skyrocketed as many manufacturing plants relocated. On top of that, pollution from transporting goods long distances increased.

Even though the policy had lofty goals with clearly expected positive benefits, the utilitarian judgement of NAFTA's implementation is anything but clear-cut. The complex mixture of positives and negatives, along with the constantly unfolding long-term consequences make calculation of NAFTA's overall utility a difficult – or even impossible – task.

Affordable Care Act

The Affordable Care Act (ACA), commonly known as Obamacare in the United States, was a piece of legislation that resulted in a major regulatory overhaul of the U.S. healthcare system, signed into law in March of 2010. It included major changes to the existing system, such as mandates to make sure everyone was covered by insurance, expansions of eligibility for Medicaid, subsidies for low-income families, and the prohibition on denying insurance based on pre-existing conditions. By enforcing coverage, the law hoped to drastically reduce the number of uninsured Americans, while at the same time reducing costs for both individuals and the government. It was also expected that Obamacare would increase the quality and accessibility of services and address health disparities across different income and racial groups.

At first, the policy seemed like a major success, with the Department of Health and Human Services reporting the number of uninsured people dropping from 16% to 9% by 2015. Initial studies also showed that access to primary care and medication had improved, especially in states that had expanded Medicaid. It appeared to reduce premiums and out-of-pocket costs for many low and middle-income families, and the use of preventative care increased, with a study in the *New England Journal of Medicine* finding a related reduction in mortality rates[21].

However, not all of these benefits lasted. The overall size of the legislation came with a lot of complexity that resulted in pretty significant downsides, many either unanticipated or worse than anticipated. Instability and issues with regional ACA marketplaces led to insurers opting out of participation, often leading to even less choice and higher costs for consumers. With so many new people eligible for expanded medical care, increased demand put pressure on the health care system in some states, especially states that had implemented the new Medicaid provisions. Mandatory coverage thresholds for employers required participation for companies with more than 50 full-time employees, leading many businesses to cut full-time staff, hours, or even hiring, in order to try to mitigate new costs. New High-Deductible Health Plans (HDHPs) became more widespread as insurers tried to offset the new costs of regulation and of accepting people with pre-existing conditions. With the rise in regulatory and compliance costs, the ACA also led to greater monopolization in the already highly regulated industry, with an overall increase in hospital mergers and acquisitions since the legislation's enactment.

These wide-ranging effects are only a subset of the different consequences that have been unfolding, with new impacts of the law still coming to light. Even though the goals were straightforward, and the outcomes were expected to be incredibly beneficial, from a utilitarian perspective, it would be difficult to claim that the ACA was a success. The sheer size of the policy and each of the many mixed compounding results have made the utilitarian calculation of morality very difficult, even impossible.

The Three Gorges Dam

The Three Gorges Dam is the largest power plant in the world, a massive hydroelectric dam that spans the Yangtze River in the Hubei province of China. In 2021 it generated 103.649 billion kWh, providing enough power for the equivalent of ten million houses in the United States[22]. The planning, organization, and construction of the dam took almost a century after it was first proposed by Sun Yat-sen in 1919, although construction itself only took 18 years after being started in 1994.

Built to generate clean and renewable energy, every single year the dam saves an estimated 31 million tons of coal and prevents around 100 million tons of greenhouse gases, one million tons of sulphur dioxide, and 370,000 tons of nitric oxide from being released[23]. The dam was also designed to manage water levels, an attempt to reduce the devastation of floods that used to be a common occurrence in the Yangtze River Basin.

With the final generators coming online in 2012, the project was completed, providing considerable energy benefits to a self-identified developing nation, as well as incredible pollution mitigation. To date it is estimated that the dam has offset the release of over a billion tons of greenhouse gases, and its 22 cubic kilometres of water storage capacity has been effective in reducing the negative impacts of regular flooding.

Even though the dam seems like a complete success by utilitarian standards, there have also been many negative effects from the development of the project, including the planned displacement of an estimated 1.3 million people – devastating communities, homes, and livelihoods – as well as the loss of quite a few valuable historical and cultural sites. Initially, the benefits that materialized were decided to be worth the cost, however, over time there have been more and more negative impacts that have been coming to light, demonstrating the uncertain nature of effects over a longer time horizon.

The construction of the dam had a huge immediate impact on the ecosystem, with numerous species – like the baiji dolphin – being declared functionally extinct with its loss of habitat. Continued erosion and sedimentation upstream have been shown to affect water quality and fish populations in the river, and 3.6 million residents are now estimated to have been displaced, almost triple the initial projections[24]. Aside from displacement, another 54.8 million residents are estimated to have been negatively affected, leading to more than $20.5 billion USD in economic losses between 1994 and 2020[25].

Aside from those more immediate and obvious impacts, there are more worrisome concerns that the project has raised. The enormous weight of the reservoir has begun causing geological instability, with studies by the China Earthquake Administration finding that the dam was responsible for more than 3,000 earthquakes in the area between 2003 and 2009 alone[26]. Alongside other issues such as landslides, the dam is believed to be responsible for a more than 3000% increase in seismicity across the region[27].

While the current utilitarian calculations could indicate that the decision to build the dam was still beneficial overall, it is ultimately impossible to tell if the unknown long-term consequences of increased seismic activity, as well as economic and ecological impacts, will flip the balance of those calculations.

Negative Outcomes

With the aspirational goal of having every decision maximize collective well-being, you can imagine that many policies fall short of this goal. Some government action produces results that are below expectations, some have uncertain outcomes, and still others result in downright negative consequences. For the most part, this last category typically includes laws that have a wide range of either unintended consequences or failures to predict the scope of expected negative outcomes. In this final group of utilitarian examples, we'll take a look at some situations where even though there were good intentions, they ultimately failed, resulting in negative consequences and a failing grade by utilitarian criteria.

The Cobra Effect

For most of the other examples in this book, historical examples of policies were chosen that had real documented intentions and outcomes – helpful to demonstrate the differences between theory and reality. This next example is the story of the cobra effect, an anecdote with dubious origins that has been used for many years to highlight the effects of both unintended consequences and the idea of perverse incentives. Because it is commonly referenced in popular culture and many people are already familiar with the story, it is a prime candidate for this section. Particularly in the context of utility, the story will help demonstrate the difficulty involved with predicting human behaviour, especially over a longer time period.

As the story goes, in order to reduce the number of venomous cobra snakes in Delhi during the time of British colonial India, the government introduced a bounty on dead cobras, providing payment to people who killed and turned in the snakes. In the beginning, the bounty seemed to work incredibly well, and large numbers of snakes were turned in for the reward.

Over time, the number of wild snakes dwindled as expected, leaving people who had begun to depend on the new income with less and less money. But soon, the government noticed that even though populations of wild cobras had shrunk dramatically, the number of bounties being claimed was continuing to rise over time. Shortly afterwards, it was discovered that people had begun to breed cobras in order to collect the reward money.

With the fraud discovered, authorities scrapped the program, causing the cobra breeders to release their now worthless snakes, resulting in an increase in the wild cobra population, whose numbers were now larger than when the bounty program was implemented.

In this classic story of unintended consequences, the policy produced a positive net utility in the short term, initially reducing cobra populations and providing benefits and income to a disadvantaged group of people. Even though measuring the utility in the short term would have considered the program a resounding success, it wasn't until later on that the negative effects became clear, highlighting increases in cobra populations, the waste of resources, and even a loss of trust in government programs.

From a utilitarian perspective, this scenario is effective at demonstrating how the cobra bounty program resulted in more harm than good, with initial benefits being overshadowed by unexpected human reactions to the policy. These responses changed the utility calculation, consequences, and ultimately the morality of the policy. Even though the story may not be entirely based on real events, it illustrates the difficulty involved in predicting utility – especially when it can change over time.

California's Three Strikes Law

While commonly government action typically results in a mixture of good and bad outcomes, sometimes policy will simply fall flat – resulting in overwhelmingly negative consequences. In March of 1994, Governor Wilson signed AB 971 into law in California, otherwise known as the "Three Strikes and You're Out" law – an example of utilitarian policy failure. The idea was simple: if a person had been convicted of three or more serious criminal offences, the court was mandated to impose a life sentence. Policymakers expected that removing repeat offenders from society through long-term imprisonment would not only serve as a deterrent to potential criminals but it would also reduce crime overall, maximizing social well-being by making society safer. In many ways it was a fairly straightforward implementation of Beccaria's utilitarian deterrence principle.

While the implementation of the law showed a reduction in misdemeanours, robberies, burglaries, and vehicle thefts, it remains unclear what other contributing factors – like economic conditions and changing demographics – played in the decline of specific crimes over the same period.

The law also created quite a few negative effects that were unexpected. Prisons quickly became overcrowded, resulting in the early release of many sentenced inmates, not to mention drastically increased costs and quickly deteriorating conditions for inmates. The laws also had a disproportionate effect on minority groups, particularly African American and Hispanic populations in California. These negative effects spread to other areas, including communities and families, where offenders could end up receiving life sentences for non-violent crimes, a disproportionate punishment that was seen as unfair and unjust.

From a utilitarian perspective, even though there was a decline in specific crime rates, the benefits could never be fully attributed to the Three Strikes Law. Instead, the policy left a wide range of economic, social, and human costs in its wake that is believed to have far outweighed the law's predicted benefits. Since its original implementation, there have been several amendments and changes to the law alongside efforts to repeal it entirely, a clear signal that its utility didn't match expectations.

China's One-Child Policy

In one of the most expansive social engineering initiatives ever carried out in human history, in 1979 the Chinese government introduced the One-Child Policy. Over the course of the next 36 years, in an effort to control population growth, the policy restricted the majority of families in China to a single child.

Even though the policy was meant to apply equally across the population, there were a wealth of exceptions for certain ethnic minorities, people whose first child had disabilities, and more. When it came to curbing population growth, the policy was effective, with some estimating that over 400 million births were prevented during this entire period. Especially during the initial period, the decrease in growth showed promising effects on economic development, including reduced dependency ratios, increased per capita resources, and an increase in women's participation in the workforce.

Over time, however, a variety of negative outcomes began to emerge – or at least become more obvious – including a shift in the dependency ratio as the smaller working-age population was left to support the larger ageing population. This effect became more and more noticeable as traditionally strong family structures began falling apart. There were fewer children to take care of their older relatives.

Another result of the new rules was imbalance, both across sex ratios of newborns and the impact on rural farmers who relied more heavily on larger families to help with work. Cultural preferences began to shift when only one child was allowed, and sex-selective abortions became common. This resulted in a pretty major imbalance that peaked in 1999 – showing 125 male births for every 100 females – a number that is still reflected in the male to female ratio of 104:100 across the entire population today.

All of the negative effects continued to compound, as the government engaged in human rights violations against citizens who disobeyed, using economic sanctions, forced sterilization, and even forced abortions in order to enforce the law.

Eventually in 2016 the policy was reformed, changing the number of children allowed per couple from one to two, and then changed again to three, and finally removed entirely in May and September of 2021 respectively. While the policy was initially effective in its goal of population control, the long-term effects clearly pushed the utility into the negatives, leading to the eventual elimination of the policy.

Canadian Residential Schools

Our next example occurred during the 19th century, when the government of Canada – in coordination with the Catholic church – removed thousands of children from their First Nations, Inuit, and Métis communities. The children were forced into the Canadian residential school system in an effort to provide skills training and education, convert them to Christianity, and ultimately assimilate them into Euro-Canadian culture.

For almost two centuries, more than 150,000 children between the ages of four and 16 were forced to attend these schools, with administrators believing it would solve the socio-economic challenges that affected indigenous communities. Even though this system lasted for more than 160 years, the expected outcomes never materialized, instead leaving a legacy of abuse and neglect. In most cases the indigenous children and their communities were in worse shape than they were to begin with.

While it is difficult to measure the full extent of damage to the affected people and groups, their forced introduction into the residential school system has been linked with the loss of languages, cultural identities, and traditions, has been rife with physical, emotional, and sexual abuse, and has been tied to increases in substance abuse, poverty, and mental health issues in many of these communities.

From a utilitarian perspective, despite the intentions of national unity behind the policy, the Canadian residential school system was an unmitigated failure. The policy completely and utterly fell short of its intended benefits of cultural assimilation, improved education, and greater inclusion into the nation and workforce, instead causing untold damage that remains visible to this day.

3

Natural law in Practice

Unlike the increasingly popular and widespread utilitarian view of modern government as a tool for improving society, the influence of natural law in different societies and civilizations has varied over time. Even though natural law theory itself wasn't formalized until much later, many different ancient empires and kingdoms over time had rules, laws, or cultural practices that reflected different aspects of the theory – especially in the form of natural or at least individual rights.

Over thousands of years, ideas centred around human nature, inherent value, and natural justice have been shared by religious scholars, secular thinkers, legal philosophers, and political theorists – influencing the development of each one. Even though pieces of the theory have been incorporated into these different fields, in Western philosophy the two areas that have been most affected are legal and political thought. With natural law being a theory defining ethical boundaries between human interaction, it would make sense that the real-world application of the ideas would naturally fall into these two buckets.

The use of legal "rights" to protect against arbitrary justice and authority is one of the most common expressions of natural law throughout history, making appearances as far back as ancient Mesopotamia. And although many individual rights are related or derived from one another, we will try to touch on many of the most essential rights and their unique echoes in the real world. With that said, let's jump into the most fundamental aspect of natural law – the right to life.

Right to Life

To quickly recap the idea, the *right to life* references the belief that every single individual – by virtue of being human – has a right to their own life, and by extension has a right to protect themselves from harm or actions that threaten their existence.

This right is considered the most fundamental right of all, and can generally be seen represented, at least in some way, in almost every legal system around the world. The natural right is most commonly protected in the form of laws against murder, reflecting the basic value of human life and the arguments behind the natural right.

Even though they predate the formal development of natural law by thousands of years, laws against homicide – in support of the right to life – have been a part of human history since the first recorded laws in ancient Mesopotamia. Dating back to between 2100 and 2050 BCE, the Code of Ur-Nammu is one of the oldest legal codes ever discovered, and it includes rules against taking the life of another person, explicitly distinguishing between accidental and intentional killing. These types of laws exist in almost every major culture and civilization over the next four millennia, an empirical reflection of the natural value of human life to social cooperation.

After being explored and discussed by theologians during the Middle Ages, the ideas of natural law were later refined and popularized during the Enlightenment, where the natural right to life became a fully fleshed-out concept, one that would later be included in many standards, founding documents, and global agreements that outline and detail recognized human rights – on both national and international scales. One of the most famous references can be found in the US's foundational documents, particularly the Declaration of Independence in 1776, which states the following.

> *We hold these truths to be self-evident, that all men are created equal, that they are endowed by their Creator with certain unalienable Rights, that among these are Life, Liberty, and the pursuit of Happiness.*

Several of the amendments to the U.S. Constitution also relate to or reference the right to life, including the Fifth, Eighth, Fourteenth, and most famously the Thirteenth Amendment, responsible for the abolition of slavery. More recently, in 1948, the Universal Declaration of Human Rights (UDHR) was adopted by the UN's General Assembly, a milestone for human rights on an international scale. In the document, Article 3 states, "Everyone has the right to life, liberty and security of person." This passage has since been referenced many times around the world.

In response to the events of WWII, in 1949 a series of treaties called the Geneva Conventions were signed. These international rules set out to govern and protect the rights of sick or injured combatants, prisoners of war, and civilians. They were designed based on the guidelines provided by the UDHR, and contained a central theme that civilians who are not a part of hostilities should have their rights to life protected by both sides during armed conflict. Since then, many other countries have incorporated the natural right to life in documents that attempt to enshrine human rights into law, including the Canadian Charter of Rights and Freedoms in 1982, the Brazilian Constitution's Article 5 in 1988, the South Africa Constitution's Bill of Rights in 1996, the UK's Human Rights Act in 1998, and others around the world.

However, even with the widespread implementation of laws and acknowledgements protecting people's natural right to life, there have been plenty of occasions over the past few centuries where – even in countries that recognize the right – laws or policies have been enacted that directly conflict with its core principles. An example of this is the prevalence of slavery in the United States for almost 90 years after the Declaration of

Independence made its noble claim of all men's rights to life, liberty, and the pursuit of happiness. Even though the natural right to life was being recognized in law, in order to gain support from the various states in the war, the institution of slavery was overlooked, with the founders even cutting a passage against slavery out of the original declaration.

This moment marked one of the first major utilitarian compromises of the country, a trade between upholding natural law and winning their freedom. And this compromise was far from the last. Another one came not long after in the form of conscription into both the Continental Army, and different state militias, a move that would force all able-bodied men to serve in the defence of the new nation – a blow to their natural rights to protect themselves from harm.

In the hundreds of years since the Revolutionary War, conscription has been implemented in the U.S. in five more conflicts, the Civil War, World War I, World War II, The Korean War, and again in Vietnam. Each time, the natural rights of individuals were suspended in utilitarian calculations that would send hundreds of thousands of draftees to their deaths for some – often murky – greater good. And many other countries around the world have used conscription as well, including countries like Finland, Greece, and Switzerland, whose policies of compulsory military service are still in place today.

Even though conscription officially ended in the United States in 1973, there are still plenty of other historical and ongoing laws, policies, and actions, at home and around the world that violate the right to life. Incidents of collateral damage during war, the use of extra-judicial killings, and the use of death as a punishment for non-violent offences or crimes are only a few of the ways that this right is commonly suppressed.

As you can see, although the most fundamental right to life is enshrined as one of the most important natural rights across most of the world, it is often ignored or put aside in many cases when there is seen to be a great enough need.

Right to Self-defence

As we touched on in a previous section, the right to self-defence is usually considered an extension of the right to life from the perspective of natural law theory. Once you have accepted that an individual has a right to their own life, it follows that they must be able to preserve and protect their life from others.

Similar to laws against murder in order to protect the right to life, laws upholding the use of self-defence have been around since the dawn of human civilization. These laws can be found spanning many different cultures and nations from the present day all the way back to Sumeria and the Code of Ur-Nammu more than 1,000 years ago. The code not only outlined punishments for people who harm others, but also explicitly referenced and recognized the right of individuals to protect themselves.

Laws referencing these rights of self-preservation and self-defence continued to show up around the world for millennia, including in the Babylonian Code of Hammurabi in ~1750 BCE, in Roman law around ~100 CE, where the legal maxim *"Ubi jus, ibi remedium"* (where there is a right, there is a remedy) enabled the protection of self and property, and even in the ancient Chinese Tang Code, among others.

Throughout the Middle Ages, specific laws outlining justifiable self-defence were more explicitly recorded in several sets of laws, including ones that would turn out to be major contributors to the foundations of Western legal systems. An example is the Magna Carta in 1215, which set out rules recognizing the individual's right to defend and protect both themselves and their property. In the 17th century, an idea called the Castle Doctrine was established by Sir Edward Coke in his work *The Institutes of the Laws of England*, which asserted that individuals could use force – including lethal force if necessary – in order to protect their homes from intruders. The concept of the home as a place of security and refuge became an essential aspect of English common law. As Coke stated, "For a man's house is his castle, *et domus sua cuique est tutissimum refugium* [and each man's home is his safest refuge]." Some of the ideas behind Coke's Castle Doctrine have remained a part of legal systems in western nations ever since.

In the many years since, the right to self-defence has been subject to different restrictions and limitations that have been raised by both natural law theorists and others. While most legal systems recognized the right to self-defence, they usually outlined expectations that the use of force was not unlimited, incorporating concepts like the proportional use of force, the obligation or duty to retreat before using force, and even punishments and criminal liability for using excessive or retaliatory force.

With the Enlightenment came the solidification of natural law theories around natural rights, including the right to self-defence. Natural law theorists argued that people had these rights by virtue of being human, and philosophers like Locke explicitly argued for the individual's right to use force in defence of their life when faced with a threat. The use of reason and the perceived relationship between justice, society, and natural rights also reinforced the belief in the importance of proportionality, advising the use of restraint when using force.

In many ways the Enlightenment thinkers – particularly Grotius and Locke – also began to consider the concept of self-defence from a larger social and political perspective. Grotius's theories extended the use of natural rights, especially self-defence, to nation states instead of just individuals. Locke on the other hand, extended the ideas of self-defence to political authority and autonomy, developing the Right of Revolution – the belief that people are able to protect their rights from authoritarian and tyrannical rulers through armed resistance and the overthrowing of government.

In modern times there are a wide range of different views and legal standards across the self-defence spectrum. For example, some states in the U.S. allow for almost unlimited self-defence without a duty to retreat – often known as "stand-your-ground" laws. In many other Western countries like Canada or the UK, laws exist that permit self-defence under "reasonable circumstances." On the other side of the spectrum, countries like Japan strongly discourage use of force in self-defence, and acts of self-preservation can even land you in prison. Most often, there is a basic level of recognition for the natural right to protect oneself, a reflection of human nature and the evolutionary urge towards self-preservation.

Another aspect related to the right to self-defence is the ownership of weapons. It is commonly argued that if you are being prevented from accessing, owning, or employing tools that allow you to protect yourself effectively, you are more vulnerable – being placed at a disadvantage that can cost your life. Historically there have been a wider range of views concerning individual and collective ownership of weapons and their link to self-defence. For example, in the Bible's Old Testament, in the book of Samuel, the Philistines are said to have prevented occupied Israelites from blacksmithing in order to stop them from making weapons, removing their ability to defend themselves on a national scale.

There are many examples of legal weapon ownership as a form of defence in the Middle Ages, including parts of English common law. One of the first Western examples was as early as 1181, when King Henry II issued a proclamation that all freemen must privately own and maintain weapons which they could use in defence of the realm. "Hue and Cry" was a legal concept first referenced in 1275 that enabled individuals to raise an alarm and use force – including weapons – in order to apprehend criminals or defend themselves. In 1328, the Statute of Northampton made it illegal to carry arms secretly, with an explicit exemption for individuals who carried weapons for the purpose of self-defence, and in 1628, the Petition of Right document was brought before parliament in order to reaffirm individual rights, including the right to bear arms for self-defence.

In 1776, influenced by English common law along with the other natural rights protected by the U.S. Constitution's Bill of Rights, is the right to possess weapons, both for personal and national self-defence.

When written, many of the founders, including Thomas Jefferson, Samuel Adams, and George Mason, believed that disarming the people would only lead to the loss of liberty, and eventually their other rights. This idea can be seen in the following quote by George Mason in 1788.

> *To disarm the people... [is the] most effectual way to enslave them.*

Even with its close relationship to the right to self-defence, in modern times many Western nations either have very strict laws governing or restricting the ownership of weapons, or even explicit bans on the ownership of weapons for the purposes of self-defence. The United Kingdom, Canada, Australia, the Netherlands, Norway, and many others do not accept self-defence as an acceptable reason for owning firearms. Often, firearm possession in these countries is heavily regulated, scrutinized, and subject to many different regulations, including requirements for transport, storage, and more, in an effort to restrict ownership and usage to "acceptable" purposes like hunting and sports shooting.

While each of these countries legally recognizes the right to self-defence, their laws against carrying weapons for self-defence sometimes even extend past firearms, including the prohibition of carrying knives, deterrents like bear or pepper sprays, batons, or sometimes any other tools, effectively making self-defence a difficult prospect.

Since the beginning of civilization, the idea of self-defence as a natural human right has been a widespread part of both legal codes and social rules. With the Enlightenment exploring and codifying concepts surrounding natural law and individual rights, self-defence has become more officially recognized by both Western nations and international bodies relating to human rights. In spite of this recognition, many countries have placed restrictions on the principle of self-defence, especially the situations and contexts in which it's deemed acceptable. Expanding on these restrictions, even more nations continue to tightly control access to the tools that enable effective self-defence, a controversial and distinctly utilitarian departure from the origins and history of the natural right.

Right to Liberty

Unlike many of other more defined natural rights, the right to liberty is one of the most expansive, open-ended, and misunderstood natural rights in modern society. It can be described as the inherent right of every individual to personal freedom and autonomy – essentially the right to be free from arbitrary interference, coercion, and oppression from other people or authority.

Since liberty is a more general concept than life, property, and speech, there are many other forms of liberty that are often included in the same conversation. Some examples of these are the right to privacy, freedom of movement, the right to choose a career, the right to education, the right to voluntary interactions with others, and overall, the right to make decisions about how you want to live your life without pressure from authority. Since each one of these examples has its own nuances, arguments, and real-world impacts, we will touch on some of the major themes without focusing on each one in depth. It is also worth noting that many modern cultural interpretations of individual rights and liberties have diverged from the original concepts in natural law. These differences are covered in a later chapter, where we will look at the cultural shift from rights based in natural law, towards the utilitarian "rights" proposed by John Stuart Mill. With that being said, let's take a look at liberty – both protections and violations – throughout history.

One of the most obvious, shameful, and persistent violations of liberty in human history is the example of slavery. For thousands of years before its eventual abolition, almost every diverse civilization on Earth had some form of slavery, including the ancient Romans, Greeks, Egyptians, Chinese, Koreans, Japanese, Aztecs, Incas, pre-colonial Indigenous, the

Ottoman Empire, the Umayyad and Abbasid Caliphates, Maurya, Gupta, and Mughal in the Indian subcontinent, and many different African kingdoms.

In the 1st century BCE, the Romans enacted the Lex Petronia, a law that made it illegal for a master to sell his slaves into gladiatorial schools without "reasonable" cause – a strange balance between slavery and the right to life. The Abrahamic religions also put restrictions on the practice, with Islamic law condoning slavery, but also encouraging slaves to be freed as an act of piety and atonement for some sins. Like the Torah and the Old Testament, Islamic law forbids the kidnapping of free people to make them slaves – an infraction with a penalty of death.

But slavery isn't the only way that liberty has been trampled throughout history. Over the past several thousand years there have been a plethora of laws and actions by authority that have both supported and infringed the principles of individual liberty. During the Vedic period in ancient India between 1500-1000 BCE, a rigid caste system emerged that segregated the population, enforcing strict controls on people based on the group they were born into. Following this classification, members were forced to marry within their group, were only allowed to have specific occupations, or were even prevented from accessing education entirely.

In ancient Egypt – and later across the Atlantic in the Inca Empire – violations of liberty were common through the requirement of citizens to provide manual labour. The Inca's *mita* system was essentially a labour tax that required subjects to supply physical labour to state projects, including the development of roads and buildings, and resource collection like mining. Ancient Egyptians had similar labour programs and were expected to contribute work on construction projects like quarries, roads, or canals for a designated period of time.

The ancient Greeks, in a paradoxical combination, began to embrace both slavery and principles of democracy in 5th and 6th century BCE, recognizing the rights of citizens, and the premise that they should be equal under the law. But even though these principles were based on early concepts of liberty and equality, they applied only to a subset of the population, excluding non-citizens, women, and of course slaves. But it was during this same period that the Athenian statesman Solon helped to reform a variety of Greek laws – with the explicit purpose of increasing equality in Athens. His reforms effectively eliminated debt-based slavery for Athenians and removed restrictions on regular citizens getting involved in the judicial and political process, effectively giving a huge chunk of the population more control over their legal institutions.

Around the same time in the infancy of the Roman Republic, the Romans were also beginning to make changes to their legal system in order to remove arbitrary restrictions on individual freedom. In the 5th century BCE, the law Lex Canuleia removed the prohibition on marriages between nobles and commoners. A couple hundred years later in the 3rd century BCE, the Hortensian Law further empowered the plebeian council – the commoners – in order to give the working class an equal voice and more influence.

During the Middle Ages in medieval Europe, the use of slavery declined from its height in the Roman Empire, although it still existed to a lesser extent in the other form of the feudal system. The rise of feudalism marked a period where many people were serfs or vassals, essentially peasants who were tied to the land they lived on and were unable to leave. The repressive hierarchy also commonly led to controls over their personal decisions about marriage or occupation. Eventually with the introduction of the Magna Carta in 1215 CE and its eventual affirmation, there came a resurgence in the recognition of many natural rights, providing a basis for English common law and setting limits on the arbitrary power of authority.

The idea of liberty as a natural right is a relatively new concept in the scope of human history. Even though individual freedoms and rights were considered in some capacity by ancient thinkers like the Greek stoics, it wasn't until St. Thomas Aquinas that the concept of liberty began to take shape, before being more thoroughly defined by the Enlightenment thinkers like Locke, Rousseau, and Voltaire.

The Enlightenment came with a flood of different thinkers who helped expand the ideas of natural rights, with John Locke being one of the first to recognize the individual's right to "life, liberty, and property" in his 1689 work *Two Treatises of Government*. This idea of liberty and people's right to be free of arbitrary authority was one of the cornerstones of his philosophy, leading to his arguments on consent and the right of individuals to overthrow authority that violated these natural rights.

Over the next century, other Enlightenment thinkers like Rousseau, Voltaire, Montesquieu, and Kant shared and expanded on these ideas. In his 1785 work *Groundwork of the Metaphysics of Morals*, Kant made the case that every person has an inherent right to make their own choices based on reason and moral law, a separate – but parallel – argument for natural liberty.

The flourishing of philosophy and theory on individual rights during the Enlightenment, especially the natural right to liberty, was directly responsible for the end of slavery in the West. At the beginning of the French Revolution, Liberty was a central theme, being the first word in the motto "*Liberté, Egalité, Fraternité*" and appearing throughout the Declaration of the Rights of Man and of the Citizen. The document contained passages that declared the equality of all men, and echoed their natural rights to liberty, property, and security. Within five years of the start of the revolution, the movement's values based on natural rights led to the abolition of slavery in French colonies.

But it wasn't long before the French First Republic's foundation on natural rights began to erode, and the young movement began to put self-preservation over its founding ideals. The "Reign of Terror" between 1793 and 1794 saw the use of extrajudicial executions, the suppression of speech and assembly, conscription, and persecution based on religious views, policies that would violate almost every natural right it was meant to protect. Within a decade, the Republic would end, and Napoleon would rise – reinstating slavery across the French Empire.

Like the less successful movement in Europe, Enlightenment ideas on natural law and liberty also had a major impact on both the founding and later the abolitionist movements in the United States. Even though the end of slavery in America wouldn't occur for another 90 years post-independence, John Locke's work on liberty and natural rights was a direct contributor to the founders' beliefs. This included the Declaration of Independence's claim that "All Men Are Created Equal," a claim that provided popular abolitionists – like Spooner – arguments that slavery was in direct contradiction to the country's core principles.

Even with natural law as a driving force behind the new union, the United States was not immune from utilitarian reasoning. In 1862, during the civil war, Lincoln was already willing to compromise the fight against slavery and the principle of natural liberty in order to serve what he viewed as the greater good. He stated the following in his now-famous *Letter to Horace Greeley*:

> *My paramount object in this struggle is to save the Union, and is not either to save or to destroy slavery. If I could save the Union without freeing any slave I would do it, and if I could save it by freeing all the slaves I would do it; and if I could save it by freeing some and leaving others alone, I would also do that.*

In the end, the American War of Secession was quashed, and slavery was abolished. Spooner believed this outcome was both a massive win for individual liberty with the elimination of slavery, and ironically a resounding loss to the right of self-determination on a political level. He saw the result as the suppression of the Southern States' right to leave the union, a direct violation of their consent to be governed.

Jumping forward to the 20th century, the natural right to liberty – along with other natural rights – became internationally recognized and incorporated into documents like the Universal Declaration of Human Rights in 1948. However, even alongside the increased recognition of natural rights in international law, the opportunities for utilitarian compromise seemed to grow in equal – or greater – measure.

For example, passed in October of 2001 in the wake of the 9/11 attacks, The USA PATRIOT Act granted a wide range of power to authorities. It was argued that its violations of rights were necessary for the protection of the people. Its provisions contained violations of several natural rights, including mandates to invade privacy without warrants through data collection, the use of wiretaps and warrantless searches, the suspension of due process, and even the circumvention of judicial oversight. And the public infringements of privacy were only the tip of the iceberg.

In June of 2013, a former National Security Agency contractor named Edward Snowden leaked a huge trove of intelligence documents to journalists, revealing the massive scope of data collection and surveillance programs that had been operating for some time. Many of these programs not only violated the privacy rights of American citizens, but of people from countries all around the globe. Since then, many other Western nations have either been discovered to have their own surveillance programs or have passed similar laws, including Canadian Bill C-51 in 2015, Australia's data retention law in 2015, and the UK's Investigatory Powers Act of 2016.

But the steady decline of modern liberty isn't limited to violations of privacy. Especially during periods of crisis, modern authorities are often quick to trade away the citizen's natural rights – especially liberty – in their various forms. As economist and political philosopher Friedrich Hayek put it in his three volume *Law, Legislation and Liberty* published in the 1970s:

> *'Emergencies' have always been the pretext on which the safeguards of individual liberty have been eroded.*

Beginning in early March of 2020, many different countries across the world began to implement restrictive policies in response to the newly declared pandemic, COVID-19. With shutdowns first appearing in northern Italy on March 7th of 2020, the country was one of the first European nations to implement restrictions, with a full nationwide lockdown being instituted just days later. Within a month, Poland, Spain, Czech Republic, France, New Zealand, UK, India, Canada, and the US, all had either national or regional lockdowns in full effect. While the duration and severity of these lockdowns varied by country and region, many areas continued with lockdowns and other strict restrictions for well over a year, some even well into 2021 and 2022.

For over three years until the WHO officially declared an end to the pandemic on May 5th of 2023, billions of people across the planet were affected by these restrictions, which effectively dismissed their natural rights in the face of the crisis. Individuals were prevented from exercising their liberty – and other rights – in a variety of ways, including the suppression of freedom of movement with the use of stay-at-home orders, travel restrictions, mandatory (and in some countries forced) quarantine, and curfews.

The right to freedom of association was violated through the implementation of restrictions on gathering sizes, bans on guests and visitors at homes, bans against family and holiday gatherings, and the restriction of interactions between individuals in the form of closures of non-essential businesses and places of worship. Some areas even sacrificed the individual right to privacy through the implementation of mandatory contract tracing or tracking apps that would ensure compliance with stay-at-home orders.

Even freedom of expression was curtailed as government policies began to enforce compliance with bans against disinformation, with individuals being banned from public discourse or punished for spreading information – some of which would later turn out to be accurate – or even for criticizing government COVID policies. Perhaps most crucially with respect to natural liberty, the right to bodily autonomy was entirely overlooked with the implementation of vaccination mandates that included punishment for non-compliance – an echo of the smallpox mandates of the early 1900s.

In some sense, the COVID-19 pandemic – like all emergencies – was a test of how Western society's foundations in natural law hold up under pressure, and the results were dismal. In spite of centuries worth of philosophical arguments that led us to recognize natural rights as a cornerstone of liberty and justice, the neglect of our founding principles resulted in the failure to restrain policymakers during the emerging crisis. These pandemic policies marked a sustained period of coordinated utilitarian trade-offs across the world, calculations weighing expected lives saved against the devastating blow to natural rights and individual liberty. But while Hayek's quote from over four decades ago has again been proven true, emergencies are simply the most obvious form of rights violations that appear during policymaking.

A more gradual, persistent, and common type of policy throughout history are laws aimed at preventing individuals from participating in activities that are deemed "immoral" by some cultural, religious, or community standards – often referred to as morality laws. In many cases these rules take the form of victimless crimes, prohibitions on activities between consenting adults, or simply bans on activities that are frowned upon, violating individual liberties in order to uphold notions of public virtue or decency.

A very widespread example of morality laws throughout history were the laws against homosexuality or "sodomy laws." For example, between the period of 1533 and 1861, the Buggery Act in the United Kingdom prescribed the death penalty for those convicted of sodomy, and although death as a punishment was repealed in 1861, the act remained a criminal offence in England until 1967.

While laws against homosexuality began to face public opposition over the past century, the last 60 years in particular have seen a surge in legal changes, beginning with the state of Illinois in 1962. Soon afterwards decriminalization caught on, occurring in Canada in 1969, New Zealand in 1986, Australian states between 1975 and 1997, and eventually a U.S. Supreme Court ruling in 2003 which invalidated laws in the remaining 14 American states. Even today many other countries continue to repeal laws or otherwise decriminalize homosexuality, with Nepal upholding the rights of LGBT individuals in 2007, India following suit in 2018, Bhutan in 2021, and more. Since then, many other morality laws have recently been subject to scrutiny in nations around the world, including prohibitions on drug use and possession, the sale of sexual services, gambling, and laws against blasphemy.

The relationship between adherence to natural law and its influence on the founding principles of our liberal democracies remains a rocky one. Even though natural rights have been tightly incorporated into many of the legal and political philosophies that inspired Western nations, the legal recognition of rights hasn't been enough to prevent utilitarian policies from eroding the ideas of liberty – especially in a crisis.

Right to Property

Often associated with Enlightenment philosophers John Locke and Grotius, the right to property is another idea that is often closely related to the right to life. Locke, in particular, believed that property rights were tied to labour and that ownership was transferred when labour was mixed with natural resources – known as Locke's *labour theory of property*. In a modern context, property rights are commonly still based on Locke's original ideas, often defined as an individual's right to acquire, keep, and exchange property that is the result of their effort – without interference from others. As property can take many forms and can be exchanged between these forms, the focus on natural resources and land has declined in favour of other forms of property, including money. Because property ownership is viewed as a result of labour, natural law philosophers view property as an extension of the person, since a portion of a person's life and effort was spent to acquire the property.

Unlike many of the other natural rights, there is less consensus around what property rights are, and how property rights should be applied in practice. Many of the disagreements or different opinions are centred around taking Locke's concepts and applying them to modern phenomena like intellectual property, money, non-physical services, the application of technology, and complex financial instruments that have arisen in modern times.

Although these topics start to dive heavily into economics, an example of these concerns can be seen in debates about financial speculators in futures markets as "rent-seekers." Some, especially Proudhon-type anarchists, consider them non-productive labour, arguing that this type of profit violates natural ownership. Many economists, on the other hand, argue that speculators provide risk mitigation and liquidity, valuable services for markets. Aside from these debates on implementation, the right to own property itself is seen by many as an indisputable part of human nature.

At least some form of recognition of property rights has existed since the beginning of recorded history, well before thinkers in the Age of Reason refined natural law into a concrete ethical theory. Just like some other natural rights, the first legal protections for property ownership appeared over 4,000 years ago in the Sumerian Code of Ur-Nammu. The early legal code had explicit rules against stealing property, fraudulent transactions, and protections for home ownership, inheritance, and even restitution for farmers whose land was damaged by neighbours.

Around 450 BCE, when the legislation known as the Twelve Tables came into effect in ancient Rome, it outlined specific rights around land ownership, as well as rules for property and boundary disputes. Over the course of the Roman Republic and the later Roman Empire, more laws in support of property rights continued to appear, laying the groundwork for many of the concepts used by later legal systems and philosophers. Some of these other Roman laws included *Dominum*, which enforced an individual's absolute ownership of their property; *Usucapio*, which combined both squatter's rights and "finders keepers" to uphold the idea that public and continuous use of property – or goods – for a period of time transferred ownership; as well as the concept of *Servitudes*, a way to permanently transfer certain entitlements to the land, similar to modern laws separating ownership from logging, mineral, or other land use rights.

Outside of the Western schools of thought, property rights were also an important idea in other cultures. Ancient Hindu legal texts from around 200 BCE, the Laws of Manu, laid out rules related to ownership of property, transactions between individuals, and inheritance – around the time that Hannibal was crossing the Alps towards Rome. Indigenous groups throughout history also had different levels of recognition for property rights, and even though they were primarily based around the idea of communal or tribe-based ownership of land, the Mesoamerican Maya and Aztec civilizations both had complex systems of land ownership that included both group-owned land and land that was privately held that could be traded, sold, or inherited.

For much of the Middle Ages, the rise of the feudal kingdoms of Europe saw a decline in respect for property rights along with other natural rights. For hundreds of years, the restrictive system of nobility and obligations to higher lords suppressed the ideas of absolute ownership that arose in the Roman era. However, with the affirmation of the Magna Carta during the 13th century, property right protections were reintroduced into law, placing new restrictions on the power and authority of the monarch. These legal protections made sure that individuals were not subject to excessive fines, that their property could not be seized without fair compensation, and that they were given due process, preventing the arbitrary confiscation of their goods, services, or land. This charter of rights later became the basic foundation for English common law and helped preserve many forms of natural rights for centuries afterwards.

In his book *On the Law of War and Peace*, pre-Enlightenment thinker Hugo Grotius linked the concepts of property rights with the potential legitimacy of war, arguing that reclaiming unlawfully taken property was a valid and natural reason for conflict. Grotius also developed ideas that would be carried forward by others, including the belief that application of labour – or direct use – to public resources was a justified reason for ownership. With the Enlightenment came new additions to the theory and the concepts behind natural rights, with property rights receiving quite a bit of attention. Locke took many of Grotius's beliefs and expanded on them, formalizing his views into the *labour theory of property* mentioned earlier, in his 1689 work *Second Treatise of Government*.

Alongside his arguments related to property, Locke argued that one of the main roles of a legitimate government is the protection of both individual rights and their property. Even though Locke's work is commonly used as a basis for modern arguments for individual rights, the positions on property rights often selectively overlook his views against the unlimited accumulation of resources. Locke believed that there were moral limits on wealth through his argument for the "spoilage limitation" – a suggestion that people should only be able to acquire as much as they can use before it spoils or goes to waste. Of course, with the use of currencies and other types of resources as the basis for trade, the idea of spoilage and moral limits can be hard to translate or re-apply.

Issued at the beginning of the French Revolution in 1789, the Declaration of the Rights of Man and of the Citizen built heavily on Enlightenment thought, containing passages upholding property rights for all people in both Article 2 and Article 17. The first article explicitly references "liberty, property, safety, and resistance against oppression," and the second more directly raises property ownership as a sacred and inviolable right, forbidding the arbitrary seizure of property without due process and compensation. The French Revolution's impact on property ownership was considerable, leading to the immediate abolition of the French feudal system. In effect, this ended the system of peasantry and special privileges for the nobility, making all people – and property holders – equal in nature.

However, just like the new Republic's recognition of liberty, these protections didn't last long as the new nation began to crumble. Within a couple of years, the Jacobins began to destroy and confiscate the property of people who were perceived to be enemies of the revolution. This included vandalism and removal of Church property, forcing people who were considered "too wealthy" to loan money to the government, and the implementation of price controls that crushed both farmers and producers, worsening shortages of food and goods. Eventually after the fall of the Republic and the rise of Napoleon Bonaparte in 1804, the legal system was overhauled, and the Napoleonic Code was introduced. This new code reintroduced the right to property across France, re-establishing a land registry, respecting the inheritance of property, protecting individuals against seizures, and in a move reminiscent of Roman law, affirmed that ownership of land was absolute.

Like other natural rights, the right to property and the influence of Locke can be seen in the results of the American revolution as well. In its founding documents the new nation encoded direct support for natural rights, including the individual right to property. The Fifth Amendment of the U.S. Constitution's Bill of Rights defines protections against individuals being "deprived of life, liberty, or property," a parallel to the views of Locke and the French Revolution, meant to enforce due process and fair compensation for any property that was taken for any reason. Since independence, the effects of natural property rights have been reflected in several other notable historical policies.

For example, the Homestead Act in 1862 allowed any American to request a quarter section – or 160 acres – of federal land at little or even no cost, based on the Enlightenment idea that by actively working and improving the land, you assume ownership. The Mining Law of 1872 was very similar, enabling individuals to claim minerals on public land without paying any royalties, based on the idea that the application of labour is what grants ownership. The result of these types of policies was a major push across the continent by settlers, escalating western expansion.

These concepts of ownership that were defined by Enlightenment philosophy ultimately clashed with many of the indigenous cultural practices of the time. Many of the social systems in these North American tribes were based on both communal ownership and traditionally nomadic lifestyles, and some believe that the concepts of permanent claims to specific areas of land were not fully appreciated – despite tribal land boundaries being common.

An example of this cultural clash was the Manhattan Island Sale, where in 1626 the Dutch were said to have paid 60 Dutch guilders – roughly $24 U.S. dollars – for the entire island of Manhattan. According to historians on the subject of law and American history, the concept of absolute ownership of land is believed by some to be foreign to the Native American people at the time, and it is speculated that they would have understood the outcome of the transaction to be joint use of the property.

In the century after the Manhattan Sale many treaties were signed with different tribes, some of which ceded massive areas of land to individuals, states, and the United States Government, including the Treaty of Fort Stanwix, Treaty of New Echota, and countless others throughout

North America. In modern contexts, these treaties have been used as examples in debates about whether or not there are ethical obligations to make sure everyone involved in an agreement understands its implications.

In the middle of the 20th century, property rights became more recognized on an international level with the adoption of the Universal Declaration of Human Rights in 1948. The 17th Article of the declaration affirms that:

> *Everyone has the right to own property alone as well as in association with others. No one shall be arbitrarily deprived of his property.*

This article has since been used to argue cases around the world on inheritance, intellectual property, expropriation and eminent domain, and land rights. However, even though it has been recognized as a right in most Western nations, this hasn't been enough to prevent many of these same governments from infringing the property rights of their citizens.

In a particularly grotesque violation of this right, both Canada and the United States have laws that enable civil forfeiture, a practice that allows the property of suspects to be seized without charging the owner of a crime. These laws allow authorities to bypass the fundamental natural law concepts of due process and presumption of innocence, usually requiring the property owner to prove that their property was *not* involved in criminal behaviour – otherwise their assets could be sold to fund government programs.

Although ideas on eminent domain aren't necessarily incompatible with traditional theories of natural law – assuming fair compensation, it remains a controversial policy among supporters of natural rights. Enlightenment-era thinkers like Locke believed that while property should not be taken without consent, exceptions should be acknowledged for property to be taken for public projects, on the condition that just compensation is provided, a view that has been since echoed by the U.S. Constitution's Fifth Amendment.

But the modern utilitarian idea of public good can be an inconsistent metric, and in the controversial Supreme Court decision of *Kelo v. City of New London* in 2015, the court upheld the use of eminent domain to take land from a private individual in order to give it to another private owner for the purpose of "economic development." This decision was a shift from previous use of eminent domain in order to serve public interests through infrastructure or public works projects, effectively changing the previously established concept of public use to justify the transfer of wealth between private individuals. This was a major step away from the ideas of Locke and the justified exceptions accepted by natural law, and an even further shift away from more hardline views on absolute ownership. This less compromising view was summed up by American founding father John Jay in the following address to the people of Great Britain in 1774:

> *No power on earth has a right to take our property from us without our consent.*

Our last two examples of modern compromises of natural property rights include land use regulations – like zoning laws – and housing regulations, like rent control. From the perspective of natural law, land use rules restrict a property owner's ability to use their property as they would like, a violation of principles of absolute ownership that enforce limits on what people can build on their land, restricting certain types of economic activity or businesses that can operate, and even putting minimum or maximum sizes on structures that are allowed to be built.

An example of a modern housing regulation is the *Mietpreisbremse* policy that came into effect in Germany in 2015. The policy limited increases on rent both by location and caps on changes over a specified period of time. Similar policies that attempt to limit rental increases have been put in place around the world, including in New York, California, Sweden, Canada, and more. In some rarer cases policies take the form of rent caps, determining maximum amounts that can be charged for rent based on area and type of property, like in France's policy of *Encadrement des Loyers*. These policies interfere with the principles of natural law, particularly the concepts of absolute ownership and the right for people to receive fair value from their property.

Despite being generally recognized and respected across most of the world, violations of property remain a common occurrence. These infringements are often packaged into utilitarian policies that make the case that these actions will help the wider population. In modern times, rent control, zoning laws, and other property use restrictions conflict with the core principles of property ownership as an absolute and inviolable right, beliefs that have been traced back before ancient Rome.

Right to Property vs. Taxes

A somewhat controversial aspect of the natural right to property that is worth separate discussion, involves conversations around the legitimacy of taxation by authorities. There are a wide variety of beliefs on this subject, ranging from individuals like Spooner, who claimed that taxation was non-consensual and therefore a violation of natural law, to thinkers like Aquinas, who believed rulers had the right to impose taxes, as long as they were fair and proportional.

Thomas Aquinas argued in *Summa Theologica* – written in the late 13th century – that taxation was a moral obligation, the duty of every person to support the common good. During the Middle Ages when Aquinas wrote his thoughts on these duties, the brunt of taxes was usually paid by the peasants in the form of both monetary and labour contributions. More often than not, these tax collections were not regular like they are today, instead being subject to the whims of both local landowners and monarchs. The situation was described in stories of the era like Robin Hood, the classic outlaw who fought back against the unjust taxation by the Sheriff of Nottingham and the noble class – who extracted taxes from those on their lands.

In John Locke's *Second Treatise of Government*, he argued that the social contract included taxation as a necessary part of maintaining civil society. His view was that taxation was included under the umbrella of the few freedoms that citizens gave up to their governments in exchange for the protections of their greater natural rights. Like Aquinas, Locke also believed that these taxes had to be fair and reasonable, and that citizens were able to withhold their consent and overthrow governments that abused their powers – including taxation. During Locke's lifetime, taxation had grown pretty significantly, and even though taxes were still lower than today, England was introducing many different forms of taxes like land taxes, excise taxes, tariffs, pleasure taxes, and more.

Just under a century later, across the ocean in the American colonies, the increases in taxation were one of the defining reasons for the U.S. War of Independence. In what became a rallying cry for the colonies, "No taxation without representation" encapsulated the Lockean idea that legitimate government requires consent, and that by paying taxes without protection of their rights in return, the social contract was being invalidated. To this end, the colonists were willing to pay some taxes, but in return insisted on having a say in tax rates and where the money was used.

Excessive taxation and the rising influence of Locke and other natural law thinkers also helped set the stage for the public outrage behind the French Revolution. After heavy taxes were imposed on the peasants in France, the people were angry at the monarchy and the widespread state of poverty in the country. So when a severe winter led to food shortages and higher prices, the country erupted.

In the early 19th century United States, overall tax rates were incredibly low, with very few direct taxes. The majority of taxation during this period happened in the form of tariffs and excise taxes on a federal level, with property taxes making up a large percentage of taxation at the state and local levels. However, even almost a century before income tax was implemented, Lysander Spooner argued that taxes in any form were a direct violation of individual property rights. He was a staunch advocate for voluntary association, and he believed that every public interaction should be voluntary, even arguing that the U.S. Government itself was illegitimate because of their use of non-consensual taxation. Similar views on taxation's status as a non-consensual wealth transfer, often declared through the slogan "Taxation is theft" continue to persist in modern anarchist and natural law circles today.

Even though not all subscribers to natural law share this absolute approach, modern forms of taxations seem to violate the principles of just and proportional levels, even by the standards of Locke, Aquinas, and others. Since the start of the 20th century, tax levels across their multitude of forms have grown, leading to much higher tax burdens in Western nations today than in the past. In 1913, the United States introduced the Sixteenth Amendment, instituting a federal income tax that ranged between 1-7% depending on income level, a move that would be followed by France in 1914, Australia in 1915, Canada in 1917, among others. These income taxes were intended to be small or temporary, but have instead grown to unprecedented levels, with federal rates in the United States ranging between 10-37% as of 2021, and even up to 45% in Australia, France, and Germany.

In addition, these federal taxes only account for one of the many forms of direct taxation, alongside property taxes, state or regional taxes on income that range up to 13% in U.S. states like California or up to 25% in the Canadian province of Quebec, regional consumption taxes like GST/HST in Canada that reach 15% in several provinces or the VAT in France that is 20%.

And while these are the most noticeable types of tax, there are many other forms that are much less visible. These indirect forms of wealth transfer to the government lead to higher prices and the erosion of purchasing power and can include excise taxes and sin taxes on specific types of goods, import taxes and tariffs that artificially drive up costs of foreign goods, corporate taxes, employment taxes, mandatory insurance, inheritance taxes, and even monetary policy that causes inflation. While it can be difficult to calculate and account for the impact of every different form of tax on individuals, cumulative taxation has undoubtedly grown drastically throughout the 20th and 21st centuries. From the perspective of natural law and even the founding fathers, this raises serious questions about the legitimacy of excessive and ever-expanding modern tax policies. As Benjamin Franklin once said in his 1758 essay *The Way to Wealth*:

> *It would be a hard government that should tax its people one-tenth part of their income.*

Just imagine his reaction to rates of taxation in 2023 that can reach over 56% in California when only accounting for sales tax (7.25%), state income tax (up to 12.3%), and a federal top rate of 37% – not even counting most indirect taxes.

Aside from the sheer volume of taxes extracted from the average citizen across Western nations – many of which are even higher than the U.S. – there are other arguments against taxation as a violation of natural rights outside of violations of property. One of these is the use of discriminatory taxes or taxes that disproportionately impact subsets of a population based on specific ethnic, religious, or social situations, a clear violation of the right to equal treatment under the law. Examples include taxes on menstrual products, indirect taxation of same-sex couples through prohibition of common law tax status, and especially poll taxes that were common during the Jim Crow era.

The natural right to liberty is also often affected by taxation, especially through "sin" taxes or other morality taxes. These are another form of discriminatory taxes that are meant to prevent individuals from consuming goods or services that have been considered by authority to be either immoral or harmful to society. These types of taxes, whether on tobacco or alcohol, traditionally use coercive pricing to violate the individual's liberty – in this case the ability to make purchasing decisions without interference from authority. These policies are effectively a utilitarian consideration that aims to improve social well-being by reducing usage or consumption of taxed goods or services, or at least an attempt to offset perceived costs of consumer choices.

Finally, perhaps one of taxation's most abstract natural law violations is against the individual's freedom of conscience. By using the people's funds to promote policies or programs that directly oppose individual taxpayers' cherished beliefs, it makes every taxpayer an indirect participant and financial supporter of actions that they disagree with.

In the end, even though natural law theorists like Locke and Aquinas often promoted taxes as a necessary or at least tolerable policy, thinkers like Spooner believed that the use of force makes taxes non-consensual and a direct violation of individual property rights. However, even when accepting Locke and Aquinas's support of reasonable taxation as a part of the social contract, it would be hard to argue that the extensive levels of taxation in place today are anything but a violation of natural law. And aside from property rights themselves, the implementation of taxation to enforce social behaviour and the use of tax money for war and other unethical behaviour demonstrates how modern taxation can also be seen as a violation of other natural rights as well.

Freedom of Conscience and Expression

One of the first recorded laws in support of freedom of conscience can be traced back to the Persian king Cyrus the Great in 539 BCE. Inscribed on an ancient cylinder of clay, the Cyrus Cylinder documents the conquest of Babylon and the following orders by Cyrus. These new edicts included the restoration of shrines, allowing displaced people to return to their lands, and removing earlier restrictions on religious practices that prevented the freedom to worship freely in their own way. For over 200 years until it was later conquered by Alexander the Great around 330 BCE, the Persian (Achaemenid) Empire continued their religious tolerance – at least relative to other powers of the time.

During the centuries that followed, the Macedonians and other Hellenistic kingdoms commonly suppressed religious freedom, merging their Greek religious practices and deities with the local traditions of conquered people, and at times banning specific religious practices – like Judaism – altogether. In 399 BCE, Socrates, one of the most prominent philosophers of his time, was tried and sentenced to death on multiple charges including "refusing to recognize the gods recognized by the state," and "corrupting the young," a reflection of attitudes towards both freedom of conscience and expression at the time.

The Roman Republic and later Empire followed suit, continuing that strategy of merging their religion with those of conquered regions, although they often actively suppressed religions that refused to conform, most notably Christianity and Judaism.

In 313 CE, the Roman emperors Constantine and Licinius Augustus came to an agreement which is now known as the Edict of Milan, a proclamation that provided state protection to Christians after centuries of interference and persecution. This led to a major cultural shift, and over the next 70 years Christianity grew rapidly, eventually becoming the state religion of the Roman Empire in 380 BCE with the Edict of Thessalonica. With the rise of state Christianity and a variety of offshoots, before long religious tolerance once again started to decline. By the end of the 4th century, practices that were viewed as pagan – including other Christian sects like Arianism – faced active suppression and punishment.

It was during this time that St. Augustine began his work on many of the concepts joining nature and the divine, laying the foundation for Aquinas and others to build more formalized ideas on natural morality. Augustine famously struggled with the ideas of religious freedom, at first believing that persuasion was the key to resolving religious differences. By the end of his life, his beliefs had shifted away from ideas of peaceful tolerance and he adopted a more utilitarian approach to salvation – justifying the use of coercion and state power in order to force conversions and bring salvation. Over the next 1,000 years, religious freedom continued to decline across Europe alongside the routine suppression of people who were deemed heretics, pagans, and dissenters over the Byzantine and Carolingian Empires, and the fragmentation of the empire in the period that followed.

Between the late 12th and the early 18th centuries, violations of religious freedom and expression continued to grow, with the establishment of several European Inquisitions, which aimed to root out heresy and enforce dominant Catholic views. Beginning with the Episcopal Inquisition in 1184 CE and followed by the Papal Inquisition of 1231, the suppression of religious views that were considered heresy increased in intensity. In 1251, the papal edict Ad extirpanda authorized the use of torture in the inquisitions, followed by the direct targeting of Jewish and Muslim converts to Catholicism in 1320. Inquisitions continued to grow in popularity across Christendom, with the Spanish launching their famous inquisition in 1478 that eventually led to the expulsion of the Jews from Spain in 1492, the Portuguese establishing an Inquisition in 1536, and finally Pope Paul III establishing the Roman Inquisition in order to combat Protestantism in 1542. Many of these movements directly incorporated the utilitarian arguments produced by Augustine centuries earlier, weighing the cost of coercion and violence against the salvation of the converted.

In 1579, several northern provinces in the Netherlands formed together into the Dutch Republic through the Union of Utrecht, a treaty aiming to combine their military might to resist Spanish aggression. Article 13 of this document contained a groundbreaking stance on religious freedom, allowing complete religious freedoms for individuals and member states, one of the first policies documented of its kind.

Even though the Spanish and Portuguese Inquisitions would not be formally abolished until the early 19th century, the widespread influence of Enlightenment philosophies during the 17th and 18th centuries were responsible for dealing significant blows to their power and influence. The liberalism movement had a profound impact on the acceptance of freedom of conscience as a natural right, with Grotius and Locke influencing other Enlightenment thinkers that came afterwards like Voltaire and Montesquieu. In 1689 Locke published *A Letter Concerning Toleration*, where he directly advocated for religious tolerance and the idea that the government should not have authority over an individual's conscience. Voltaire was also a strong believer in freedom of conscience and thought, and his stance on freedom of expression is often represented in the following quote commonly misattributed to him:

> *I disapprove of what you say, but I will defend to the death your right to say it.*

With the French Declaration of the Rights of Man and of the Citizen in 1789, natural rights – including the right to freedom of conscience and expression – were recognized in the public sphere, with Articles 10 and 11 of the French Revolution's founding document guaranteeing freedom of thought, opinion, expression, and religion. Although it didn't take long for the French Republic to abandon these ideals as the new nation fell apart, the influence of these Enlightenment ideas had also stretched across the sea to the United States.

Shortly after the end of the American Revolutionary war in 1786, the *Virginia Statute for Religious Freedom* was written by Thomas Jefferson to abolish the Church of England in Virginia. This statute declared that all individuals had a natural right to freedom of religion free from coercion, a groundbreaking move for natural law, and a move that would later be the basis for the U.S. Constitution's First Amendment. In 1791, the Constitution's Bill of Rights was ratified, containing ten amendments, the first of which enshrined the rights to freedom of conscience and expression in the following statement.

> *Congress shall make no law respecting an establishment of religion, or prohibiting the free exercise thereof; or abridging the freedom of speech, or of the press...*

Overall, while the U.S. Supreme Court has upheld these rights in many different circumstances since the 18th century, there are a few notable exceptions and policies that violated them. One of the first notable examples took place in the 20th century with the Espionage Act of 1917. This policy was a significant blow to the natural right to free expression, a utilitarian trade-off that put in place sweeping rules against supporting those considered enemies of the United States during WWI. This law and the later addition known as the Sedition Act in 1918 made it a crime to speak out against the government, to disparage or interfere with the war effort, and even to criticize the U.S. Constitution, the military, or the flag, effectively decimating freedom of expression.

Many anti-war activists, socialists, and anarchists of the era, including Emma Goldman, Eugene V. Debs, and Charles Schenck were arrested and thrown in prison for their activities in opposing the draft, a clear violation of their First Amendment rights. However, just like in other times of perceived crisis, when the cases of both Debs and Schenck went before the U.S. Supreme Court in 1919, their convictions were upheld. These cases marked some of the first major legal blows to freedom of conscience and expression since the nation's founding over 140 years earlier.

In 1948 the Universal Declaration of Human Rights was adopted by the UN General Assembly, and like many of the other natural rights, it officially recognized the right to freedom of conscience on an international level. The document's Articles 18 and 19 contained the following declarations in support of these rights.

> *Everyone has the right to freedom of thought, conscience and religion; this right includes freedom to change his religion or belief, and freedom, either alone or in community with others and in public or private, to manifest his religion or belief in teaching, practice, worship and observance.* – Article 18

> *Everyone has the right to freedom of opinion and expression; this right includes freedom to hold opinions without interference and to seek, receive and impart information and ideas through any media and regardless of frontiers.* – Article 19

Even though religious freedom has faced a wider level of acceptance in many Western nations over the past century, freedom of expression has not always shared that same status. Over the past several decades, the United Kingdom, in particular, has faced criticism for the introduction of laws that restrict freedom of expression in the name of public good. In 1986, the Public Order Act was passed, criminalizing several forms of protest, placing restrictions on public assemblies, and preventing insulting or abusive materials from being displayed publicly – a series of rules with broad interpretations.

The UK also passed the Communications Act in 2003, containing Section 127 which makes it an offence to send messages over the internet that could be considered "grossly offensive or of an indecent, obscene or menacing character." This legislation has led to the prosecution of individuals for social media posts, internet comments, and jokes online – a clear violation of the right to freedom of expression.

In 2022, the Police, Crime, Sentencing and Courts Act came into force in the UK, placing limits on protests that are deemed by authorities to be too noisy, that could cause "intimidation or harassment," or even "unease, alarm or distress" to bystanders. The Act also expanded the definition of "public assembly" to apply to groups as small as a single individual, a broadening of definitions that allows almost anyone to be targeted for any public speech. And unfortunately, these modern violations of natural expression are not limited to the UK. Many other countries like Canada, Germany, France, Sweden, Spain, and Australia have implemented laws against "hate speech," an often poorly defined term that has led to the prosecution of individuals for using racial slurs on private telephone calls, for making comments that showed scepticism towards racial self-identification, and even comedians making jokes about offensive topics.

Over the course of human history, the right to freedom of conscience has been one of the least acknowledged or recognized aspects of natural law, second only to freedom of expression. Most of history up until the Enlightenment consists of a wide range of groups suppressing the belief systems of other groups to varying extents, with small breaks of tolerance in between. Since the Enlightenment and the identification of these rights as a part of natural law, they have seen a popular rise in support in Western nations. This has led to the recognition of religious tolerance and freedom of speech on both national and international levels, though the right to expression has continued to face increasing limitations.

Freedom of Association

For most of history the right to freedom of association was not seen as an explicitly unique right and would have been considered another aspect of the right to liberty, or even the right to freedom of religion covered in the previous section.

Public associations known as "collegia" first appeared between the 6th and 3rd centuries BCE in ancient Rome. They often took the form of trade guilds, religious groups, political movements, or even social clubs. Over the course of the Roman Republic and Empire, the right to form these collegia was regularly restricted or promoted, depending on the political climate at the time. An example of these laws was the Lex Julia de collegiis in the late 2nd century BCE, which restricted the formation of groups, followed by the Lex Clodia in 58 BCE, which re-established the right of formation, before it was restricted again by Augustus in 7 BCE.

Centuries later during the Islamic Golden Age, the Abbasid Caliphate was known for its role in encouraging philosophical thought between the 8th and 13th centuries. Although the period saw other rights with a mixture of support and restrictions, the right to association was relatively well respected, and there was a flourishing of scholarly, religious, and spiritual associations. Many of these groups played significant roles in the formation of Islamic society, doctrine, and law.

Throughout the Middle Ages in Europe, freedom of association was stifled by the feudal lords, heavily restricting the peasants and serfs in their ability to associate with others, move around, or even change their allegiances. This suppression was often enforced by law, like the Statute of Northampton in 1328, which banned unlawful assembly, or the Statute of Laborers in 1351, which prevented labour movements in the wake of the bubonic plague. The purpose of these feudal laws was generally to control dissenters and to prevent workers from benefiting from increased wages, especially after there was a shortage of workers caused by the plague. These types of violations and more were incredibly common for centuries, including legal restrictions on guilds, like the Statute of Artificers in 1563, effectively an early form of occupational licensing that allowed the crown a level of control over workers' guilds. This law enabled the state to determine the terms of entry into guild apprenticeships, and even forced individuals into certain lines of work – like agriculture – depending on the occupation of their parents.

In fact, it wasn't until the Enlightenment and the associated workers movements based on natural rights that freedom of association became recognized as a natural principle. Even during this period, many of the Enlightenment thinkers believed that freedom of association was implicitly included in the rights to freedom of thought, religious freedom, and of liberty. For example, Locke, Rousseau, Montesquieu, and Voltaire all believed that the formation of associations, public groups, and assemblies was a prerequisite for people to participate in political and social life. John Locke's work on contract theory stated that the formation of consensual societies and even governments required both voluntary association and mutual agreement.

In 1789 with the French Declaration of the Rights of Man and of the Citizen, the right to association was first proclaimed in Article 2, stating "The aim of all political association is the preservation of the natural and imprescriptible rights of man." However, as with most other natural rights, freedom of association also didn't last long in the First French Republic. In 1793, the government passed The Law of Suspects, enabling the revolutionary government to arrest individuals suspected of being enemies of the revolution or of opposing the Republic. This law often targeted individuals based on their friends and their membership in groups, first aimed primarily at dissenters, and later expanding to target factional supporters of the revolution and even members within the Jacobins – the radical political group responsible for much of the later turmoil.

Only a few years later with the ratification of the Bill of Rights in 1791 in the U.S., the First Amendment was primarily focused on the freedom of religion and expression, but it has since been interpreted by the courts to protect the right to assembly and association. However, although the right was recognized in the U.S. Constitution, infringements of the right have been common over the centuries, especially in the suppression of unions and labour organizations. Interestingly, from the perspective of natural law, unions are a unique concept, one whose modern implementations often fall on both sides of the principle of freedom of association.

While the ability to collectively bargain and negotiate with employers as a group is a perfect example of freedom of association and the formation of mutually beneficial bonds, union requirements have also been used to suppress this right. In cases where unions require mandatory membership and payment of dues as a condition of employment, there are clear restrictions on the right for individuals to participate in voluntary association. These restrictions may also prevent individuals from exercising self-representation or independent bargaining, making membership a necessary precondition of industry employment.

In 1914, the Colorado National Guard attacked a camp of striking miners in Ludlow, Colorado, killing more than 20 people and leading to a nine-day period of violence between the two groups. Alongside many other instances throughout history, the use of force in order to break up the miners' collective action was a clear violation of their right to freedom of association on behalf of private enterprise. As a result of the Ludlow massacre and other events, in 1935 the National Labor Relations Act was passed in the United States, protecting the rights of employees to form, join and assist labour unions, as well as affirming employee rights to engage in collective bargaining. Just under 20 years later with the passing of the Universal Declaration of Human Rights in 1948, the right to freedom of association became explicitly acknowledged and protected in international law in Article 20. Since then, the European and American Conventions on Human Rights, the African Charter on Human and Peoples' Rights, and others have included the right, in addition to being incorporated into the constitutions and legal frameworks of many countries around the world.

Even though it was controversial and strongly disliked by labour organizations and workers' rights movements, right-to-work laws have also become an important protection of freedom of association. These laws first appeared in the United States after the passing of the Taft-Hartley Act of 1947. They aim to ensure that participation in unions remains optional, respecting individual autonomy and the right to choose membership, and preventing compulsory payment of dues. This allows individuals to separate from groups that often take political stances they may not agree with, and even allows workers to break from unions whose benefits are not valued by the individual. Opponents of right-to-work laws, on the other hand, argue that freedom of association weakens workers' rights by undermining collective bargaining power. Although allowing individuals the freedom to choose their own membership might weaken these movements, these arguments are entirely utilitarian in nature, weighing the loss of the individual's natural right to association against the increased power of collective worker movements.

Even though freedom of association is most often viewed through the lens of employment and workers' rights, it can also be seen in other ways that humans form bonds, groups, and personal relationships. Between 1956 and 1971, the Counterintelligence Program – also known as COINTELPRO – was a series of covert and often illegal activities enacted by the FBI, aimed at the surveillance, infiltration, and discreditation of American political organizations. The targets of these actions were often left-leaning and civil rights organizations, and this program was used to subvert and violate the integrity of these groups. The use of coercion by authority to interfere with group participation is by Locke's standards, the very definition of illegitimate government action and a clear violation of natural rights. Thankfully, once it became public the program was shut down, but the illegality of these and similar activities were never officially tested in court.

Right to Family and Procreation

Like the right to freedom of association, the right to family and procreation was not entirely defined until the Enlightenment era, although similar historical ideas like the ability to marry outside one's social class or rules detailing family rights and obligations can be found incorporated into historical laws.

The ancient Babylonian Code of Hammurabi from ~1750 BCE contained a few rules that defined different family rights, including inheritance, the obligations of fathers to their children, and rules governing divorce. Even though these laws weren't to the same scope or scale as modern family laws, they aligned with ensuring that individual's families were protected from arbitrary authority.

Between 1500 and 1000 BCE, as mentioned earlier, there was a caste system that arose during the Vedic period in ancient India. This was a strictly enforced system of cultural segregation that dominated almost every aspect of a caste member's life. Among other restrictions, cultural rules prevented members of these groups from marrying outside of their caste, and marriages were often arranged by relatives instead of personal choice.

Although not as pervasive as the Indian caste restrictions, the Roman Republic also had strict restrictions on marriage between social classes, up until the passing of the Lex Canuleia in 445 BCE, which legalized marriage between nobles and commoners. This seemed like a major step towards recognizing family rights in ancient Rome. However, in 18 BCE the Lex Julia was passed in an attempt to increase the birth rate, a law that implemented penalties for Romans who did not marry and rewarded those who had more than three children. This law was followed by the Lex Papia Poppaea in 9 CE, building on the Lex Julia and adding more severe penalties, including the forfeit of half of one's estate if they were unmarried or childless by a certain age. These utilitarian laws aiming to increase the declining population were a major blow to the right of Roman people to choose their family structures, pressuring individuals into relations that they wouldn't have otherwise chosen. Although enforcement declined over time, both laws remained in place for centuries until the fall of Rome in 476 AD.

In the 7th century and over the course of the Golden Age of Islam, family rights faced a mixture of support as they intersected with both religious and cultural traditions. Although Islamic law technically required the consent of both husband and wife for a marriage to be considered valid, in practice marriages were very often arranged between the parents for political, social, or religious compatibility. Even though forced marriages were technically forbidden, the expectations of family and social pressure didn't leave much room for individuals – especially women – to choose their own partners. Islamic law itself also enforced limitations on choice, and Muslims were prevented from marrying people from select religions. Women, for example, were restricted to marriage with other Muslims, and men were prevented from marrying women outside of the "People of the Book," limiting choices to Jews, Christians, or other Muslims.

During the same and later periods in Europe, the feudal system was also a major setback for individual rights related to family. Overall, individuals lost significant control over their own relationships including common requirements for both vassals and serfs to ask their lord's permission in order to marry. In many situations these subjects had to purchase their right to marry from their lord by paying fees – called merchet – or were even outright banned from marrying outside of the lord's lands.

With the rise of more formal Catholicism, control of marriage began to move away from the feudal lords, falling more and more under the jurisdiction of canon law – the legal system of the Church. With the Fourth Lateran Council in 1215 came official church rules around marriage, including the implementation of public announcements – called banns – of upcoming marriages, a rule that was put in place to prevent secret marriages and provide the opportunity for public objections. One of the main goals for the Church's marriage rules was to reduce the arbitrary and oppressive marriage restrictions by feudal lords, as well as ensuring that marriages conformed to religious principles. In 1563 at the Council of Trent, individual marriage rights were expanded even further – in parallel to Islamic law – reinforcing the idea that marriage required the consent of both spouses to be valid.

With the rise of Enlightenment and the shift towards greater recognition of natural law, the right to family and other parental rights were expanded and refined by thinkers like John Locke and Voltaire. Consistent with his other work, Locke highlighted the need for mutual consent in marriage, reinforcing the idea that it was a voluntary and consensual union between individuals. He also argued that parents' natural authority over their children covered both protection and education but came with the unconditional obligation to respect the inherent rights of their children. Many of these views were echoed by others of the era like Voltaire and Rousseau, who also believed that individual choice was the most important consideration when it came to family and relationships.

At the outset of the French Revolution, there were massive reforms in both marriage and family laws, focusing on individual freedom and autonomy. These changes included the introduction of civil marriage and the legal recognition of divorce, a move partially aimed at reducing the authority of the Church over the personal lives of French citizens. Family laws were also impacted, by granting illegitimate children rights that were similar to those for legitimate ones, and introducing the concept of adoption, allowing families to choose children outside of blood relations. These changes made the French Republic one of the first countries on Earth to incorporate these types of protections for the right to family.

Early in the 20th century across the ocean, the United States Supreme Court ruled that the Constitution's principles of freedom of religion, speech, and assembly also covered parental rights and family life in the rulings *Meyer v. Nebraska* in 1923 and *Pierce v. Society of Sisters* in

1925. These rulings recognized parents' rights to educate and provide moral guidance to their own children, upholding the Enlightenment ideas of Locke and others.

Leading up to and after WWII, natalist laws similar to those of ancient Rome made a reappearance in the Soviet Union and some of its satellite states. As a result of falling birth rates, policies were implemented that included both penalties and financial incentives in order to boost population growth. By 1944, soviet military and civilian casualties from WWII are estimated to have reached upwards of 25 million people. As a result, the Soviet government put in place even more policies meant to help replenish the population, including support for families with more children and taxes on childlessness – echoing the laws of Ancient Rome. These pronatalist benefits often came in the form of generous maternity leave, child allowances, as well as awards, recognition, and even priority housing for large families. Much like our assessment of the earlier Roman policies, these laws created undue pressure on individuals to have families they didn't want and punished individuals who exercised their natural rights.

With the Universal Declaration of Human Rights in 1948, the right to family received international recognition in modern society, with Article 16 stating the following:

> *Men and women of full age, without any limitation due to race, nationality or religion, have the right to marry and to found a family. They are entitled to equal rights as to marriage, during marriage and at its dissolution.*

The document inspired many other national and regional claims of human rights, and the inclusion of family rights was instrumental in helping to end restrictive laws around the world, including prohibitions on same-sex marriage and interracial marriage. Another effect of these international recognitions of family rights was the end of eugenics movements throughout the Western world. Up until the mid-70s, the United States, Canada, several Nordic nations, and Switzerland, all had laws in place that allowed people to be forcibly sterilized under certain conditions, including individuals who were declared to have mental disabilities or who were deemed "unfit" to reproduce.

Over the past few decades, the natural right of individuals to pursue relationships of their choice has seen increased acceptance. These changes include continued movements to decriminalize, legalize, or otherwise give equal rights to same-sex relationships; decreases in forced marriages, arranged marriages, and child marriages; and even the increase in equal protections for common law relationships.

However, in spite of the many improvements and the rise in acceptance of these natural law rights in Western nations, many areas of the world still engage in arranged and coercive marriages, dispute the legitimacy of relationships using religious or cultural standards, and even attempt to restrict the guidance and influence of parents on their children's education.

Right to Equal Treatment

The right to equal treatment under the law is perhaps the most essential part of any natural law system and is based on the core principle that natural rights are universal to all people. In essence, it ensures that each of the other rights are extended to everyone equally, fairly, and without discrimination – underscoring their ties to human nature, not cultural context.

Like so many of our other rights, the first examples in law can be traced back to the ancient Babylonian legal code from around 1750 BCE, the Code of Hammurabi. It included laws and edicts that applied to every person regardless of social status. Even though punishments for some crimes were sometimes unequal based on the social status of the individuals involved, the implementation of this common set of laws that applied to everyone was quite unique by historical standards.

More than 1,200 years after their appearance in Mesopotamia, the ideas of legal equality resurfaced, this time in ancient Greece. At the height of Athenian democracy in the 5th century BCE, a series of laws and legal procedures were established to provide equal rights for all citizens. The goal of these reforms was to flatten the social hierarchy and allow all citizens to participate in assemblies and legal processes. Even though these reforms did in fact reduce the power imbalances between aristocrats and the commoners, restrictions on citizenship itself still prevented political equality for many people, including women, slaves, and even people without two Athenian parents.

Like Greece and many of the other early empires, the Roman Republic and later Empire was heavily broken into different social classes, from the patricians – or aristocrats – down to the plebeians – or commoners, with the slaves at the bottom. Around 450 BCE the laws of the Twelve Tables were implemented, containing the first written legal code of Rome. These rules were public and applicable to all citizens, although the noble class was still heavily favoured. Until the 3rd century CE, there were many different attempts to reform Roman inequality and corruption, and even though they sometimes led to greater equality for the plebeians, reforms in ancient Rome very often led to widespread political instability and violence.

Hundreds of years later during the Islamic Golden Age between the 7th and 13th centuries, treatment under the law was still rarely equal, depending on which religious group individuals belonged to. Members of non-Muslim Abrahamic religions were required to pay a special tax – the *Jizya* – in order to receive legal protection and the right to practise their religion. Alongside women and slaves, at various times over the course of the period, non-Muslims also faced social and legal discrimination that included wearing specific clothing or symbols to mark their status. Other legal inequalities included the prevention of non-Muslims from holding many types of public office, limited inheritance rights, and a diminished legal status in court testimonies.

The next major step towards legal recognition for equal treatment came in 1215 CE with the signing of the Magna Carta, laying the foundation for much of English common law. The document effectively declared that the king and his authority were no longer above the law, and that the rights of citizens should be protected in a variety of different ways. The Magna Carta established the rights of all individuals to access equal forms of justice, provided avenues for people to address injustice or improper treatment, and overall ensured that everyone was bound by the same principles.

With the rise of Enlightenment values in the 17th century, arguments in support of individual rights, autonomy, and equality became common and the principles of equal treatment under the law were carried forward as a core aspect of natural law. Thinkers like Locke and Voltaire championed egalitarian values, and Kant's arguments for the treatment of people as ends instead of means helped to clearly define and highlight the inherent equality of every individual.

These principles of equality were also echoed by both French and American Revolutionaries, with the U.S. Declaration of Independence's bold statement that "all men are created equal" and its references to their individual rights, and the French Declaration's proclamation that "Men are born and remain free and equal in rights." The French Revolution, in particular, began with a pure vision of equality for all, illustrated by the famous motto *"Liberté, Egalité, Fraternité."* It had the noble goal of dismantling the feudal system's privileges for the nobility and the church, abolishing slavery, and striving for equality of women and the marginalized. However, as mentioned earlier, in spite of these noble goals, the end of the Republic saw the focus on equality fall apart, and the rise of Napoleon and the First French Empire saw slavery and the suppression of women's rights make a swift return.

Like the French Republic, the United States was also established on many of the principles of Enlightenment thinkers including the ideal of equality for all. Unfortunately, with the founders' compromise allowing for the continuation of slavery, equal treatment under the law was still elusive in practice. With the rise of the abolitionist movement based on the arguments of natural law and the promise of fulfilling the country's founding ideals, equality once again became a central theme.

In the mid-20th century, in the wake of WWII, equal treatment under the law was among the rights explicitly recognized in the Universal Declaration of Human Rights in 1948. In this document, Article 7 clearly stated that:

> *All are equal before the law and are entitled without any discrimination to equal protection of the law.*

As with other rights, these principles of legal non-discrimination helped to influence articles in other human rights movements, including the European Convention on Human Rights in 1950, as well as the civil rights movement in the United States. In 1964, the U.S. passed the Civil Rights Act, outlawing discrimination based on race, colour, religion, sex, or nation of origin, and marking the official end of "Jim Crow" laws. This move towards legal equality was also followed by the Canadian Charter of Rights and Freedoms in 1982, which promised equal protection under the law, and the United Kingdom's Human Rights Act in 1998, a law based on the European Convention that addressed the equal treatment of individuals.

While it might seem like Europe and other Western nations have fully embraced these ideals, they have not always been upheld. For example, in recent decades the Roma people in Europe have continued to face persecution and discrimination – both legal and otherwise – in many regions. Between 1966 and 2007, the states of Czechoslovakia and later Czech Republic actively engaged in the forced sterilization of Roma women, almost 60 years after the passing of the Universal Declaration of Human Rights. After decades spent in segregated schools and camps on the edges of cities, in 2008 the Italian government implemented a policy to fingerprint all Roma people in their camps, including children. In 2010, the French government forced the evictions of many Roma camps and deported thousands of individuals out of France to Romania and Bulgaria, underscoring the staggering lack of equality and continued discrimination faced by some ethnic groups in Western nations.

Despite these horrendous violations of equality, over the past 100 years laws around the world have continued to shift closer to the Enlightenment views on natural law. A large part of this movement has been the acknowledgement and correction of legal disparities between different groups. However, with efforts to correct and compensate for historical wrongs to subsets of the population, an increasingly common social and legal approach has been the inversion of discrimination against groups that previously faced legal prejudice. This utilitarian approach proposes new reductions in equality in the form of preferential treatment in order to promote policies that would improve the well-being of these historically challenged groups. While the idea behind these policies is to address racial or gender imbalances across a variety of outcomes – an idea known as "equity" – the implementation of policies that apply unequal treatment based on these (or any) criteria directly conflicts with natural law's requirement of legal equality.

In recent times, many countries have implemented laws or specific policies that are in line with this new approach to addressing racial or gender disparities, including Canada, Australia, the United Kingdom, the European Union, and the United States. Introduced in 1961 by President John F. Kennedy, the term *Affirmative Action* was originally focused on non-discrimination and ensuring equal treatment "without regard to their race, creed, colour, or national origin" – words that echoed the Enlightenment concept of equal treatment. As mentioned, however, over time these policies began to evolve to focus on preferential treatment instead.

Passed in Australia in 1975, the Racial Discrimination Act allowed for "special measures" to be applied in order to advance racial or ethnic groups in an effort to achieve equality. In a similar ruling, in 1999 the Supreme Court of Canada ruled that Canadian courts must take the unique circumstances of Indigenous offenders into account during sentencing, effectively creating a tiered system of justice contingent on the race of the offender. Other examples of policies that have been implemented in order to benefit specific minority groups include the provision of services at reduced or even no cost, unique access to subsidies, low-cost loans, and tax breaks.

Although the right to equal treatment is still upheld as a core value of Western justice, there has been a steady rise in these policies over recent decades. Spread across different countries, each example is a product of a utilitarian calculation, dealing a blow to the natural right of equality in exchange for perceived gains in racial equity. Even so, when compared with the legal inequalities that have persisted for much of human history, the principles of equal treatment remain stronger than ever.

4

The Gap between Theory and Practice

Over the past few chapters, even though we took different approaches to observing the two moral frameworks on their own terms, we can immediately notice a couple of interesting things. The first is that utilitarianism can be a difficult ethical system to get right in real life, and the second is that many laws supporting natural rights have come and gone throughout history.

With respect to utilitarianism, there are a variety of reasons for these difficulties, especially the theory's focus on outcomes instead of the actions themselves. It can be difficult to predict the results and effects of your actions, especially in situations involving complex moral calculations of potential causes and real effects that are not always obviously assignable to a single policy or action.

It can also be difficult to identify which benefits policymakers were predicting in many situations, since they neglect to record their expectations when it comes to many laws and policies. Either that or they use post-hoc attributions of success, effectively claiming "we meant to do that" if the law has beneficial outcomes, and "it was their fault" if outcomes fall flat.

On the natural law side, we saw how many of the most essential natural rights can be observed to different degrees across almost every society since people first began forming social bonds. Many historical civilizations and cultures including ancient Mesopotamia, Greece, Rome, Europe, and Caliphates of the Islamic Golden Age incorporated varying ideas on personal liberty, justice, and equality – albeit to a lesser degree than we do today.

With the rise of Enlightenment thinking, natural law theorists like John Locke combined with other thinkers of the era like Rousseau, Voltaire, and Kant helped to raise natural law theory and individual rights to philosophical and political prominence. These views highlighted concepts of absolute rights, the focus on individuals instead of collectives, and political theories around justice, equality, and the legitimacy of authority.

The direct effects of these ideas were monumental, including widespread social shifts in support of natural rights, as well as both the French and American Revolutions. Each of these movements were based heavily on natural rights and Locke's notion of "consent of the governed," justifying what the revolutionaries saw as overturning unjust and oppressive authority. Since American independence and the failed First French Republic, natural rights have become more and more recognized across both Western nations and international law, inspiring bills of rights, charters of human rights, and other codifications of these principles.

But these increases in formal recognition have not been enough to completely preserve natural rights in practice. Over the past century, we've seen an increase in utilitarian trade-offs and policies, as well as new forms of violations that have started to emerge, enabled through rapid increases in both taxation and spending by governments. Even aside from the arguments against excessive taxation as a violation of property, the use of taxation has been shown to violate freedom of conscience by funding controversial social programs, activist movements, and wars, actions that are often at odds with the beliefs of people being taxed.

Because of utilitarianism's default role in modern governance, we explored some select examples of policies that examined both utilitarian effectiveness – or how the results of the policy aligned with net utility – as well as a look at both intended and unintended consequences. Grouping our examples in this way highlighted one of the major gaps between the theory and practice – the difficulty involved in predicting utility. In the case of utilitarianism, whose entire moral system relies on outcomes instead of intentions or actions, this focus seems particularly apt.

Overall, both natural law and utilitarianism showed us mixed effectiveness in the real world, but for largely different reasons. While utilitarianism's goal of "greatest good" seems wholly reasonable in theory and on the surface, there are plenty of issues that pop up in the prediction and execution of these actions. These issues also highlight how difficult it can be to calculate the real utility after an action is taken – becoming exponentially more difficult as both the scope and the time horizon of the policy increase.

Natural law, on the other hand, has mixed effectiveness not because it is difficult to predict and execute, but because it is often put aside for the sake of expediency. But as we saw over the course of these chapters, many of the concepts keep reappearing over and over, popping up repeatedly in diverse civilizations and societies.

Now that we've had the opportunity to see how these two theories translate into real-world policy, we've begun to see their cracks, caveats, and complications. These examples and the preceding concepts have laid the foundation for this book's final part – the arguments both for and against each of these moral frameworks, and the ultimate conclusions we can draw from them.

PART IV

GREATEST GOOD

1

Arguing Morals

It was the early hours of April 15th in 1912, and one of the worst maritime disasters in history was unfolding; the RMS *Titanic* was sinking. The ship was carrying just over 2,200 people when it set sail from England and within three hours of hitting the iceberg more than 65% of them – 1,503 souls in all – were gone, consumed by the watery depths.

Unfortunately, the "unsinkable" vessel only had lifeboat capacity for less than half of the passengers, and as the Titanic filled with water the allocation of lifeboat seats was looking grim. Because of the prioritization of women and children – known as the Birkenhead drill – and first-class passengers, survival rates were heavily stratified by both class and gender. Women in first class were more than twice as likely to survive as women in third class, and six times more likely to survive than men in third class.

Outside of the situational panic, in many ways the priority for survival was based on moral utilitarian rules that attempted to even the outcomes for vulnerable members of the population, as well as implicit moral calculations that first class passengers were "worth more." While it's easy to look back and assign moral judgements over 100 years later, could you have made better utilitarian decisions if you had been an officer in charge of loading a lifeboat?

Would you have been able to evaluate each person and attempt to assess their value to humanity in the panic of the moment? Could you have known if the person you just turned away may have been the next Einstein, or Thomas Edison, or one of the Wright brothers? What are the unknown ripple effects of these simple in-the-moment decisions? As you can see, even though the ideas we have looked at may seem intuitive and straightforward so far, there are plenty of ethical boogeymen lurking in the shadows still waiting to be dragged into the light.

After identifying both the underlying concepts and some real-world applications of these theories in detail, we see the arguments that have started to form – both in favour and against. Some of these arguments have been around for a long time, initially raised by thinkers we covered in our first section like Hume, Kant, and Aquinas. Over this next section, we are going to look at a range of rationale, including concerns about democratic rule, a theological argument for secular natural law, and examples of unequal utility across individuals.

But aside from these historical debates, there are newer ideas presented here that consider the two moral systems from a modern perspective. These new arguments incorporate studies, concepts, and examples that were not necessarily available when the theories were first developed – a benefit of hindsight and the age of technology. Both natural law and utilitarianism have limitations in how they approach moral decision-making, and by looking at the following arguments in detail, we can reach conclusions on appropriate use, and when they should be avoided.
With all of that said, let's begin by looking at the case against natural law, with perspectives by Hume, Kant, and others who reject the theory either in part or entirely.

2

Opposing Natural Law

Even though the result of the Enlightenment was widespread support for natural law ideas, the theory wasn't unopposed. Many philosophers of the era were contributing to metaphysics, epistemology, and empirical thought, resulting in debate and arguments against natural law and related concepts. Thinkers we have already looked at, like Hume, Kant, Bentham, and others like Descartes and Hegel, each questioned the foundations of natural law theory in different ways.

An example of this is Immanuel Kant's argument against natural law. As you will recall, Kant was grouped with natural law theorists earlier in the book, largely because of the sizeable overlap between natural law and his ethical work on moral absolutism, moral autonomy, and other similar ideas. However, Kant's hyper-focus on rationality in ethics led directly to his critique of natural law. The root of his argument was that natural law relied on empirical observation, which he rejected in favour of morality based on pure reason.

He believed that human behaviour had the capacity to change over time, and in those circumstances moral systems based on that behaviour would become inconsistent and irrational. Alongside these concerns, Kant argued that natural law was flawed because it assumes that the natural order is inherently moral. For these reasons, Kant's ethical system, deontological ethics, was developed as a moral guide based entirely on pure reason, an attempt to be truly universal, consistent, and absolute.

This concern about the assumption of nature's morality was shared by other thinkers as well, like Thomas Hobbes. In his work *Levia-*

than, Hobbes stated his belief that nature is a state of war and that without a powerful centralized government to keep order, life would be "solitary, poor, nasty, brutish, and short." The same concern was raised – thought in a different way – by David Hume through his "is-ought problem," also commonly known as Hume's Law. In essence, it challenges the idea that just because the state of nature *is* a certain way, that doesn't automatically follow that we *ought* to use it as moral guidance.

An example of the problem being applied to natural law is as follows. A natural law theorist may attempt to argue that since humans have a natural motivation to preserve their own lives, it follows that we should aim to preserve human life. Hume's Law argues against this idea, claiming that the existence of natural human instincts for self-preservation does not automatically dictate that humans have a moral obligation to preserve the lives of others.

While Hume's law is an important consideration, unlike some older less defined versions of nature and morality like Aristotle's concept of *telos*, natural law theorists rarely jump straight from *is* to *ought*. Instead, like utilitarianism's use of utility to bridge the gap between the two, natural law commonly uses natural social cohesion as the bridge between human nature and natural rights. The argument for self-preservation above would instead present the idea that the existence of natural human tendencies for self-preservation results in a moral obligation to respect the lives of others *in order to preserve natural peace, innate justice, and social cohesion*.

So Kant rejected natural law for its basis in empiricism instead of rationality, and Hume raised concerns about the validity of its empirical foundation – despite Locke being one of the founders of British empiricism. German philosopher Hegel, on the other hand, believed that morality wasn't absolute or fixed and challenged the universality of natural law, claiming that empirical evidence is dependent on both social and historical context. He also argued that natural rights and duties were overly reductionist, condensing fundamentally social beings down to a collection of individuals. However, from the perspective of natural law, the recognition of the individual is precisely what makes the greater social groups function.

With the rise of utilitarian theory, Bentham famously dismissed natural rights as "nonsense upon stilts." He believed that laws should be based on his new concept of utility, and that human nature couldn't be used to discover universal moral truths. Instead, he focused the development of utilitarianism on measuring the happiness of tangible outcomes. Although the revolutionary events of the 18th century would prove him wrong, he believed that natural law was too abstract, and therefore not practical for creating legal and political systems.

The opinion that natural law is not practical was also shared by Rousseau in his work *The Social Contract*. In his case, he argued that even though humans might be good by nature, natural laws were not robust enough to practically govern complex societies. This could lead to situations where fundamental rights conflict with each other, leading to ambiguity in moral action.

While moral absolutism and universality are central features of natural law, critics argue that as society, technology, and philosophy progress, unchanging principles can be easily misapplied to new ethical situations. An example can be seen in the widespread adoption of the internet and the capacity for instant duplication of information. While there are natural law arguments both for and against intellectual property laws, the advent of new technology raises questions around the right to the product of one's own labour, especially when software can take years of effort to produce but can be duplicated and resold in moments.

In these unprecedented situations, traditional views on nature and rights can be difficult to interpret or reconcile, leading to confusion, disagreement, and inconsistent approaches to enforcement. This also demonstrates one of the ways that natural law is sometimes considered unintuitive. Utilitarianism might approach this situation and create rules based on what outcome would be best, natural law could come to unintuitive conclusions about legitimacy – or lack thereof – of owning digital information created through labour.

Natural law's lack of intuition in certain situations also isn't limited to the complex intersection of technology and traditional rights. For example, according to a study published in *PNAS* in 2020 which collected data from across 42 countries and 70,000 total participants, more than 81% of respondents endorsed the utilitarian action of killing one person in order to save five others[28]. This high level of similarity in moral judgement around the world implies an underlying level of moral intuition that is clearly at odds with the approach of natural law. Unique ethical dilemmas like this lead to opponents of the theory claiming that the restrictions that natural rights place on society are not morally intuitive and are difficult to follow, especially in times of crisis or impending threat.

The restrictions of natural rights also raise another major concern about practicality when it comes to politics, particularly the mixed compatibility with democratic processes and ideals. In a nutshell, the relationship between natural law and democracy is complicated. On the one hand, it provides a political mechanism for individuals to exercise political autonomy and influence social outcomes, and on the other hand, the democratic principles of majority rule directly conflict with natural rights.

Through the use of voting for representatives and referendums, individuals are provided with some level of influence in their government, granted it is usually a very limited form of consent. Still, without this ability to express their preferences, Locke's ideas of consent of the governed would be difficult to achieve. Because of this, the constant struggle between natural law and democratic ideals often boils down to either diluting the will of the people in order to prevent violations of rights or respecting the choices of the majority at the cost of individuals.

In even more stark contrast, anarchists like Lysander Spooner argued that even the existence of authority – democratic or not – contradicts natural law. He outright rejected the idea of the social contract, believing that natural law only legitimized voluntary interactions in every single situation, and authority could not exist without coercion.

Although there were also arguments against natural law by socialist and communist thinkers of the 19th century, some of them simply revolved around aligning natural law views with the interests of the "ruling class" in order to dismiss them. Philosophers like Marx and Engels instead thought that morality was inseparable from the material conditions of society – largely reducing morality to categorizing people as exploiters and exploited according to their perceived class.

However, their arguments against prevailing legal and moral theories – including natural law – as a tool of economic exploitation is a fundamental mischaracterization of the theory. The purpose of the work by Locke and Spooner, for example, is entirely the opposite: emancipation from authority and systemic exploitation. This was demonstrated by the American and French Revolutions, centred on the principles of returning power and justice to the people.

In the past few centuries, there have been many different moral theories that have questioned the legitimacy of natural law's foundations. Kant's work, although parallel in many ways – criticized the theory for being empirical instead of purely rational. Hume on the other hand, criticized the theory's basis in reason, arguing that morality was based on emotion and was subjective. This ironic tug-of-war between explicit empirical and rational viewpoints has left natural law in the centre, a mixture of two philosophical approaches to morality.

Aside from these disagreements, opponents have also raised claims that the simplicity of natural law is impractical in developed society, a suggestion that complex problems require complex solutions. Since it ignores outcomes and focuses on moral action, natural law has also been labelled unintuitive by utilitarian thinkers – who reject the sanctity of the individual in favour of the collective.

In the end, disagreements with the underlying concepts behind natural law have existed since ideas joining natural order and moral behaviour first emerged. That being said, many of these concerns have been addressed, and the case for natural law remains strong as we will see in the next chapter.

3

The Case for Natural Law

With ideas that have extended back thousands of years, some of the fundamental concepts of natural law have since appeared in almost every civilization around the world. Whether they surfaced in the form of laws that protect individuals from authority, each other, or through cultural beliefs in innate human value. Even though not every natural right was respected by each nation, empire, or group, the ideas can be seen to surface over and over again. In the past chapters we looked at some of the major examples that helped influence modern thought, making up only a few of the countless instances throughout history that align with these basic principles.

In essence, the widespread persistence and emergence of these views across unrelated cultures is an independent validation of natural law's core claims, and a powerful argument for the theory. It demonstrates that these ideas are common to human nature and social interaction and highlights the themes of natural justice which underpin human bonds.

Although in the vast majority of situations these related laws weren't directly tied to explicit theories like natural law, they are derived from human nature through the use of reason – the process that defines the theory. These moral rules and laws going back as far as ancient Mesopotamia – and likely further – acknowledge, encode, and protect the *natural rights* that make up our most essential human properties and goals.

Some of these rights are a consequence of natural biology, like the right to self-preservation or reproduction, which are not unique to humans but almost all forms of life. Others are derived from uniquely human traits, such as the capacity for rational thought, leading to the right to freedom of conscience and expression. Others still are a reflection of our social nature, providing guidelines and guardrails for interactions with others, such as protections from arbitrary authority in the right to liberty and the right to property. And finally, other aspects like the right to equal treatment under the law, natural justice, and the Lockean social contract, help define the parameters of how we enforce and resolve disputes in a way that respects all rights in order to maximize natural peace and justice.

Because of the widespread reflection of these rights throughout human history and the belief that rights are observable in nature by everyone, supporters believe that natural rights are self-evident. This can be seen in the natural law inspired U.S. Declaration of Independence, which includes the following as a part of its second paragraph.

> *We hold these truths to be self-evident, that all men are created equal, that they are endowed by their Creator with certain unalienable Rights, that among these are Life, Liberty and the pursuit of Happiness.*

Although the document only lists a few specific rights, others were later included in the U.S. Constitution's Bill of Rights, capturing many of the natural law beliefs that were prevalent at the time. Defined and analysed during the Enlightenment, each of these rights is the result of rational analysis of these human or natural properties, a codification of inherent human rights – or what Lysander Spooner called the "science of justice."

As we've already seen earlier on, the rights themselves are only a part of natural law. Over the past few centuries, much of the political work during the Enlightenment by Locke and others explored the implications of these rights, extending the concepts to far reaching conclusions about legitimacy of government, the obligations of citizens, and human interactions on both local, national, and even international levels.

Ultimately however, even though many of these greater political concepts are integral to Western thought, philosophy, and society, they aren't exclusive to the West. Whether it is called natural law or something else, the principles of natural rights can be derived by any culture or civilization through an analysis of human nature, as we have already seen. This gives natural law the unique benefit of being a universal moral system built on concepts that any human can discover for themselves, regardless of location, social context, and culture.

One of the implications of this is that unlike morally relative approaches, natural law provides a globally applicable moral benchmark that can measure human action regardless of location or circumstance. It can be used to judge violations fairly and equally in modern culture, historical societies, and isolated tribal communities in equal measure. This idea was clearly conveyed by writer, historian, and politician Lord Acton in the following quote.

> *Moral precepts are constant through the ages and not obedient to circumstances.*

This universality of natural rights also creates an immutable foundation for the idea that all people, by virtue of their humanity, have inherent worth, respect, and dignity that must be recognized. These natural law arguments were the primary driver behind the abolition of slavery both after the French Revolution and in early America, as well as many later women's rights and civil rights movements in the 20th century.

Even though the influence of natural law has declined in recent times, these principles still help guide moral behaviour across cultures and between different groups of people. In the international sphere, while it can be difficult to separate geopolitical ambitions from humanitarian forms of interventionism, international communities will often attempt to step in to prevent extreme human rights abuses in foreign nations. An example can be seen in the Western intervention in Kosovo during the ethnic cleansings that occurred during the late 1990s.

Although foreign intervention is a contentious subject among modern supporters of natural rights, in the case of Kosovo both Grotius's and Locke's respective works support the move by international communities. Locke's work in particular highlighted how violations of natural rights were grounds for invalidation of government authority and sovereignty, in this case representing a fundamental failure of the Yugoslav government to fulfil its primary function of protecting its citizens – leading to the protection of rights by external forces.

Another effect of the theory's universality and basis in nature is the implication that natural rights and morality are absolute. Since these "rules" are embedded in the natural order of humanity, they are not subject to change, regardless of situation or cultural values. Even though opponents and subscribers to moral relativism categorize this as an inflexible defect of natural law, it is not a flaw but instead a feature. Unlike competing ethical systems like utilitarianism, the moral absolutism provides a fixed point of reference for all human behaviour, reducing moral uncertainty and avoiding confusing and complex justifications for action.

Aside from the simplicity of decision-making based on natural rights, it allows individuals to make choices that are less impacted by personal biases in the calculation of outcomes, evaluating actions on whether they violate rights or not. By refusing to condone actions that violate rights, it ensures the protection of all people's natural rights instead of gambling them for the chance at a subjectively "greater" outcome.

Moral absolutism – whether Kantian ethics or natural law – provides certainty, stability, and a high-trust framework that allows individuals to live without fear that their inherent value as an individual will be arbitrarily compromised for any reason. This means that no matter who decides that an action is in the best interests of society, they cannot legitimately violate your rights to life, liberty, or property in order to give it a try.

The breakdown of natural law into granular rights is also a major benefit to the theory, providing a simple and practical toolset for judging action. Unlike utilitarianism, which requires complex moral calculations no matter the situation being considered, natural rights provide explicit restrictions against certain behaviours. This allows rights to be upheld in complex situations with incredibly intuitive and straightforward considerations of whether the potential action violates individual rights.

The focus on individual rights and the effect of actions on a personal level also helps identify and hopefully prevent direct and indirect violations of natural law. An example of this can be seen in the use of taxation in order to collect funds from the population. By a utilitarian standard, the collection of taxes is a compromise of individual property in order to fund programs that benefit society at large. But once taxes are collected, even utilitarian moral calculations become blurred, and the effects are abstracted away from the costs to individuals. So when government spending results in a mixture of both positive and negative outcomes, the costs to the taxpayer are already factored out, and we often simply look at the program's effects, rarely in relation to their full costs. But examining those same policies through the lens of natural law, we can identify government violations of the individual's property rights through excessive taxation, and then the use of those same funds to violate the right to liberty or freedom of conscience, etc.

Having the individual and their natural rights as the root focus of all moral action provides a clear and intuitive expectation of what inherent human dignity means for both yourself and others. This simple understanding of what others – whether people or authority – cannot legitimately do to you is also a prerequisite for ensuring that everyone's rights are equal under the law. After all, if you don't understand what protections and expectations apply to you under a complex legal system, is it even possible to ensure that you are treated fairly under the law?

This moral foundation based on individuals and their interactions also emphasizes personal moral autonomy, making it clear that individuals are directly responsible for their own lives and their actions in relation to others. This cornerstone of ethical behaviour prevents the delegation of morality to others – including authority – who may decide that violations of rights are in the interests of society or even themselves. It enforces the idea that moral behaviour is tied to action and respect for natural rights, **without caveat.**

This contrasts with utilitarian systems, where some level of hierarchical moral delegation is required in complex situations. If a decision is made by positions of authority that certain actions are best for social well-being, people in lower positions with less information are required to trust that the decision will result in moral outcomes, being unable to validate, assess, or predict outcomes themselves.

To demonstrate, let's imagine the classic trolley problem. In this situation, you are the operator in charge of switching trolleys on tracks and are receiving instructions via radio from your supervisor. You are able to see one of the two tracks, the one with the single individual tied to it. A call comes in requiring that you switch the trolley to the track with a single person in order to save lives. The natural law approach means that you wouldn't change tracks, whether or not you were aware of the five people currently tied in front of the vehicle, but the utilitarian situation is unique. If you choose to evaluate the situation yourself, doing nothing would appear to have the greatest utility. However, by delegating moral decision-making to authority and "just following orders," you will save the lives of the other five people – the moral action by utilitarian standards.

Although this example seems contrived and somewhat farfetched, the idea translates to complex modern government policies that have wide-ranging effects. These government actions are rarely fully understood or predictable at an individual level, whether by a member of the public or even a front-line government employee – our trolley operator. Circling back, unlike the potential for participation in unknown moral circumstances, the application of natural law is inseparable from the personal responsibility of direct action.

Even though natural law is considered to be inflexible because of its many restrictions on potential action – as seen in the example above, in different ways the theory provides greater flexibility. When considering cultural and social values, utilitarianism makes demands of society for action that leads to optimal outcomes regardless of whether the required action conflicts with cherished beliefs. Natural law, on the other hand, steps back and lets individuals, communities, and religions retain traditions and values – as long as the rights of others aren't negatively impacted.

In other words, the gap between prescriptive and restrictive guidance is left unfilled by natural law, leaving space for individuals to make personal choices. Whether you are a Confucianist, atheist, Christian, or Muslim, you are able to effectively build your moral system on top of natural law. This is further demonstrated by the history and spread of natural law views, which saw contributing philosophers distributed across cultural and religious borders, from ancient China to the Abbasid caliphate during the Golden Age of Islam.

A key factor to this flexibility is that in order for both secular and theological belief systems to be compatible with natural law, it is necessary that moral principles be discoverable without religious guidance. This idea was supported by Locke, Grotius, and even the religious scholars Aquinas and Qadi Abd al-Jabbar. Tying back to the idea of nature and universality, they believed that since moral codes were empirical and derived from nature, they didn't depend on religious interpretation.

In fact, one of the most compelling theological arguments for natural law results in the conclusion that the theory is secular. This argument was provided by St. Thomas Aquinas in his magnum opus, the *Summa*

Theologica, published 200 years after his death, and can be summarized in the following way.

Given the following premises:

1. An omnibenevolent and just God would desire humans to live in accordance with his divine order and moral laws.

2. God gave human beings the capacity for reason, observation, and the use of logical inference.

3. Nature is an expression of God's eternal law and can be evaluated with the cognitive tools given to humans.

4. Scripture has not been universally accessible to every human being.

5. It would be unjust for God to require humans to adhere to moral laws they have no way to discover.

In his famous work, Aquinas used these essential premises to conclude that:

- Since God is just, he must have provided human beings with a way to discover his moral will through a natural law, derived from the application of reason and observation to nature.

In the 750 years since his death, Aquinas's work has become a cornerstone of both Catholic and greater Christian theology, being adopted as an authoritative source of many different theological and philosophical issues even today.

From the secular perspective, the argument for natural law effectively skips the assumption that nature is a reflection of divinity, instead focusing purely on human nature. Whether the conclusions are drawn from biological imperatives, social foundations, or other mechanisms, the "source" of humanity or nature isn't considered as a factor in the resulting moral principles. In essence, the secular theory is the *what* of the moral system; Aquinas is simply providing a *why* through a theological lens. Overall, the case for natural law is incredibly strong. The emergence of similar natural principles across the world in almost every time period and culture since the dawn of civilization is a strong validation of natural rights and their relationship to human nature. The empirical nature of the theory, and the resulting universal principles that have arisen provide a constant, stable, and just foundation for all human interaction. The theory allows for individual preferences and beliefs, neglecting to make demands that are unreasonable or restrictive, instead simply reflecting human properties that pre-existed the theory as a formalized system of ethics. But that isn't to say it is perfect. As we saw, there is plenty of opposition and even alternate ethical theories that have arisen. In the next chapter, we will take a look at the case for natural law's primary contemporary alternative – utilitarianism.

4

The Case for Utilitarianism

Just like natural law, utilitarianism has also had a wide range of supporters, contributors, and critics since it was first developed by Bentham a few centuries ago. Even though the historical legacy of the theory isn't as rich and deep, recent society has more than made up for utilitarianism's lack of influence in the early eras of human history. Especially since the early 20th century, there has been a steep increase in adoption of utilitarian rationale alongside rising support for centralized authority, collectivism, and a broader role for government in society.

To this end, we have to ask – why and how did utilitarianism become such a prominent decision-making paradigm? Although the how will be touched on a little later, the why fits nicely into this chapter. One of the major benefits of utilitarianism is the moral validation of political expediency. In essence, utilitarianism allows policymakers a huge range of flexibility in assessing problems, solutions, and their expected outcomes. No matter the situation at hand, if there is a chance that outcomes can be improved, there is a path forward. While natural law's answer to the question "Are the costs worth it?" is almost certainly a resounding **NO**, utilitarianism instead responds with its own question – "What do we get in return?"

In theory, by enabling any action that improves outcomes, not only do you have more flexibility in terms of available decisions, but every decision should result in net positive outcomes to social well-being and the common good. The other related benefit is that it provides actionable moral guidance. To make this benefit clearer, let's take a look at an analogy.

Imagine you are visiting a national park, and your goal is to take the best photograph possible. Our two characters in this example are a natural law conservation officer and your utilitarian local tour guide. If you ask the conservation officer where to get the best photo, he'll likely shrug his shoulders, but what he can do is give you a list of the areas of the park you should avoid for safety or environmental reasons.

On the other hand, the tour guide will be able to advise you on locations for the best photograph, but it might involve entering a dangerous or protected space. If your goal is to take the best photograph, the tour guide will likely help evaluate the risk of these protected areas, making a decision that accounts for the best combination of risk and potential reward.

These two roles reflect the approaches of the two theories to moral guidance. Natural law will prohibit access (actions that violate rights) regardless of outcomes, and utilitarianism will balance the risk and reward (net utility) in order to suggest optimal outcomes.

Utilitarianism is able to approach and provide guidance not only in the realm of policy or law but in many different areas of life, though always within the context of maximizing utility. Whether you are aiming to donate to charity, choose a career, decide which product to buy, or determine foods to eat, utilitarianism can help guide your choices based on which outcomes are best for society. It also includes a mechanism for resolution for complex situations, since if there are several options available, theoretically the moral one is the one that has the greatest net benefit.

This also helps make utilitarianism incredibly intuitive – at least on the surface. By having the flexibility to take almost any action as long as it results in net good, the theory provides a system of decision-making that is what most would consider common sense. Simplified, it aligns very closely with natural intuitive human empathy; if it makes lots of people happy, it is likely moral, if it increases suffering, it is likely immoral.

This is demonstrated again by the 2020 study referenced earlier in which more than 81% of 70,000 people across 42 countries chose the utilitarian option in a simulated trolley problem. This level of widespread alignment on moral action across different cultures and beliefs reveals that the intuitive moral response in certain situations is closer to utilitarianism than natural law. Based on these results and the intuition behind the action, it is likely that as the calculation shifts further and further towards greater outcomes, even more would choose the utilitarian option, despite the costs.

Another aspect of the intuitive nature of utilitarianism – or more accurately consequentialism – is the focus on results. Judging actions based on tangible outcomes is intuitive because it aligns with the practical way that we make most decisions. Since most human action is centred on achieving specific goals, the theory is easy to understand and apply for most people.

For example, lying is almost universally considered immoral, however, lying in order to spare someone's feelings is a common action that is seen as moral. Although a simple example of utilitarianism, you can see how a moral trade-off can be entirely justified based on the measurable outcome – in this case, not hurting someone's feelings.

The measurable aspect of judging outcomes is also highly beneficial compared with other forms of intuitive decision-making. Since individual intentions and desires are difficult – if not impossible – to verify and measure, consequentialism aims to use empirical evidence in order to objectively determine morality based purely on results. This gap between intentions and outcomes was captured by French Abbot Bernard of Clairvaux in the 12th century, with the following now-famous quote.

The road to hell is paved with good intentions.

Even though reliance on outcomes is a double-edged sword, it does allow the theory to be grounded in real-world impacts instead of a theoretical and abstract philosophy like Kant's deontology.

Another practical aspect of utilitarian thought is the theory's compatibility with modern political systems – particularly democracy and the expansion of government. With regards to democracy, the utilitarian goal of maximizing well-being for the most people, aligns closely with democracy's mechanisms of majority rule. Even though it isn't always perfect, it allows the majority to choose their preferences and advocate for their own desires. Citizens are able to advocate for policies and services that match their wishes, and the government can fulfil its role to execute the will of the people.

The expanded role of government as both protector and provider is not only compatible with utilitarianism, it is a direct result of utilitarian views – as we will cover in more detail shortly. This is largely because of utilitarianism's view that inaction is tantamount to negative action, effectively creating a moral burden to solve problems. This has led to the view espoused by many that the role of government is just that – improvement of society. As more and more inequities or suboptimal outcomes are identified, utilitarianism continuously demands action to improve the situation, a role that modern policymakers are more than happy to fulfil.

This requirement for moral action is also seen by many as a major benefit. By demanding positive change, utilitarianism theoretically should always result in a constant stream of net improvements in the lives of every person – or at least society. Over time, this should lead to less suffering, resulting in a better experience for every human, and less indifference since morality requires them to act.

Overall, utilitarianism presents a powerful and compelling moral theory, one built on the idea of a measurably better world. It has proved to be intuitive, aiming to maximize good with every action, actionable – with guidance for every situation, and expedient – never shutting down action, simply considering the cost. Although the modern adoption of many of these ideas seem like a validation of the theory's complete success, the question remains – how far does the theory hold up? Next up, we will take a look at many of the downsides, the gotchas, and the arguments against utilitarianism, both old and new.

5

Opposing Utilitarianism

Since the time of Bentham and Mill, utilitarianism has faced heavy criticism in a number of different areas. Concerns about political, economic, and unrealistic aspects of the theory have been common over the past few centuries, highlighting both practical and theoretical failures. Many of these issues have become especially visible over recent decades as the Western world has increasingly embraced and escalated the use of utilitarian policymaking. In this chapter, we will take a look at some of the more traditional arguments against utilitarianism, supplemented by studies, arguments, and information that has emerged in recent times.

One of the first building blocks of utilitarianism that comes under fire is the central tenet of impartiality in decision-making. Although natural law also requires impartial behaviour, its form of impartiality boils down to not violating rights equally, more of an implicit standard. Utilitarianism, on the other hand, is centred on proactive guidance that requires the impartial evaluation of impacts on individuals. Although in theory utilitarians have the ability to measure the happiness of strangers using the same scale as those of family and friends, practically speaking this is unrealistic.

Even though in the trolley problem study we referenced earlier we showed how some utilitarian decisions are naturally intuitive, studies also demonstrate that familial preferences are almost always weighed significantly more than those of strangers. A study published by Burnstein et al. in the *Journal of Personality and Social Psychology* in 1994 confirmed these preferences, demonstrating that people were more generous towards close family than others, and weighed distant family over strangers in life-or-death situations, among other natural evolutionary preferences[29].

Another example can be seen in a 2018 study in the journal Plos One, which showed that individuals are more willing to donate organs to relatives than non-relatives or anonymous recipients[30]. These studies, alongside many others, contradict the fundamental expectation in utilitarian decision-making that we can consider every person's well-being in equal measure.

This subjectivity also isn't unique to our treatment of individuals. Another of utilitarianism's most significant failures appears when comparing different people's goals. Even though the subjectivity of value in the economic sphere is indisputable, utilitarianism as a system still relies on the flawed idea of objective moral outcomes. This often presents itself as an inherent bias in the decision-maker's evaluations of which outcomes are good or bad, leading to the potential for different individuals to judge the same situation in different ways. You don't have to look far to find differences in opinion on whether a policy has been beneficial or not, let alone any number of personal desires or preferences.

And the difference in evaluating positive and negative outcomes is only the start of utilitarianism's subjectivity problem. Even in a hypothetical world where everyone shares the exact same standard for determining happiness or suffering to a high degree of accuracy, not everyone values happiness to the same degree. Many individuals would prefer autonomy, dignity, purpose, or virtue over simple happiness, highlighting the subjectivity of goals as well, not only calculation.

A simple example can be observed with the ancient Greek and Roman stoics, whose belief system revolved around self-control and the suppression of emotions they viewed as destructive. Buddhism, Confucianism, Spartan Culture, Monastic Christians, and other movements throughout history have also centred their philosophies on self-control and the overcoming of hedonism, instead often holding certain virtues as the highest good.

With the work of John Stuart Mill and other utilitarians, there have been attempts within the theory to solve these problems, but often with adverse effects. For Mill, he believed that the solution was the application of different weights assigned to different types of activities or outcomes. Even Mill attempted to incorporate his personal preferences into utilitarianism, using them to evaluate the well-being of others who may not have shared these values. This is demonstrated in the following quote from his 1863 work *Utilitarianism*.

> *It is better to be a human being dissatisfied than a pig satisfied; better to be Socrates dissatisfied than a fool satisfied.*

Although this quote clearly validates the concerns of critics, others within the theory have tried to introduce changes and variations in order to mitigate these problems. With the development of preference utilitarianism, attempts were made to use utility to measure the preferences of every person, a way to account for subjectivity.

However, even this falls significantly short of its goal. The potential for conflicts between diverse individual preferences can make calculations exponentially more difficult, especially when people's preferences can be counter-intuitive or morally questionable, including preferring destructive or negative outcomes. Collecting and reconciling preferences is also a daunting task, and even though there are modern processes like referendums, surveys, and polling that can help gather individual desires, they are often limited in scope and cannot capture the wide ranges of public opinion.

Another issue that arises from preference utilitarianism is that people are generally not very good at predicting what choices will make them or others happy. An example of this is a study by Daniel Gilbert on

Affective Forecasting in 2003, where it was shown that people often overestimate both the positive and negative impacts of future events on their happiness[31].

Effectively, the subjectivity and diverse nature of people's happiness, goals, and values, present an almost impossible barrier to the practical calculation of utility or implementation of moral policy, especially on decisions that involve complexity, large scope, or interactions with other people.

Related to the issue of subjectivity in a different way is one of the thought experiments raised by Robert Nozick in his 1974 book *Anarchy, State, and Utopia*. This experiment, *the utility monster*, presents a challenge to the idea of maximizing overall happiness or utility, especially in the context of subjective individual values. In it, Nozick imagines that there is a hypothetical creature, the utility monster, that gains more utility from each unit of a resource or from an experience than anyone else.

Just like two people eating the same dessert might receive different levels of happiness or satisfaction from it, the monster would gain more happiness from it than all other beings. According to the principles of classical utilitarianism, society would be morally required to give most, if not all, resources to this monster, because it would maximize total utility.

Even though some critics argue that this scenario is hyperbolic and discounts the nuance of real-world utilitarian applications, in the 50 years since Nozick's experiment was published there have been observable examples that we can point to. One of these examples is the utilitarian arguments for trickle-down economics that have been made by some groups. Supporters of the policy claim that every dollar distributed to a wealthy individual or corporation (our utility monster), will have a greater impact (utility) through investing and employment, than it would by giving that same dollar directly to a regular citizen.

Although some policies like bank bailouts, increased taxation, and specific subsidies can also be seen as overt examples of this valuation, in effect, every single dollar that is spent from public coffers uses similar reasoning. Recipients of public money are selected with the belief that a dollar spent there will have a greater impact than in other places. So even though Nozick raised these issues as a theoretical thought experiment, many policies are built on the idea of unequal distribution that can consume more than their "fair share" with moral sanction in order to maximize outcomes.

Another related criticism of utilitarianism is the calculation problem. In the example above, we encounter the problem of being able to identify and predict impacts of public resource allocation relative to other options. The problem of calculation applies to almost every centralized system that operates on a large scale, whether that is economics or utilitarian moral decision-making. While in small and self-contained situations calculations might not be too complicated, the theory requires that every action is evaluated against alternatives in order to maximize utility. This leads to constant prioritization of potential options, including the weighing of one's own needs, and those of one's family, against the greater good.

Take, for example, a utilitarian out at a restaurant with friends who is deciding whether or not to order dessert. The money spent on the luxury could be given to someone less fortunate, donated to a charity, or have a greater moral impact in many different ways. Are they less moral for not choosing to maximize happiness in small and potentially trivial situations? Is there an obligation in every aspect of life to pursue moral outcomes?

Calculating the morality of outcomes is made even more difficult when time preference is taken into account. Long-term outcomes are inherently more difficult to predict, and sometimes short-term suffering can lead to the greatest long-term outcomes. An example of this is current approaches towards environmental stewardship and resource consumption. While there is little doubt that we should reduce pollution and work towards reducing our environmental impacts in the long term, there are significant short-term pains that would result in immediate action.

In effect, the calculation problem has a variety of facets, including the subjective evaluation of potential and real outcomes, the complexity of analysing alternate options, missing information, and the measurement of utility across different time preferences. Each of these, and more, present unique challenges to the calculation of utility – whether based on happiness, preferences, or collective well-being. In some situations, these calculations also fail to account for random or external variables, resulting in moral judgement based on happenstance, or what some critics call *moral luck*.

The concept of moral luck was popularized by philosophers like Bernard Williams and Thomas Nagel. In an example put forward by Nagel to illustrate the principle, he discusses two different drivers. One driver speeds recklessly but makes it home safe, while the other one is driving in the same way but the driving leads to a car accident. Although both of the drivers took similar actions, the outcomes were vastly different, leading to different moral judgements for each one.

The results of this circumstantial guilt can even lend itself to modern arguments that much – if not all – of our own behaviour is outside of our control. After all, if those that came before us hadn't set the world on this course, we wouldn't have reacted the way we did, and our actions wouldn't have the outcomes that they did.

As a real-world example, we can look at the cases of Edward Snowden in 2013 and Daniel Ellsberg in 1971. Both Snowden and Ellsberg leaked classified government documents to the public, with Snowden releasing information about illegal NSA surveillance programs, and Ellsberg releasing details about illegal government behaviour in the Vietnam war. While Snowden was charged under the Espionage Act and was forced to flee the United States, Ellsberg's charges were eventually dismissed.

Both of these acts were very similar in scope, however the public and legal moral judgement of these two cases differ greatly, in large part because of public sentiment and the political climates at the time. With the high degree of complexity involved in predicting outcomes, the ability for similar actions to have radically different outcomes can often make utilitarian moral judgements inconsistent and unpredictable.

In *Anarchy, State, and Utopia*, Robert Nozick also introduced another thought experiment that was aimed at countering ethical theories based on hedonism, like utilitarianism. In the *experience machine*, Nozick wants us to imagine a hypothetical machine that could give us any experience we could imagine if we plug ourselves in. With just this machine and no other external needs, anyone could experience their entire life filled with maximum pleasure and fulfilment, even though the experiences themselves would be simulated and not real. According to classical utilitarianism's focus on pleasure and pain, plugging in would unequivocally be the moral choice, a conclusion that was dismissed by Nozick and others.

Even though the situation is hypothetical, this thought experiment also has parallels to modern day experiences, such as video games, as well as the use of increasingly potent drugs in order to experience pleasure through chemical escapism. In this instance, there are two specific arguments at play, one that synthetic or simulated experiences are inherently worth less than authentic ones, and another argument that escapism and pleasure-seeking are not positively related to overall fulfilment and well-being.

While the first argument is philosophical in nature, research in the field of VR has found that even though it can evoke strong emotional responses, most participants often view these experiences as less meaningful or valuable compared to real-life experiences, particularly because of the lack of real-world consequences involved.

With regards to the second argument, studies on recreational drug use show negative long-term consequences and worse mental health outcomes, including a study published in 2020 in JAMA Psychiatry that found decreases in mental health outcomes for recreational cannabis use[32]. Interestingly, in contrast to substance-based escapism, in the case of video games, a recent study published in *Royal Society Open Science* in 2021 found that time spent playing video games was positively associated with overall well-being[33]. These two different methods of escapism, while neither proving nor disproving Nozick's concerns, certainly provide an interesting avenue for considering the thought experiment.

One of the next arguments against utilitarianism is related to one of the proposed benefits of the system, the inherent compatibility with democracy. As we talked about in the last chapter, forms of direct democracy align with preference utilitarianism, providing the majority of individuals with the ability to advocate for their own wishes. However, both preference and classical utilitarianism, like democracy, are often criticized for their potential for the oppression of minorities in order to serve the interests – or happiness – of the majority.

Warnings about fulfilling the desires of the majority can be traced back to Aristotle and his work *Politics*, where he argued against the concept of pure democracy. He believed that the rule of the majority often came at the expense of the minority, and that the majority's pursuit of their own interests led to injustice. These views were shared by many throughout history, and in 1835 the term "Tyranny of the Majority" was coined by French philosopher Alexis de Tocqueville in his work *Democracy in America* to capture this idea.

Although in the modern age Western liberal democracies are usually restrained by a combination of legal protections for individual rights and prohibitions on types of policies, as we have seen in previous chapters, these restrictions are not absolute. Rule utilitarianism parallels these restrictions through the implementation of guidelines for actions that lead to optimal outcomes. However, situations tend to arise that lead to the circumvention of these rules in order to serve the greater good, like government action in times of crisis.

One of the most straightforward examples of the compromise of the few for the benefit of the many takes us back to the trolley problem, a situation where utilitarianism actively prescribed the death of an individual in order to save the lives of five others. But while the utility calculation for the trolley problem is clear and the outcome is limited in scope, more open-ended or complex calculations may not be so clear-cut.

This type of problem can be extrapolated to other forms of extreme sacrifice and trade-off for utility. Let us imagine a town of 100 people that has 98 farmers, as well as one resident doctor and one baker, both of whom are nearing the age of retirement. If there are no alternatives available when these two people retire, is there a utilitarian case for forcing them to continue working against their wishes?

If the doctor quits, almost a 100 people will face potential negative consequences in the case of medical emergencies, but if she is compelled to continue, assuming all else is equal, only she faces the negative consequences of being forced to work. This case for the doctor being required to continue has overwhelming utility, resulting in her sacrifice for the greater good of the community. On the other hand, although the baker may bring happiness to the other residents of the town, likely the negative utility of using force to prevent his retirement would not be balanced by the positive impacts he brings to the community.

This idea has also been popularized in works of modern fiction. Taking the idea to an even greater extreme is a short story written by Ursula K. Le Guin in 1973, titled *The Ones Who Walk Away from Omelas*. The story presents a utopian city that only remains perfect because of the eternal misery of one single child kept locked in a dark, windowless room in a basement. The story questions the morality of sacrificing even a single person for the happiness of many, a clear parallel to this common argument.

In the real world, policies that reflect the will of the majority are common, even though they might result in increased suffering for some minority groups. Examples abound on both small and large scales, including Jim Crow laws, restrictions on same-sex marriage, religious majority laws, and language enforcement laws.

Just like our consideration of the doctor in a small town, these examples demonstrate that utilitarian ideas have the potential for trade-offs that result in drastic treatment of individuals and minority groups in service of the majority. The following quote by economist and historian Ludwig von Mises, published in his 1957 work *Theory and History*, sums up the idea in relation to natural rights.

> *The struggle for freedom is ultimately not resistance to autocrats or oligarchs but resistance to the despotism of public opinion.*

And many of these attitudes and majority preferences are still common around the world today. In a 2013 survey for the *Global Attitudes Project*, more than 90% of respondents in Jordan, Egypt, Indonesia, Pakistan, and Nigeria believed that homosexuality should not be accepted by society[34]. Given these statistics, direct democracy, preference utilitarianism, and likely other forms of utilitarianism would support the banning or repression of homosexual behaviour in those countries. With a focus on the outcomes of these laws, if a case was to be made that the benefits of increased social conformity and stability outweighed the costs to a small group, restrictions would not only be permissible but morally obligated.

This use of ends (outcomes) instead of means (actions) as the basis of morality has also faced opposition in the past century. In *The Road to Serfdom* in 1944, economist and philosopher Friedrich Hayek argued that the core principle of consequentialism, that the end justifies the means, results in "the denial of all morals" for individuals. Although aimed originally at collectivist ideas, his arguments are equally applicable to utilitarian principles.

In essence, his argument states that in systems of ethics where achieving the greatest good for the greatest number is the requirement for moral behaviour, if there exists an action to serve the greater good, you are morally obligated to make it. Logically then, any cost is permitted, no matter how horrible, as long as it results in this greatest good.

Hayek's argument can be presented in the following way.

- Utilitarianism asserts that the most moral action is the one that maximizes overall utility.

- Utility is calculated purely through evaluation of consequences.

- Intent and intrinsic morality of actions do not contribute to utility.

- Utilitarians have a moral obligation to maximize utility.

- Therefore, utilitarians have a moral requirement to take any action that results in maximization of utility.

The exploration of extreme utilitarian actions and morally questionable means in order to justify a greater, often misguided end, is also a common theme in modern popular culture. This trope can be found throughout books and movies, often demonstrating a villain's attempt to justify great tragedy with arguments that it will result in a utopian or preferable outcome.

In the recent Marvel's *Avengers*, the audience is presented with a villain named Thanos, whose aim is the elimination of half of all life in the universe, a move that he justifies with the claim that it will prevent suffering due to overpopulation and resource scarcity. *I, Robot* was a 2004 film based on works by Isaac Asimov that sees an AI attempting to imprison and control humanity in order to prevent their self-extinction. *The Watchmen* (2009), *Kingsman* (2014), *Inferno* (2016), and many other films rooted in older source material, all draw on similar themes, demonstrating the real underlying argument about maximizing utility at extreme costs.

These examples of modern media, while hyperbolic, highlight key issues in utilitarian thinking, including the focus on outcomes instead of actions, and the maximization of utility at any cost. Unfortunately, extreme trade-offs under the guise of the greater good are not exclusively confined to works of fiction.

Aside from the historical examples of collectivism that inspired Hayek's argument against these principles, in August of 1945, the United States dropped atomic bombs on the two Japanese cities of Hiroshima and Nagasaki. Despite the high number of casualties that were expected, the justifications of a swift end to the war and a dramatic reduction in Allied casualties were believed to be worth the cost. Ultimately, the bombings resulted in the deaths of between 100,000 and 300,000 people across the two cities, marking the most devastating single military attack in history.

Even today, the use of atomic bombs to end the war is still seen as morally justified by many across the West, illustrating that even horrific acts can be seen as morally acceptable when the stakes are high enough, a perfect demonstration of Hayek's concerns.

So, even though it is one of the most influential and prominent ethical theories of the modern age, utilitarianism is contested by many critics, and is riddled with flaws. Based on the impractical idea that human moral judgement can be entirely objective and impartial, it demands the suppression of human nature. These issues are compounded by utilitarianism's most fundamental requirement – the calculation of happiness.

Without the ability to quantify and calculate the potential outcomes of every single option, all while accounting for the desires, impacts, and goals of every individual, calculation is impractical at best, and impossible at worst.

These shortcomings present major barriers to the practical application of the theory, but the failures don't end there. With a basis entirely on outcomes, the effects of actions or circumstances outside of our control can result in moral judgements on our behaviour, an escape from responsibility. As Hayek pointed out, the focus on outcomes instead of action is also tied closely to the dissolution of individual rights. After all, if you are not willing to maximize the welfare of the collective for the sake of a single individual, the core tenet of utilitarianism –maximization of utility – is ignored.

Even though many of these traditional arguments in opposition to utilitarianism are convincing on their own, there are some areas that we can evaluate in even greater detail. Over the next chapter, we will look at some more unique challenges to utilitarianism as a practical theory.

6

Escalating Arguments

Building on the criticisms of the last chapter, let's look at some more specific and detailed criticisms that attempt to combine novel – or at least reimagined – arguments against the theory. Here we will dive into the concerns of calculation in much greater detail, alongside arguments that touch on concepts like the surprising utilitarian morality of lobotomies, putting the causal cart before the horse, and the delegation of morality.

Even though this chapter will identify and even name specific arguments for quicker reference later on, many of these challenges have likely been raised by others through centuries of debate on utilitarianism and its variations. With all of that said, let's jump into our next argument against the idea of utilitarian calculation – Moral Chaos.

Moral Chaos (Theory)

While the difficulty in predicting and evaluating long-term consequences is a common criticism of utilitarian ethics, I believe that the complexity problem has been drastically understated, especially as the scale of the action is increased. Since utilitarianism is focused solely on the consequences of actions, it is worth exploring the concept of empirical calculation of outcomes in greater detail.

Chaos theory in mathematics and physics is a field of study that examines the behaviour of dynamic systems, particularly how small changes or choices can lead to large and unpredictable effects. Often referred to as the "butterfly effect," one of the core notions of chaos theory is presented as a situation where the flap of a butterfly's wings can cause a tornado on the other side of the world. In effect, the theory presents the possibility that even small actions can cause significant effects, a chain reaction of unanticipated and often hidden ripples that can be vastly larger than the initial action.

With utilitarianism's entire system of morality based on evaluating outcomes, the idea of chaos theory and the sensitivity of effects to initial conditions raises questions about our ability to understand, let alone effectively evaluate morality using this approach.

However, even when ignoring the unpredictability of chain reactions of events, when investigating the connections between actions and outcomes, we should also be aware that not every cause has a single effect. While some actions may be straightforward and have a single action result in a single effect, oftentimes an effect will have multiple causes, or even multiple causes will all contribute to multiple effects.

An example of complex causality is the 2008 housing market crash in the United States. Policies on subprime lending, widespread speculation by investors, bundling of risky mortgages into securities, and relaxation of regulatory oversight were just some of the trends that contributed to the crash. The crash also consisted of a wide series of effects, including impacts on the banking sector like bankruptcies and bailouts, a rise in foreclosures and a collapse of house prices, reductions in consumer spending in retail, rising unemployment, increases in government debt, and significant declines in international trade around the world.

Given the complexity of causality and the unpredictability of outcomes that we have just discussed, how do we even begin to assign *morality* to an action? In the example of the 2008 housing crash above, how do we assign morality to the many initial causes? Are they each held responsible for the sum total utility of final outcomes, or is the resulting moral judgement split evenly across each of the initial causes? And how should we assign judgements in a causal chain, where actions and effects iteratively trigger more effects; are we held responsible for the decisions of others that were prompted by our own?

By now, we can begin to see the full scope of difficulty involved in measuring moral outcomes and associating them with actions, before even accounting for other issues like personal subjectivity or the weighing of diverse categories of effects like overall well-being, literacy rates, economic uncertainty, or many other variables.

In the end, despite arguments attempting to highlight the difficulty involved in utilitarian calculations, the full impact of the calculation problem appears much more significant than one would have imagined. The chaos and unpredictability inherent in any action makes the usefulness of outcomes alone an unstable metric for morality, not to mention the sheer difficulty of calculating the outcome in the first place.

When considering complex causality, such as effects with multiple causes, multiple causes intermingled with multiple effects, or even causal chains, tracing and identifying the source of short-term effects can become impractical. For long-term effects, it can become next to impossible.

However, even in a utopian world where all these causal relationships can be traced and understood to a high degree of empirical accuracy, we are left with the problem of calculating the utility of a single action. Each effect needs to be weighed and valued differently based on each of the many impacted individuals across a variety of contributing metrics such as happiness, long-term well-being, education and literacy, economic certainty, food and resource security, and many other factors over different time periods.

With these concerns in mind, it seems quite clear that the *true* extent of any outcome is guesswork at best. Ultimately, this suggests that the effectiveness of any consequentialist system – including utilitarianism – is not only speculative but unknowable.

Schrödinger's Morality

Another one of the most significant failures of consequentialist – and by extension, utilitarian – reasoning is the underlying principle that moral judgements should be based on the outcome of actions. As we have seen with the argument of moral luck and chaotic outcomes, there is the potential for external impacts on outcomes, and therefore moral judgements on our actions that are outside of our control.

In a lighthearted parallel to the popular thought experiment of "Schrödinger's cat," a situation where a cat in a box is supposed to be both alive and dead until an observation is made, utilitarian moral action is subject to similar constraints. Because only the true impacts or outcomes of an action determine its morality, until an action is taken and the effects are observed, there is no way to truly judge the action's morality beforehand.

From the complete reliance on the effects in order to validate the initial cause as a moral one, we are left with the following deductive argument.

- Actions are deemed moral by their consequences.

- Consequences can be predicted, but not known until after an action is taken.

- Therefore, the morality of an action cannot be known when it is being made.

So in effect, while consequences may be predicted and net utility calculations of actions may use these predictions, utilitarian actions can never be determined to be moral in advance. This fundamental limitation of utilitarian decision-making reduces its value as a tool for guiding moral action.

Equilibrium Pill

Let's imagine a new drug is created that can eliminate both positive and negative emotions when consumed, a hypothetical scenario inspired by the plot of the 2002 film *Equilibrium*. In a world where emotion can be limited or eliminated, it raises significant questions about the moral approach of utilitarianism.

With these tools at our disposal, should we compel its use in people with depression, whose negative emotions weigh much more than their positive ones? Or people who repeatedly commit crimes, in order to prevent their creativity or independent ability to commit crimes? Or perhaps the victims of violent crimes and those with trauma? Or how about simply people who disagree with government policies, causing social and political strife? Or as the government's argument in the movie suggests, should everyone be required to take these pills in order to prevent war, suffering, and all pain?

With the greatest happiness for the greatest number as the guideline for moral action, the answer to most of the above questions could likely be yes. A complete elimination of emotions for people whose utility is chronically negative would be an absolute moral improvement by utilitarian standards. Negative utilitarians may even choose to remove the emotions from every person, since it would effectively eliminate all negative emotions entirely.

The question might even become: To what extreme would utilitarian morality allow us to push treatment of those who have taken the pills? If we could remove the negative emotional effects of forced labour or even slavery, would the net utility of these actions be positive?

While this hypothetical seems extreme, some medical conditions with parallel effects to this drug do exist, such as anhedonia, a condition causing the complete inability – or drastically reduced ability – to feel pleasure, or even the effects of lobotomies. In a more direct parallel to the equilibrium pill, modern medications like antidepressants also exist that can cause "emotional blunting," a reduction in emotional response.

These situations raise ethical questions about treatment of these individuals in utility calculations, and utilitarianism's potential lack of regard for autonomy. So while the thought experiment remains largely hypothetical, the questions are relevant to specific subsets of humanity and to the application of existing medications.

Zeno's Moral Action

In the 5th century BCE, ancient Greek philosopher Zeno of Elea devised a series of philosophical problems centred around the concepts of motion and space, now generally known as *Zeno's paradoxes*. One of these paradoxes is the Dichotomy Paradox, which presents the following idea.

> *Imagine you want to walk to a nearby park. In order to reach your destination, you must first reach the halfway point. Then from that location, you must reach the halfway point of the remaining distance, and so on. Logically, it takes a finite amount of time to cover each half, and there is an infinite number of halves to cover, so you can never actually reach your destination in a finite amount of time.*

Zeno's paradox challenges our understanding of motion by suggesting that movement is impossible, even though in practice we obviously do reach our destinations. The criticism of utilitarianism presented in this section is an extrapolation based on applying the idea of Zeno's paradox to utilitarian decision-making.

In essence, the concern about moral action can be presented as follows.

- Utilitarianism requires that if an action can be taken that increases net utility, there is a moral duty to take it.
- Every complex action in the real world results in some combination of both positive and negative consequences.
- As negative consequences arise, new actions are required in order to increase utility, resulting in more positive and negative outcomes.
- Therefore, in a parallel to Zeno's paradox, the more actions we take towards utility, the more actions we are obligated to perform in order to address new negative outcomes. In this sense, it seems as though utilitarians never actually "reach their destination" or generate any pure contributions to net utility.

While this argument may seem rather abstract, it attempts to highlight two major issues with utilitarian action. The first is the compounding effect of actions or policies that contain trade-offs and compromises in order to maximize utility, and the second issue is with utilitarianism's approach to continuous moral demands for action compared to other ethical systems like natural law.

The first of these, the compounding effect of action, can often be seen in real-world policies whose outcomes may not have matched positive expectations, or when negative outcomes were more varied or widespread than expected.

A perfect example of this is the United States Tax Code, traced back to the ratification of the Sixteenth Amendment, and the following Income Tax Act in 1913. Over more than a century, continuous changes have been made that attempt to increase positive outcomes through the use of provisions, deductions, credits, and incentives that have aimed to provide public services, increase education rates, close loopholes, entice charitable giving, and encourage spending on social concerns like green initiatives.

This has led to constant modifications and additions, ultimately bringing the total size from its initial 400 pages, to over ten million words, estimated at over 70,000 pages in length. This complexity has led to massively increased compliance and enforcement costs, not to mention the public cost of legal loopholes that many regular citizens do not have the expertise to identify or use.

And tax policies are not unique in this regard, with the size of regulatory codes increasing across financial, healthcare, education, environmental, and other industries. As we continue to take action to introduce new policies in order to improve outcomes, the negative effects also compound, creating chaos, inequality, and complexity, obligating more and more government action to compensate.

Intuition and Cognitive Bias

Even though we just talked about intuition as a benefit of utilitarian ethics, in many ways it also presents one of the system's greatest weaknesses. When morality and intuition are aligned, it makes it easier for us to take moral action, reducing the effort, calculations, and self-control required to make simple or straightforward decisions. The goal of the greatest happiness for the greatest number is also an intuitive outcome, and one that most people can grasp and accept with little extra reasoning required. The major difference is that while the outcomes are often intuitive, getting to them is most certainly not.

Since utility can only be determined after an action is taken, utilitarian decision-making relies on a complicated problem, intuiting potential moral outcomes. Over the past several decades research has further explored the relationship between intuition, predicting outcomes, and effective decision-making, ultimately leading to conclusions that intuition is very often flawed or misleading.

The expanding field of research into cognitive biases attempts to identify and categorize common patterns of thought that limit objective analysis in different ways. There are currently over 180 cognitive biases that have been identified and named since the concept was first introduced by Amos Tversky and Daniel Kahneman in their 1972 paper titled *Subjective Probability: A Judgement of Representativeness*.

Even though most of these biases impact our ability to objectively interpret and predict moral outcomes, we can't hope to cover every one. For that reason, we will explore just a few examples to help demonstrate their effect on utilitarian decision-making.

One of the first examples of cognitive bias that most people will be familiar with is *Confirmation Bias*. In effect, this relates to people's natural tendency to find, interpret, weigh, and use information in a way that confirms their pre-existing beliefs. Real-world examples of this bias can be seen in many ideologically charged policies such as the War on Drugs, where policymakers often chose selective data on seizure rates and arrests, despite studies showing the policies' ineffective reductions in drug use rates.

Another example is the *Sunken Cost Fallacy*, which refers to the tendency to continue or double down on ongoing actions, primarily because of previous investments of money, effort, or time. For almost two decades, the United States Military was involved in the Vietnam War, a bloody conflict that is estimated to have cost $168 billion, or $1 Trillion after adjusting for inflation. Despite declining public support and increasingly questionable strategic value, the continued commitment to the war was in large part due to the lives and resources already spent.

The *Affect Heuristic* is a bias that relates to the impulse to make decisions based on emotion and affective responses instead of logical or objective analysis. Policies based on this type of bias are one of the most popular representations of cognitive bias and are often seen in response to isolated tragedies or events whose frequency or impact aren't statistically proportional to the public reactions. Examples of this bias can be seen in most emotionally driven policies, including the Patriot Act after 9/11, and public policy and reactions to nuclear power following the Chernobyl disaster in 1986.

Self-serving Bias is another common habit of attributing successes to your own actions, but attributing failures to external factors or others. A relatively recent example of this bias can be found during the COVID-19 pandemic in relation to the spread of the virus. Quite often, positive effects like successes in controlling the virus or reductions in cases were attributed to government policies, but when cases rose, external factors like public compliance or viral mutations were frequently blamed.

A final example that perhaps touches more on preference utilitarianism than other varieties is the *False Consensus Bias*, the tendency to overestimate the number of other people who share our beliefs or values. This can result in policymakers assuming widespread support for a proposed initiative, even though it contradicts the wishes of the public. An example of this is marijuana criminalization in the United States, which is still classified as an illegal substance by the federal government despite support for legalization reaching over 68% in 2024.

Although there are so many great examples of cognitive biases to choose from, these examples seemed particularly impactful, common, and likely relatable to most of us. The theme of most of the biases and policies mentioned above revolve around the suspension or circumvention of objectivity, both in evaluation of the current situation, as well as in relation to prediction for utility of outcomes.

Moreover, in addition to the cognitive biases involved, there is the fundamental problem of the complexity of large-scale social processes. Earlier we briefly discussed the intersection between "chaos theory" and large-scale ethical decision-making. It is often unclear which actions or social decisions lead to which, and this makes it prohibitively difficult to assign blame or success, making judgement ripe for biased evaluation. This, in conjunction with the biases expressed above, stands as a powerful blow to ethical systems grounded in intuition-based decision-making.

Overall, we can summarize in the following way. The ultimate goal of utilitarianism is intuitive, aiming to maximize overall well-being or happiness for the greatest number of people. However, the use of intuition in actual decision-making or calculations is counterproductive to this goal, often leading people to make choices that don't result in the predicted outcomes.

Moral Surrogacy

The increased scope of government as not only protector but provider and arbiter of collective well-being has led to an increase in what I would call moral surrogacy. In essence, this is a situation where individuals have not only ceded their natural rights to the state but have also outsourced moral decision-making, moral responsibilities and moral action itself.

The reliance on authority for moral guidance is by no means a new phenomenon, with plenty of examples to see throughout history. This moral decision-making has been provided by monarchs, religious leaders, populists, democratic governments, and any number of other movements.

For example, in 1215 the Fourth Lateran Council under Pope Innocent III decreed that all Christians must confess their sins at least once a year and receive Holy Communion during the Easter season. This moral guidance and other examples of religious customs, societal norms, public behavioural guidance and even civic education have been common throughout history, making decisions for the populace on what is considered moral behaviour.

However, one of the novel aspects of modern moral surrogacy, especially from a collectivist perspective, is not only the delegation of which actions are considered moral, but moral responsibility itself. While moral decision-making by an authority will prescribe what decisions people should make, just like the requirements for yearly confessions, the outsourcing of action results in a shifting of moral obligation from individuals to the moral authority, such as the government or collective.

Entitlements and government services are an example of this shifted requirement, putting the onus on authority to fulfil utilitarian outcomes, instead of attempting to maximize the good of our own individual choices. In effect, the delegation of moral action to authority allows individuals to abandon personal accountability towards their social responsibilities and the greatest good.

The concept of moral surrogacy may also be related to the psychological and sociological phenomenon known as *Diffusion of Responsibility*. Diffusion of Responsibility is a concept where the individuals are less likely to take responsibility or action as the number of other people present increases. This principle has been widely observed in cases like the bystander effect, where people are less likely to help a victim when other witnesses are present.

In the case of utilitarianism, the delegation of moral action to the government may lead to diffusion of individual responsibility, where individuals feel less responsible for social and moral outcomes – believing it is the government's role to address these problems.

The prevailing trend towards this transfer of moral responsibility to authority, usually the government, can be seen reflected in the public's attitudes towards the role of government and the obligations of individuals. A direct example of this is a 2020 poll conducted by the Pew Research Center, where over 59% of American adults believed "government should do more to solve problems," firmly placing responsibility for moral action on authority[35].

To further support this argument, the belief in collective moral responsibility tends to have a correlation with one's political preferences. It should be emphasized that the studies point only to *correlation*, as opposed to *causation*, and it is still unknown exactly which factors and components contribute to the correlative dynamic. Moreover, in introducing these points I am not attempting to make any political claims. Nonetheless, this correlation is supported by several different sources, which help draw a clear connection between utilitarianism and the view that moral action is a collective responsibility, not a personal one.

In 2016, a study by Hannikainen, Miller, and Cushman demonstrated that conservatives tended to consider intrinsic moral value of actions, as compared with the liberal emphasis on expected consequences or utilitarian outcomes[36]. This utilitarian preference and the resulting moral surrogacy can be seen in the data from the 2020 poll mentioned earlier, where the statement "government should do more to solve problems" was supported by over 82% of Democrats, compared with only 32% of Republicans.

Given the relationship between delegation of moral action and utilitarian views, we would also expect to see a greater correlation between charitable giving and the view that moral action is a personal obligation, instead of being the responsibility of authority or the social body. Published in 2000 by the Roper Center, data collected on charitable giving shows results that conform with our expectations. Those who self-identified as "conservative," despite having a lower overall household income, give 30% more than their "liberal" counterparts[37].

Another study published in *Nonprofit and Voluntary Sector Quarterly* in 2018, also further confirmed this dynamic, demonstrating that rates of charitable giving were higher in Republican counties, and rates of taxation – and therefore the delegation of moral action through redistributive policies – were higher in Democratic counties[38].

Unlike natural law or other ethical theories that focus on the intrinsic moral action, utilitarianism is uniquely susceptible to the evasion of individual moral responsibility. In part, this may be because it provides active guidance on a larger social scale, and because it is heavily dependent on complicated predictions – which require information that may not be immediately available to individuals.

In contrast, natural law's role in prescribing moral limits on agency is universal and absolute, and the restrictions on action itself cannot be delegated. To put it simply, you cannot delegate the morality of an immoral action you've taken, but you can delegate the responsibility to make the world "a better place."

7

Utilitarian Variants

Since the introduction of utilitarianism as a unique ethical theory by Bentham in 1789, there have been many different attempts by philosophers and ethicists to propose alternate ways of maximizing utility, hoping to mitigate some of the weaknesses of the theory highlighted in the last couple of chapters.

The foremost of these variations are rule, preference, and negative utilitarianism, each with their own unique approach to solving gaps or challenges to the primary concepts. As we discovered in the first and second parts of the book, rule utilitarianism was introduced as a way to provide stability and contribute a longer time preference to utilitarian decisions. Preference utilitarianism was created as a potential way to solve the fundamental utilitarian weakness of subjective value and different perspectives between individuals. Negative utilitarianism arose in part to try to simplify calculations further and prevent some of the situations of extreme sacrifice that might otherwise be deemed moral.

While these different variations each attempted to provide solutions to the underlying problems inherent in classical utilitarianism, their focus on changing core concepts in order to solve a subset of problems has also raised many new challenges alongside old concerns. In this chapter, we will look at how some of the primary arguments against utilitarianism apply to each variant, as well as new or unique challenges that each one faces.

Rule Utilitarianism

Rule utilitarianism is the variation of classical utilitarianism first developed by John Stuart Mill and published in his 1861 work *Utilitarianism*. The essential concept of this variation is that identifying and consistently following moral rules can result in greater outcomes over the long term.

Rule utilitarianism suggests that we can identify patterns and explore historical data in order to implement rules that will create long-term stability and utility by providing clear moral guidelines for decisions and action. In theory, this should help reduce the complexity and increase the intuitive nature of moral decision-making, as well as providing more weight to long-term outcomes instead of chasing short-term happiness.

Overall, while rule utilitarianism attempts to avoid some of the concerns with utilitarian systems, it still falls prey to many of the other downfalls of utilitarian thought. As with the original system, these problems include some of the failures of practical application explored above.

Even though the difficulty in predicting utility might not be as extreme compared with determining morality for every action, it can still be incredibly difficult to predict the utility of moral rules. These rules have their own prediction challenges, such as the acceptance of short-term negative value for a greater longer-term benefit that was mis-predicted or never arrives. The struggle of tracing positive and negative effects through causation back to their original rules also faces the same problems as any other form of consequentialist evaluations.

Although the rule variant does attempt to avoid subjectivity and become more impartial, it still requires both equal application and the establishing of rules that account for a range of subjective values, a goal that has been shown to be difficult at best. Although rule utilitarianism means that actions might be less subject to cognitive bias and subjectivity by simply following predefined rules, the creation of these rules inherits the opportunity for bias instead.

Many of the other concerns or arguments raised above are also equally applicable, such as the implementation of rules that enable tyranny of the majority, the unequal emotional impact of utility monsters, and other fundamental flaws of consequentialism.

The rule variant also suffers from its own unique flaws, including problems of rule selection, rule worship, and even lack of adherence to the greatest happiness principle. When developing rules that are expected to produce the greatest happiness in the long term, the adherence to these rules can also prevent actions that may lead to the greatest overall outcome. Put simply, if a rule-breaking action would have more utility, strategists could violate the rule (which would violate rule utilitarianism), or they could continue following the rule (which would reduce potential utility and violate the underlying principles of utilitarianism).

"Rule worship" is also a concern, occurring when rules become seen as the ends instead of the means, effectively tying morality to compliance instead of positive outcomes. This can be seen in action in bureaucracies that are slow to change and is often related to cognitive biases like the *Status-Quo bias* (a preference for keeping things the way they are) and the *Authority* bias (a tendency to be more influenced by the opinions and judgements of authority figures).

Although Mill's rule utilitarianism tried to solve some of the challenges of utilitarian thought of the time, he ultimately failed to produce the perfect or utopian ethical system he wanted. Instead, by attempting to patch some of the known flaws in the theory, he revealed brand new flaws with his fresh approach.

Preference Utilitarianism

Preference utilitarianism was first introduced by R.M. Hare, and then expanded on by modern utilitarian Peter Singer in his work *Practical Ethics* in 1979. This variation was rooted in the idea that ethical decision-making should involve weighing the preferences of affected individuals, and that an action's moral status should be tied to its respect for, and fulfilment of, those desires.

The focus on preferences when calculating utility is an attempt to overcome one of the major criticisms of utilitarian thought, primarily the problem of subjectivity in the decision-making process. By working to shift from happiness to stated preferences, it aims to bypass assumptions and potential elitism involved with decisions on what is best for others.

Although Singer's fresh approach to the subjectivity problem of utilitarianism has the theoretical capacity to account for the individual preferences of affected people, it appears that many of the other flaws of regular utilitarianism become even more pronounced.

An example of this is utilitarianism's calculation problem. While preferences can theoretically be collected before actions are made and satisfaction can be measured afterwards, calculations become incredibly broad, needing to account for any number of different preferences or desires instead of simply happiness or suffering. The issues of chaos in understanding an effect's causes still apply to actions and outcomes but are made infinitely more complex through the new range of unique and often conflicting preferences that need to be weighed as well.

While it seems reasonable to collect preferences in order to act, in practice this has only been done on small and specific scales, like referendums on single issues, or even through the implementation of democratic principles, allowing individuals some limited level of choice through the political process. Unfortunately, even if full preferences could be accounted for in every decision, the likelihood of suppression of minority groups through the implementation of majority preferences becomes even more pronounced than in other forms of utilitarianism. Without happiness or well-being as a measure, there is less to stop negative effects for people whose preferences are under-represented.

A final criticism of the unique flaws of preference utilitarianism compared with other variations is its divergence from the foundations of the theory, most specifically the concepts of utility as a barometer for happiness and suffering. In effect, if the preferred choice of every person results in extremely negative outcomes, as long as preferences are satisfied it can be considered a moral action.

So in the end, even though preference utilitarianism attempts to solve the difference in subjective values and desires across a wide range of individuals in order to reduce bias and assumptions, it ultimately fails to address many of the other arguments against utilitarianism, or even makes them more pronounced.

Negative Utilitarianism

Negative utilitarianism is at its core a variety of utilitarian thought that excludes happiness from the utility calculation, focusing purely on the reduction of suffering instead. Under this approach to decision-making, the greatest happiness principle in effect becomes the "least suffering principle."

Negative utilitarianism has two primary goals, the simplification of utility calculations by focusing solely on avoiding harm and changing utility in order to prevent negative costs that could be considered moral by other types of utilitarianism.

Like other variations of utilitarian thought, the fresh perspective on utility calculations and other modifications led to new concerns, in addition to many of the previous arguments. One of the benefits of the focus on negative outcomes instead of a more holistic approach is that calculations are often simpler, completely ignoring half of an action's effects entirely. Even though this change leads to more intuitive and actionable moral guidance overall, the complexity and chaos inherent in consequentialist calculations is still present.

Many of the other issues with utilitarian thought still persist despite the shift in focus to prevent extreme sacrifice, such as the failures of human intuition and cognitive bias, the subjectivity of negative experiences, and especially the compounding effects of policies that attempt to prevent negative side effects.

Interestingly, the thought experiment corresponding to Nozick's utility monster becomes even more relevant when you consider only the negative outcomes in utility. In 2002 research titled *Serotonin Transporter Genetic Variation and the Response of the Human Amygdala*, studies of brain imaging showed that some individuals with more reactive amygdalas experienced more intense reactions to negative events[39]. These studies present us with real world "utility monsters," who objectively experience negative effects more strongly than others, bringing Nozick's thought experiment to life.

The "*Equilibrium* pill" that we saw in the previous chapter, which is able to remove emotions, also becomes a more serious consideration. In the thought experiment, by ignoring the loss of positive emotions in utility, it would likely be morally justified to force every person to take the pill, reducing all negative emotions to zero, the ideal moral outcome for negative utilitarian ethics. This thought experiment also translates well into the real world. When only negative calculations are taken into account, for those with chronic depression, past trauma, and other overwhelmingly negative experiences, even a lobotomy or a quick, painless death might be considered a moral action.

Aside from these new approaches to previous arguments, critics also argue that the so-called negative approach to utility ignores happiness, fulfilment, and other values that make life worthwhile. We can see a demonstration of this argument in a forced choice between the following two options, where we will assume the ability to calculate utility with perfect accuracy. The first option will result in the happiness of 1,000 people, but it will require that five people suffer greatly. The second option will not result in any happiness, but only four people will suffer an equal amount. Applying negative utilitarianism would result in choosing the second option in order to reduce suffering, effectively trading away the happiness of 1,000 to mitigate the suffering of one.

As with other variations we explored, although negative utilitarianism attempts to solve some flaws with classical utilitarian thought, it opens up new arguments and concerns, trading old downsides for new ones.

8

Distilling the Theories

So far, over the course of this book, we have explored these two theories in depth, covering history, influential figures, core concepts, real-world applications, and finally a range of arguments that examine both their strengths and major flaws. Some of these concerns were practical in nature, demonstrating how difficult it is to bring consequentialism to bear outside of theoretical situations. Others involved exploring the limits and approaches of the theories, considering how they respond to interesting thought experiments and extreme situations.

On their face, both utilitarianism and natural law seem like rational approaches to ethical decision-making. If people generally strive to be happy, utilitarianism's system of moral guidance that aims to maximize happiness for everyone provides a reasonable basis for decision-making. And with natural law, both the secular and theological arguments are logically sound, resulting in principles that separate morality from ideological or political beliefs, basing it in raw human nature and experience. However, after considering the wealth of analysis we just covered, we can see that the two theories are not as equal as they first appear, especially when it comes to executing their core concepts.

Intention vs. Outcome

Natural law overcame Hume's is-ought problem, bridging descriptive and prescriptive statements by accounting for social order and natural human relationships. Utilitarianism, on the other hand, is unable to escape the flaws of consequentialist theory, especially the arguments in previous chapters, such as *Schrödinger's Morality* and *Moral Chaos*. If morality depends on outcomes, and outcomes are the result of action, it is impossible to know your choice is moral until after it is made, an illogical foundation for an ethical system. At this point, utilitarians can either choose to acknowledge moral intentions behind the action – conflicting with consequentialism's reliance on outcomes – or simply accept and then attempt to overcome these limitations through further "moral" action, running into the concern we raised earlier called *Zeno's Moral Action*.

This flaw between intention and outcome is further revealed by the argument of moral luck, which builds on the uncertainty of utilitarian action. Since the outcome determines morality, two actions or decisions that act on the same information in similar situations may have very different outcomes due to external circumstances, resulting in radically different moral judgements for the same choice. This lack of consistency is a direct result of the dependence on outcomes and presents us with an ethical system that produces potentially arbitrary moral judgements.

The Calculation Problem

The next fundamental failure of utilitarianism is the theory's foundational reliance on calculating the morality of outcomes. Although it might make sense in a theoretical vacuum, the astonishingly difficult – even impossible – calculation problems that are required to accurately quantify and weigh the utility of options and alternative actions make the theory's goals impractical. Perhaps even unachievable.

As we saw earlier, if we wish to accurately calculate utility, we need to overcome the problem of subjectivity in both the evaluation of outcomes and the prediction of preferences, the inherent chaos and unpredictability of causation at the very least. In essence, in order to be able to perform utilitarian calculations in a way that perfectly achieves the "greatest good for the greatest number," every decision must be made with full omniscience in a deterministic universe. Unless of course, we are willing to compromise the core principles of the theory and accept intention as a substitution for actual positive results.

We can also see this need to compromise in order to be applicable outside of pure theory in the way utilitarianism handles unique and extreme situations. This can be observed through the *Equilibrium Pill* argument raised earlier, where a case could be made for lobotomizing people who suffer from chronic pain or depression, along with the negative utilitarian case for total human extinction, as well as both of Nozick's thought experiments.

In particular, Nozick's utility monster is a blow to the ideas of impartial and equal treatment of individuals, contrasting the collective good with an individual whose potential utility is always greater than others. The existence of unequal utility between individuals – an idea that we saw has a scientific basis – requires moral action to violate impartiality in order to maximize outcomes, also conflicting with the original goals of utilitarian theory.

Flexible Application

Another important aspect of ethical theories is their flexibility, the ability to adapt to a variety of different and complex circumstances that arise in human interaction. If new contexts or situations make it difficult to apply the theory, then moral action will be limited to pre-existing situations. When considering these two theories, utilitarianism is by far the more flexible system in terms of adapting to changing circumstances. This is in large part because of the complete lack of restrictions on individual actions themselves, allowing for a practically infinite number of different approaches to a problem, including applying solutions that would be considered immoral under other systems.

In theory, this flexibility provides utilitarians with the ability for optimization of outcomes in any situation, regardless of complexity or even sacrifices required. Natural law, on the other hand, provides much less situational flexibility, actively preventing certain categories of action that are considered inherently immoral, no matter what the predicted or guaranteed consequences. These differences can be seen in the previously explored trolley problems, where utilitarianism supports the killing of one to save many, and natural law prevents the killing of one, even if it would save the entirety of mankind.

Although natural law is entirely inflexible when it comes to restrictions on immoral action, the theory itself makes fewer demands from a moral perspective, providing flexibility of a different kind. As a result of the focus on preventing "bad" instead of requiring "good," traditional beliefs on natural law have been embedded into a variety of cultural and religious systems throughout history, demonstrating a much wider flexibility in terms of ideological compatibility.

Predictability

Ethical systems must also be predictable and reproducible, otherwise the system becomes arbitrary, reducing trust and stability among individuals and society. By ensuring consistent and predictable application of principles, people can be sure that the actions taken are moral, and that all interactions are backed by common rules. While flexibility may be an underlying utilitarian strength, unlimited flexibility carries downsides, including the potential for inconsistent and unpredictable approaches to moral decision-making depending on context.

For example, let's imagine two versions of the classic trolley problem, with a person on one track, and five others facing imminent death on the other track. In the first version, the single person is an average individual, and in the second version, the person is a researcher on the verge of a medical breakthrough that could save thousands. Although the immediate situations are directly comparable, the calculation of utility may result in two different choices, the choice in the first situation leading to the sacrifice of the one, and the choice in the second situation not to intervene.

Earlier we covered the significant calculation problems involved in utilitarian actions, which make even the simplest decisions potentially inconsistent and unpredictable. With moral judgements subject to chaotic and generally unpredictable outcomes – especially at scale – anticipating moral outcomes can be highly inconsistent.

Unlike its ethical peer, natural law's morality does not fall victim to the whims of causality as a product of its core concepts. When considering natural law from the perspective of consistency and prediction, its high level of rigidity provides a series of very repeatable and reproducible ethical mandates, like those of other morally absolute systems. In essence, this means that the actions that natural law sees as immoral are not subject to context and are not arbitrarily considered moral as situations and contexts change.

The stability and predictability of moral decision-making is another element of the fair and impartial application of the theory. If an ethical system doesn't provide an equal and consistent basis for every member of society, then the members who face discrimination are not incentivized to contribute or support social harmony, leading to conflict. This belief in equal and impartial treatment is a cornerstone of many ethical systems, and both utilitarianism and natural law are no different.

Impartiality

Utilitarian theory requires the impartial evaluation and calculation of all individuals' happiness and suffering in equal measure, aiming to maximize utility in a way that is equal, fair, and without discrimination. Although this impartiality is central to utilitarianism, Nozick's utility monster raises questions about the equality of individual's emotions and their role in the utility calculations. It allows for the possibility that calculations themselves may result in impartial or unfair treatment due to circumstances beyond the individual's control, such as the favouring of those who are more sensitive to emotional stimuli.

Utilitarianism's reliance on circumstance and outcome also has the capacity to lead to significant differences in treatment. For example, a distinguished researcher on the verge of a breakthrough and a low-income individual are the cause of two drunk driving accidents that each result in the death of a pedestrian. By throwing the researcher in prison, it might result in a failure to discover a cure for a disease, leading to many deaths. In these instances, utilitarian outcomes might be maximized by choosing to imprison the low-income individual but only fine or otherwise punish the researcher.

Natural law is also theoretically impartial in its treatment of others, but in a much different way based on its central principle of universality and the rejection of subjective morality. This sets up the natural rights of all individuals as equal and unchanging. They should not be violated, regardless of the circumstances.

Other failures of impartiality also apply to both theories, though they are not flaws with their underlying theories or concepts, but instead a problem with human nature itself, expressed through cognitive biases. After all, if we look back to the trolley problem, and a hypothetical situation in which the decision-maker's child is tied in front of the oncoming trolley, and pulling the lever will sacrifice two other people instead, how many people would let their family member die in order to be impartial or fair?

In that example, utilitarians might try to find a post-hoc rationalization for why the two people have less utility in order to reconcile their decision with their ethical system, and natural law theorists might try to claim their child's right to life or attempt a claim to familial self-defence. In this hypothetical case, despite the impartiality of the corresponding theories, the choice to save their child would probably be made anyway, a reflection of the limits of human ability to be impartial.

Practicality

Perhaps the most important criterion for an ethical theory is its practicality, both in terms of application, as well as outcomes. In essence, this means it must be both realistic and easy to apply in real-world situations. This includes the simplicity to ensure that people of diverse educational and philosophical backgrounds are able to grasp and follow its concepts. For example, if it requires complicated, convoluted or otherwise time-consuming decision-making processes, it will be more difficult to choose actions in plenty of circumstances.

Although some of the issues raised in other areas are centred around the theoretical limits of both utilitarianism and natural law, they can easily be observed as practical limitations in various real-world examples. As we have seen from both real-world examples and our arguments, utilitarianism is at its most effective and practical when implemented at a smaller and less complex scale. By reducing the scope of decisions and outcomes, we mitigate many of the impractical aspects of prediction, calculation, and moral attribution.

An example of this scope could be a utilitarian deciding which of several charities they should donate their money to. Evaluating the different options is entirely feasible and should provide guidance on which charity has the highest impact or contributes the most value to those being helped. In this example, the lack of external sacrifices also limits the ability for trade-offs to be miscalculated, ensuring that utility is positive, regardless of what the realized utility of other choices would have been.

As we have seen with previous examples and evaluations, although the principles of chaos apply uncertainty to actions of every size, our ability to calculate and evaluate outcomes accurately is indirectly proportional to the size and complexity of the actions taken. Realistically this means that as the effects of a policy are more widespread, the ability to not only predict outcomes but to even evaluate their utility after the fact becomes greatly hindered, reducing the practicality of utilitarianism at scale.

The effects of cognitive bias also play a greater role in diminishing the practicality of utilitarian decision-making because of its moral requirement to act in an impartial way, instead of simply restricting immoral action like natural law. When choosing moral actions that have the capacity to generate both suffering and happiness, cognitive bias will inherently influence the decision-maker's predictions of utility towards personal preferences, the effects of which can have a significant impact on moral outcomes.

Although hardly immune, as a morally absolute ethical system, natural law's restrictions of action based on individual rights are much less open to interpretation, helping to protect against cognitive bias or subjective evaluations. The focus on action instead of outcomes also allows natural law to scale more easily, not concerning itself with gigantic complex calculations in order to judge morality.

So even though utilitarianism can be practical and effective in small-scale decisions, as the consequences of those decisions begin to grow, the knowledge and calculations required to operate according to its own principles can quickly become overwhelming and impractical.

The other side of practicality is tied to the actual impacts of moral behaviour, determining how well the theory translates into effects in the real world. If moral principles sound good in practice but consistently makes things worse when applied, anyone would be hard pressed to claim that it is either practical or successful. Not only should ethics aim to promote good and prevent harm, but systems should be evaluated for their effectiveness and efficiency in achieving their stated goals.

Positive Impact

On the surface, exploring these two ethical theories based on their positive impact is an evaluation that seems to naturally favour utilitarianism. After all, the entire purpose of utilitarianism is to achieve positive impacts or consequences, while natural law rejects the idea of outcomes as a valid method of determining morality, focusing instead on the inherent right and wrong of the actions themselves.

In a theoretical sense, utilitarianism has a quite incredible potential for positive impacts, more so than other ethical theories, since it is directed to perform any sacrifice required in order to achieve those outcomes. However, the complete lack of restrictions on action in pursuit of positive results also comes with the potential for dreadful consequences, both unintended and as a result of accepted trade-offs.

In practice, because of the sheer difficulty in truly predicting outcomes on a large scale, utilitarianism has a rather mixed track record. This results in many policies with a mixture of both benefits and drawbacks when combined with other laws. This blurring of action and effect makes it difficult to even identify and attribute effects, let alone understand moral outcomes.

Some actions and policies we discussed earlier have much clearer outcomes, like the One-Child Policy in China, forced sterilizations, the residential school system in Canada, and the War on Drugs, which have had horrific effects that far surpassed the positive outcomes that were expected. On the other side, the Clean Air Act, universal healthcare, public education, and social security programs are examples of policies that are held up as examples of great utilitarian successes, despite any negative effects that can be identified.

Theoretically, one could imagine that since natural law ignores positive consequences of action, its guidance would result in less of a positive impact. However, the substantial difficulty in breaching the divide between desire and ability has shown us that although utilitarianism aims to maximize positive impacts, the intention and the results don't always line up.

With that said, as we explored in our previous section, natural law's focus on moral action instead of moral outcomes has directly resulted in a wealth of positive impacts throughout the world. Beliefs in natural law and individual rights were pivotal in the establishment of liberal democracies, abolitionist movements, the fights for gender equality, religious tolerance, and fair and equal justice for all humans.

Realistically, the effects of utilitarianism in real-world policy are quite difficult to judge, even according to its own standard of morality. The intertwined interactions between complex policies, the difficulty of calculation, and the gap between prediction and reality, all make utilitarian impacts effectively impossible to quantify. Natural law, on the other hand, has provided relatively simple mandates and the outcomes are clearer. The recognition of religious freedom, individual liberty, consent to authority, freedom of expression, and others have had clear and enduring benefits.

Unfortunately for utilitarianism, even though on its surface the goal of maximizing happiness seems like a simple, straightforward, and morally intuitive concept to use as a basis for ethical theory, as they say – *the devil is in the details*. In this case, the details of the theory's implementation show major failures in real-world applications, as well impracticality from a theoretical standpoint.

So where does that leave our moral choices?

9

Moral Triumph

In the end, we can see the strength of natural law's foundation across a range of different criteria such as predictability, practicality, and even impact. Its straightforward approach that simply prohibits immoral action instead of concerning itself with outcomes or intentions, avoids many of the pitfalls related to calculation, bias, and predictability.

The results of our evaluation also reveal the true extent of utilitarianism's flaws, falling short in almost every single area of comparison. Under its caring and shiny surface, the theory is riddled with limitations, unpredictability, opportunities for bias, impractical calculations, and real-world results that don't match their promises. In effect, utiliarianism's requirements lie opposite to human nature, giving it fundamental flaws that are not easily addressed.

We saw utilitarians throughout history working to address these issues by adapting (or compromising) the central tenets of the theory, changing the focus towards general moral rules, considering subjectivity by accounting for preferences, and even ignoring positive outcomes altogether to try and limit negative consequences.

But even with these variations attempting to change the foundations of utilitarian principles, including the very idea of utility, the way it is calculated, and its use in decision-making, we saw that each compromise not only kept many of the old limitations, but came with its own new flaws.

Even on a theoretical level, the basic principles of the system begin to fall apart quite quickly when you consider the complexity of calculations in the real world, the great difficulty involved in predicting outcomes, and the inability to know morality before actions are even taken.

In practice, we can actively see these theoretical flaws and limitations represented in real-life policies. As we saw in a wide snapshot of major government policies, utilitarian intent to maximize positive impacts often ends in mixed results. These results themselves contain a variety of smaller positive and negative outcomes, including effects that weren't immediately obvious or were far-removed from the initial actions.

In effect, the track record of utilitarian decision-making is quite poor, and while outcomes sometimes result in the realization of positive utility, we can never know if any of the policies have maximized utility relative to other potential options. Without perfect and universal knowledge before decisions are made, we cannot hope to actually achieve the utilitarian goal of utility maximization.

A fundamental issue demonstrated by empirical analysis of utilitarian policy can be presented through the following argument.

- Utilitarianism requires the maximization of utility.

- In order to choose the action with the most utility, the outcomes of every alternative must be predictable.

- In order to accurately predict all outcomes, you must have perfect knowledge of the universe.

- The limitations of human understanding and the complexity of the world make perfect knowledge impossible.

- Therefore, human beings are unable to knowingly maximize utility – the requirement for realizing utilitarianism.

When utilitarian decision-makers are unable to maximize the utility of consequences, the greatest good for the greatest number becomes unlikely (or even impossible). The implications of this conclusion are clear.

Without compromising its basic principles, utilitarianism is immoral by its own judgement.

The pure philosophical goal of utilitarianism requires humans to overcome their very nature and to conquer the unknowable, a glorious, utopian, but ultimately impossible requirement. By rejecting both the inherent morality of actions and the good intentions behind them, utilitarianism sets a high bar for its moral judgements, while simultaneously asserting that you don't get points for trying, only for actual outcomes. This focus on utopian outcomes parallels the following quote from economist Thomas Sowell in his 1993 essay *Is Reality Optional?*

> *Much of the social history of the Western world, over the past three decades, has been a history of replacing what worked with what sounded good.*

In a perfect world without constraints or the limitations of reality, utilitarianism may have succeeded in its lofty goal of having every decision result in the betterment of the human experience. Ironically, these limitations leave utilitarian decision-makers attempting to maximize utility, without having the ability to truly validate their efforts, an unfortunate position for adherents to a theory that judges entirely on results.

In contrast to utilitarian practical failures, the directly attributable outcomes of recognition of natural law are empirically positive. These outcomes, while not the focus of natural law as a moral decision-making framework, are in essence, a validation of natural law as an expression and derivative of human nature. They also show us that even when rejecting natural law, it doesn't invalidate the underlying principles of the theory. Human nature exists regardless, and its existence implies that there are actions that, when combined with our natural tendencies, will result in increases or decreases in stability, trust, and cooperation between social interactions.

It follows that since natural law and individual rights are derived from the very nature of human social behaviours, respect for natural law will reduce the friction of human interaction, resulting in positive outcomes and less conflict. Although it may seem counterintuitive on its surface, by focusing on moral action instead of outcomes, we then end up with better outcomes. This idea was summed up as follows by Albert Camus in his work *The Myth of Sisyphus* in 1942.

> *Does the end justify the means? That is possible. But what will justify the end? To that question, which historical thought leaves pending, rebellion replies: the means.*

The real-world effects of natural law principles also clearly demonstrate these ideas to be true, as increased religious tolerance, respect for life, liberty and property, freedom of association and conscience, all contribute to maintaining personal, legal, and political stability and equality for all. Violations of these rights, even with the aim of achieving some greater good, have gone hand in hand with every one of humanity's greatest travesties throughout history.

Ultimately, the results of our evaluation become clear. The exploration of utilitarianism revealed the common problem of converting theory into practice, by no means a unique problem to utilitarian theory. The real world is the ultimate test of hypotheticals and theories, often revealing the rotten false assumptions that make up their foundational principles.

Natural law, on the other hand, starts in the real world, and derives its foundational beliefs from empirical analysis of human nature.

When its moral mandates are exposed to practical application, we can immediately see it flourish, complementing the human experience instead of demanding it change in ways that will conform to our beliefs.

In sum, natural law is practical morality.

10

The March Towards Utility

Now you should be asking, *if natural law is so much more practical, why has it declined in popularity compared to utilitarianism in modern times*? In effect – how did we get here? In contrast to the formalization of natural rights over the course of the Enlightenment, utilitarian ideas were also growing, with a focus on the general interests of the people and collective outcomes.

Between Rousseau's version of the social contract that was more focused on the common good, and Bentham and Mill's utilitarian ideas of calculating results on a societal level instead of just individuals, the new theory of utilitarianism was beginning to take shape. Mixed together with the popular concepts of natural rights and inherent equality of human beings, these ideas helped shape the public's views of the role of authority and separately helped inspire many different versions of anarchist thought in the 19th century.

The popularity of the 20th century collectivist movements, and revolutions in particular, contrasted the influence of natural rights revolutions of the 1700s. These new movements rejected individualism and human nature, focusing on the greater good of the social body, often implemented through force, and rationalized with utilitarian arguments. Much like the utopian claims of utilitarian theory, these collectivist movements sounded pure and moral on the surface, declaring they would end suffering, inequality, and injustice for all members of society.

This can be summed up and seen in Leon Trotsky's expectations for the effects of collectivism in his 1924 work *Literature and Revolution*, captured in the following quote.

> *Man will become immeasurably stronger, wiser, and subtler; his body will become more harmonised, his movements more rhythmic, his voice more musical. The forms of life will become dynamically dramatic. The average human type will rise to the heights of an Aristotle, a Goethe, or a Marx. And above this ridge new peaks will rise.*

Throughout the late 19th and early 20th centuries, many of the social reformers and progressive movements in the United States pushed for worker's rights, including addressing poverty, ensuring fair wages, and safe working conditions. Alongside the rise of collectivist concepts were two major events that helped push the ideas into prominence. The communist revolution in Russia intensified the appeal of the government's role in providing for the people's basic needs, and the start of the Great Depression in 1929, which exacerbated social and economic issues in the United States and abroad.

Although the increase in government reach is a pattern that is visible and well documented in many different countries, there are very few countries whose foundations were built and codified from the principles of natural law. This provides us a perfect microcosm for our look at society's overall shift from natural law towards utilitarian policy – the American Experiment.

Over the early 20th century, the influence of British economist John Maynard Keynes had also been growing, and his arguments for government intervention, economic management, and public spending had been gaining traction. When Franklin D. Roosevelt took office in 1933 at the height of the Great Depression, he put Keynesian economics in practice through the implementation of the New Deal, a series of programs, public works projects, and regulations designed to provide "relief, recovery, and reform." These policies included social security, unemployment benefits, and other entitlements that dramatically shifted the previous role of government closer towards many of the collectivist ideas that had been gaining traction around the world.

In 1941, the acceptance of individual rights as an extension of natural law suffered a blow, when President Roosevelt grouped "Freedom from Want" with freedom of speech and freedom of religion in his State of the Union address. This explicitly introduced the idea that economic security was a human right, marking a major shift from the natural law perspective of freedom as liberty from government, towards the idea that freedom was something that could be granted by government.

Shortly after the beginning of the New Deal, while the idea of entitlements was becoming merged with the idea of natural rights, the legal protections for natural rights that were embedded in the constitution were also being reinterpreted and stripped away. Prior to this era, the Tenth Amendment to the U.S. Constitution – stating that any powers not explicitly delegated to the federal government belonged to the people and the states themselves – had been effective in limiting the scope of federal powers.

In retaliation for a series of Supreme Court decisions which declared that New Deal policies exceeded the powers of the federal government, in 1936 FDR threatened to expand the Supreme Court, adding justices who would rule in his favour. The move successfully coerced the Supreme Court to ignore the amendment, severing the constitution's natural law principle of limited government authority and providing legal precedent for expansive government action.

By the time Western nations began to see the true face of the soviet failures and horror, the idea of government powers as a tool for providing entitlements and rebalancing inequality was already socially and legally entrenched, rapidly deviating from Locke and the founder's ideas on liberty and the legitimacy of authority. As Austrian economist Ludwig von

Mises pointed out in his 1949 work *Human Action: A Treatise on Economics*:

> *Collectivism is the "philosophy" of postulates, premises, and principles directly opposed to those of individualism.*

In the wake of World War II, with the passage of the Universal Declaration of Human Rights in 1948, more entitlements began to appear alongside the concepts of natural rights, a new hybrid concept of "Human Rights" that continued to mutate. This shift was directly in line with John Stuart Mill's arguments that utilitarianism and outcomes that resulted in the greatest good should serve as the basis for rights. In the public sphere, natural law's explicit view of rights as the protection of individuals from arbitrary authority was changed to incorporate utilitarian ideas of what individuals should be entitled to receive in a fair and just world.

These entitlements – sometimes called positive rights – such as the right to social security have since been expanded greatly, including free education, healthcare, food, and other goods and services that align with these collectivist and utilitarian principles. From the utilitarian perspective, these entitlements clearly benefit social well-being, and as a result have been a major driver behind government policies for decades. However, not only are entitlements and natural rights opposites in terms of purpose, with their focus on outcomes vs actions, they are also contradictory in terms of application.

With almost a century of examples to look back on, we can begin to see how entitlements in practice have resulted in the weakening of many different natural rights. As the concept of individual rights expanded to include these new utilitarian "human rights," the distinction between natural rights and entitlements was quick to disappear on a policy level. After all, when the right to property and the right to a service like education are considered equal in terms of status, compromises between the two become simple utilitarian calculations. This has directly led to easy justifications for further erosions in the form of taxation, for example, of the right to property in order to be able to fully provide education to the populace, alongside many other trade-offs.

The result of FDR's Supreme Court coercion and push to reinterpret the limits of federal powers was the unchaining of government power, legally indulging its role as a provider instead of simply a protector. The removal of these natural law restraints led to rapid growth of the size and scope of accepted authority, clearly demonstrated by the increase in government spending over time. From government spending at 8% of GDP in 1930 to over 20% by the end of the 30s, it continually increased to over 35% since 2009, including a peak of over 47% in 2020, as reported by the U.S. Bureau of Economic Analysis[40].

Like any invasive species with no natural predators, over the last century the federal government spread from its traditional roles into almost every aspect of life, getting involved in the provision and regulation of services, such as utilities in 1935, housing in 1965, healthcare in 1965, transportation in 1967, environmental regulation in 1969, workplace safety in 1971, education in 1979, and many, many more areas.

As a part of this radical utilitarian expansion of government into every facet of everyday goods and services, the 1960s and 1970s also saw a steep rise in the volume and scope of welfare programs, particularly under Lyndon B. Johnson's "Great Society" programs. Aimed at eliminating poverty and tackling racial injustice, programs like food stamp programs, housing subsidies, and Medicaid were implemented, followed by more expansions of social security in the form of benefits for the elderly and those with disabilities.

A study titled *The Deserving Poor, the Family, and the U.S. Welfare System* published in 2016 by Robert Moffitt at John Hopkins University found that despite common misconceptions that social services are being reduced over time, welfare spending has increased more than 240% per capita between 1970 and 2007[41].

The usage of programs like SNAP, formerly known as the Food Stamp Program, has also skyrocketed since first being introduced in 1964, rising from an estimated one million monthly participants in April of 1966, to over 15 million monthly participants a decade later in 1974[42]. Today, the number is even greater, with over 41 million average participants per month in 2022, accounting for more than 12% of the population of the United States, up from around 7% in 1974, as reported by the U.S. Department of Agriculture[43].

The other forms of social welfare mentioned have also seen similar growth, including old-age pensions, Medicaid, and disability insurance, the latter of which has tripled in enrolment since 1970, up to more than nine million beneficiaries in 2020[44].

As demonstrated through the increase in government spending outlined above, the rise of entitlements and government overhead has led to a major need for greater funding, ultimately through greater violations of property rights. These violations have taken many forms, through direct infringements such as increased taxation, as well as new types of taxes on goods, services, imports, and other actions. In many cases the violations are less direct, taking the form of monetary financing and deficit spending, leading to inflation and the erosion of purchasing power over time. Even looking back to FDR and his New Deal, in order to pay for the new spending programs and entitlements, the top marginal tax rate in the United States increased from 25% in the early years of the Great Depression to over 79% in 1935[45].

This excessive level of wealth confiscation and redistribution, outside of direct and obvious violations of property, also results in the violation of freedom of conscience, as mentioned in a previous chapter. This idea was summed up most clearly by Thomas Jefferson in his 1779 *Virginia Statute for Religious Freedom* with the following quote.

> *[T]o compel a man to furnish contributions for the propagation of opinions which he disbelieves and abhors, is sinful and tyrannical.*

Outside of these violations of property and conscience, the use of taxation for redistribution, incentives and other government programs not directly related to law and physical protection also run afoul of the Enlightenment-era principles of natural law. In his work on the social contract, Locke expressed the relationship between the citizenry and the government as a partial transfer of natural rights from the citizens, in order to empower the state to better protect the rest of their natural rights. In effect, this argues for the legitimate use of reasonable taxation to fund legal or protective services for the populace. As described by Locke, the sole purpose of these services is to ensure that the citizen's rights to liberty, freedom of expression and religion, and others, were even more secure.

Aside from the sheer scale of these utilitarian violations of natural rights, there are many economic arguments against the draining of wealth from the citizenry in order to redistribute it through entitlements, regardless of intentions to craft a more equitable world. These arguments often highlight the great and impossible task involved with rational calculation of economic needs, particularly when goods and services become divorced from prices.

In a direct parallel to utilitarianism, the knowledge requirements for effective calculation and allocation of goods and services, especially as economic centralization increases, create an entirely unrealistic and even impossible prerequisite to decision-making. These arguments are backed up by academic research demonstrating that economies with greater degrees of market freedom generally have higher growth rates, better standards of living, and more innovation overall. All that being said, there are plenty of works by economists like Hayek, Mises, and others who have covered these topics in great detail, and I will leave the in-depth economic analysis to them.

From a natural law perspective, many of these social programs and the new role of government also conflict with many of the original concepts of liberal democracy that were defined by Locke and adopted by Western nations, specifically the role and legitimacy of authority. Instead of consent of the governed, the increased presence of government and their more intrusive impacts on daily life have the opposite effect, leading to more coercion and arbitrary authority, not less.

The goals of emancipation from authority and the empowerment of the populace have also been degraded, tied to increases in dependence on government services as a result of entitlements and economic policies. This dependence can be seen in the long-term participation of the SNAP program, where a USDA study found that in 2018, only half of new participants left the program within nine months, as well as the large and continued increases in disability beneficiaries over time[46].

In 1981, Ronald Reagan became the president of the United States, promising to tackle the unchecked growth of government through a variety of approaches like tax cuts, reductions in government spending, and deregulation. Over the course of his first term, some of these promises were implemented to different degrees, though ultimately to mixed success. Many of the policies that were enacted failed to solve the underlying issues that lead to the creation of these programs in the first place.

Although Reagan attempted to scale back government involvement in everyday life, by the 1980s the cumulative momentum of 50 years of government authority and entitlements was too great to stop, and the precedent of FDR's forced reinterpretation of the limits on federal power would prove too strong to circumvent. This situation was candidly expressed through the following quote by Nobel-prize winning economist Milton Friedman in *Tyranny of the Status Quo* in 1984.

Nothing is so permanent as a temporary government program.

As government authority and mandates continued to spread, much of the government involvement in its continued role as provider now turned parent was aimed outside of the economic sphere, although the incentives put in place to achieve these goals were often economic in nature.

This role of a "nanny state," a term often used to refer to a government that has become overprotective, can be seen through overt utilitarian policies that take away people's freedom to do things that could result in negative consequences, even just for themselves. While this type of policy had always been a part of local and even state laws to varying extents, these policies were much less common on a national level before Prohibition at the start of the 20th century.

Examples of these utilitarian restrictions include laws against gambling in order to protect people from addiction, food-related regulations like restrictions on sale of unpasteurized milk and bans on importing Scottish black pudding, safety requirements such as seat belt and helmet laws, and many others. These common everyday restrictions slowly erode the ability for individuals to make their own choices, building up walls around the citizenry to protect them from their own potential choices, just like a parent would for their child.

The other authoritarian approach to influencing the behaviours of the people is through social engineering and the creation of incentives and disincentives, a common way to promote outcomes that are desired by authority. The use of financial manipulation to achieve new or changed social behaviours also cleverly conceals the relationship between the violation of natural liberty and the policy, a more subtle form of behavioural coercion than outright bans or restrictions.

Sin taxes are a common disincentive implemented in many parts of the world. As we saw earlier, these are taxes on goods and services that are seen to present health risks or undesirable social behaviours. Aside from the most common sin taxes like tobacco and alcohol, these additional fees and taxes sometimes apply to junk food, marijuana, gambling, tanning salons, firearms, and more.

Sin taxes are also similar to other forms of disincentives, adding additional costs in order to influence decision-making and promote specific initiatives on a larger scale. Examples of these types of policies include fuel taxes, carbon taxes, emissions trading, or other environmental programs, as well as recycling and fees on plastics that aim to reduce plastic waste. These environmental initiatives are also usually coupled with incentives such as electric vehicle tax credits and subsidies for the installation of renewable energy systems, like solar panels or wind turbines, among others.

Another example of positive incentives that are used to influence decisions are programs designed to increase participation in post-secondary education. In attempting to achieve the goal of a more intellectual and educated population, a wide variety of incentives are available, including subsidies and scholarships, guaranteed student loans, tax-free education savings accounts, and more.

These examples are just a small sample of the many different ways behaviour is guided by government policy, commonly through economic means. This use of financial manipulation as a social engineering technique, while effective, conflicts with the principles of natural law in a variety of different ways.

The first is through the unequal impact these financial burdens place on low-income individuals. As many different studies have shown, direct consumer taxes on goods and services, including sin taxes, gas or carbon taxes, and plastic fees, are regressive in nature, having a greater impact on low-income individuals and households than others. In a similar vein to the adage "If the penalty for a crime is a fine, then that law only exists for the lower class," the lopsided impact of using disincentives to modify behaviour reflects the inequality of these programs, a natural law violation of equal treatment under the law.

Another way in which these methods of social engineering violate natural rights is by effectively holding your right to liberty hostage and selling your ability to make specific choices back to you at a fee. While the outright banning of certain choices is a more obvious violation of liberty, requiring the payment of special fees to the government in order to acquire specific categories of goods effectively puts a price on your liberty to consume these goods or services.

Although there are undoubtedly more, the final notable way in which these economic tools violate natural rights is through the expansion of mandates of legitimate authority as defined by Locke and other natural law theorists. The increased control over everyday life and the implementation of laws that influence behaviour constitute an arbitrary application of justice and authority, far outside the legitimate scope of natural authority.

Unlike some of these specific examples above, it is common to see economists, anarchists and natural law theorists often bring up the outcomes of failed authoritarian policy when contesting utilitarianism and collectivism, pointing to failures of authority, flaws with decision-making, and impacts on the citizenry as proof that authority was misused or abused.

While these arguments against the newfound size, scope, focus, and efficacy of authority are each potentially devastating in their own right, they all ultimately fall victim to the same flaw, a focus on suboptimal or negative outcomes. By skipping past moral objections to the utilitarian concepts themselves and focusing on ends instead of means, not only have the basic principles of natural law been cast aside, but the argument becomes a utilitarian moral calculation. In effect, these arguments attempt to make a utilitarian case for why utilitarianism is wrong, instead of a case based on natural rights.

Over time, public perception has changed, and social acceptance of utilitarianism and collectivist policies has grown, with a study by Pew Research Center in 2012 showing that more than 40% of individuals contacted preferred "Bigger government, providing more services," compared with 51% who chose "Smaller government, providing fewer services."[47] In 2020, another poll showed that over 59% of U.S. adults believed the government should do more to solve problems[48], and a Gallup poll conducted in 2019 showed that positive views of socialism range from 32% to 49% across different generations of Americans[49].

While the polling results above show it hasn't occurred yet, Hayek believed that the increasing dependence on government would eventually highlight the issues of diminished natural rights, expressed as follows in *The Constitution of Liberty* in 1960.

> *Perhaps the fact that we have seen millions voting themselves into complete dependence on a tyrant has made our generation understand that to choose one's government is not necessarily to secure freedom.*

The widespread acceptance of utilitarianism demonstrated here, and in the trolley problem study referenced earlier, has seen utilitarian themes become a common theme in popular culture. Books like Kazuo Ishiguro's *Never Let Me Go* in 2005 and movies such as *Unthinkable* in 2010 and *Watchmen* in 2009, and many others have helped to normalize conversations and acceptance of utilitarian trade-offs and sacrifices for the greater good.

These radical changes in public perception of natural law represent a seismic cultural shift since the founding of American liberal democracy. Natural law theory went from a widely accepted ethical framework, one that led directly to the spawning of the United States, to being generally unpopular and even seen as controversial by many.

Modern movements like libertarianism, based on ideas of moral absolutism, natural law, and individual rights, are often seen as extreme and uncompromising instead of being aligned with the fundamental values of the Enlightenment and liberal democracy. This has led to a common view that those who strictly adhere to the principles of individual natural rights, especially property rights, are selfish and lacking empathy. This misinterpretation of natural law can be seen in a popular misquotation of John Steinbeck by Ronald Wright in his 2005 book *A Short History of Progress*.

> *Socialism never took root in America because the poor see themselves not as an exploited proletariat, but as temporarily embarrassed millionaires.*

This fundamental misunderstanding of the morally absolute position of property rights under natural law theory implies that supporters of natural law only value the theory for its relative and personal outcomes, attempting, and failing, to understand the natural law position by evaluating the concepts through the utilitarian lens.

Other critiques based on misunderstandings and false perceptions of individual rights have been common, including the incorrect attribution of natural rights to strictly theological roots, a relationship that would allow it to be dismissed alongside other religious beliefs, instead of treating it as the secular and empirical theory it is. Although many supporters of natural law believe that natural rights are a product of divine sources, Grotius, Locke, and the U.S. founders made it clear that natural law was independent, secular at its core, and inherently tolerant of different belief systems.

This shift away from the principles of natural law has also led to historical revisionism of the founding of the United States, and the attempted reinterpretation of individual rights by equating them with new widely accepted utilitarian concepts of human rights. Individual rights based on human nature became seen as valuable for their outcomes, viewed only through the lens of their value to society and humanity, absorbed into Mill's utilitarian definition of rights.

This use of natural rights as a variable in utilitarian calculations is evident in many government policies that trade these rights for other perceived benefits, an increasingly common exchange over the course of the 20th century and beyond. Aside from many of the specific violations of liberty already covered, many government actions serve to trade away or influence the ability to make certain choices in order to bring value to the social body.

As we saw in previous chapters, the right to privacy has been – and often continues to be – violated through mass surveillance programs, warrantless searches, and requirements to reveal personal information to government entities, including purchase histories and records of personal transactions. Each of these policies has traded away pieces of the natural right in order to solve some perceived social, security, or economic issue that was identified.

Policies and laws have also eroded the natural right to life through the waging of unjust war as defined by Grotius, and through extra-judicial killings. The related right to self-defence has also been increasingly ignored and even rejected by some nations, with outright bans on the use of lethal self-defence, and the prevention of owning tools, including firearms, knives, and even pepper spray for self-defence.

The natural right to freedom of expression has also faced a decline, with the rise of laws against misinformation, laws against the ever-broadening category of hate speech, restrictions on protesting and public speech, and even laws against offensive speech as seen in the UK's Communications Act passed in 2003.

The right to property, outside of the violations through excessive taxation mentioned above, has been compromised across a variety of policies such as misuse of eminent domain, civil asset forfeiture, confiscation of property through legislation, and restrictions and regulations on ownership of goods.

While these infringements and more have been commonplace in Western nations over the 20th and 21st centuries, there has also been an increase in the recognition of some natural rights, especially towards freedom of family. In 1967, the U.S. Supreme Court's decision in *Loving v. Virginia* struck down state laws banning interracial marriage, a monumental win for natural rights in the United States. Family rights also saw another series of wins starting with the legalization of same-sex marriage in the Netherlands in 2001, followed by Belgium, Canada, and Spain over the next decade. By the end of 2015, France, the UK, the United States, and Ireland also followed suit, allowing individuals from many different nations to choose and form families of their choice.

These recent realizations of family rights align with natural law principles, and although in the U.S. the legal decisions were justified with the U.S. Bill of Rights, just like in many of the other countries the changes were heavily driven by their perceived utilitarian value. The utilitarian arguments for American legalization, in particular, are visible in several ways, including a study by the Williams Institute at UCLA School of Law, which argued that same-sex marriage would generate significant economic benefits for states[50], a direct case for the positive outcomes of marriage equality. Another example is the amicus brief submitted by the American Psychological Association in the U.S. Supreme Court case in 2015, citing evidence of the positive effects of marriage on mental health for same-sex couples[51]. Alongside Justice Kennedy's opinion that mentioned the decision's social benefits of stability and inclusion, there are many examples that demonstrate the public focus on utility, rather than the natural rights to family and equality under the law.

This type of U.S. Supreme court ruling has been common since the court was first established, with more than 900 examples of laws being overturned for violations of the Constitution since 1803. In the current United States political, social, and legal climates, in many ways it seems like these actions represent the last vestige of support for natural law, a by-product of enforcing the related principles enshrined in the founding documents.

However, even the protections of natural rights offered by the constitution are under siege by the aforementioned changes in public perception and acceptance of utilitarian ideals and modern interpretations of rights. This trend is reflected in acceptance of the constitution as a "living document," with a 2020 survey conducted by Pew Research Center finding that more than 55% of Americans believing that the Supreme Court should rule based on their interpretation of what the constitution "means in current times," compared with only 43% who subscribe to the originalist approach[52].

The utilitarian public attitudes towards the legal system have also changed in relation to the ideas of justice over time, moving away from the natural law principles of restitution and even punishment, towards an overall rehabilitative approach, and even at times away from the principles of equal treatment in order to maximize social welfare.

While this shift in expectations for the justice system isn't strictly a new phenomenon, it can be tied to the shift away from traditional views that crime generally constituted a wrong against individuals, towards a view of crime as an offence against the state or social collective in general. This led to a system where the state became the primary driver behind prosecution and punishment, rather than focusing on community or individual restitution.

In the late 20th century, the Victims' Rights Movement in the United States aimed to try and improve treatment for victims of crime within the justice system, often focusing on support as well as ensuring proper compensation for victims. In 1972, the first victim compensation program was established in California, and in 1984, the Victims of Crime

Act was passed under the Reagan administration, establishing federal support for these compensation programs.

Although the justice system added some recognition for victim compensation, in most cases the criminal justice system overlooked the concept of restitution, leaving individuals to seek redress through civil litigation instead. An example of this can be seen in the fallout of Bernie Madoff's Ponzi scheme, where victims had to turn to civil actions to seek restitution in order to recover their lost investments.

The separation of law and justice from the principles of natural law has also led to situations where legal inequality becomes a property of a utilitarian justice system, rather than a flaw. Situational and disproportionate application of justice has historically been common, although the end of Jim Crow laws led to a broad increase in legal equality as a result of the Civil Rights Movement of the 1960s.

With the rise of public acceptance of utilitarian and collectivist decision-making, conversations around constitutional interpretation and the role of the judiciary in interpreting law as a way to shape policy have increased, highlighting a rise in activism in the application of justice. This rise of purposeful inequality for perceived benefits is a blatant utilitarian violation of natural law principles, specifically the right to equal treatment under the law.

An example of activism as a tool for addressing racial outcomes in a preferential capacity can be seen in a 1999 Canadian Supreme Court ruling that led to the *Gladue Principles*, a requirement for unique accommodations to be made for Indigenous offenders, considerations that do not apply to other racial groups.

Approaches to policymaking are also commonly focused on benefiting specific racial groups that are seen to be historically disadvantaged, as demonstrated in a 2023 press release by the White House on their achievements towards racial equity. The list contains many different policies and specific measures intended to assist individuals primarily based on race, including investments in black communities, initiatives around boosting wages for black federal workers, assistance for black homeowners in resolving inheritance issues, and several others. The use of targeted policies and redistribution in order to provide preferential discrimination, while culturally and politically expedient, also demonstrates a violation of the natural principles to equal treatment under the law, aiming for equality of outcome instead of treatment.

But what are the results of this drastic rise in utilitarian policy? One of the major impacts of invasive government intervention in everyday life is a growing mistrust of government, and a radical decrease in perceptions of social stability in the United States. In data collected by the Pew Research Center, polls in 1958 showed that around 75% of Americans trusted the federal government to do the right thing, "almost always or most of the time."[53] As the role of government expanded throughout the second half of the 20th century, the trust in government has been in marked decline, and since 2007, the percentage of people who trust the government "almost always or most of the time" has not surpassed 30%[54].

While trust in government is at its lowest point in decades as it continues to shift away from its role as protector of natural rights, there is also growing dissatisfaction with the cultural, political, and economic landscape in America. In mid-2022, a poll conducted by the Associated Press's NORC centre showed that more than 85% of Americans believed that the country was headed in the wrong direction, an overwhelming display of bipartisan dissatisfaction[55].

Alongside the cultural and political concerns of the population, there are growing concerns with the results and effects of the highly engineered and intrusive economic policy. Ironically, while government involvement has reached all-time highs, our study from earlier showed that the majority of Americans believe the government is doing too little to help people. And while the government's costs are dramatically increased as a result of such widespread interference, only 6% hold the view that the federal government is "careful with taxpayer money."[56]

The effects of the utilitarian and collectivist monetary policy and economic decisions can also be seen in the continual decline in purchasing power over time, especially since the rise of government involvement in industry and major entitlement programs. Over the 40-year period between 1982 and 2022, inflation has totalled more than 190%, more than 100% of which has been since 2005[57].

While many of these polls and statistics demonstrate how easily the outcomes of utilitarian policy can deviate from their intended purpose, they also serve to further reinforce arguments that highlight utilitarianism's failure to maximize overall well-being and happiness. These failures also align with the political trends of trading away natural rights, and the decline of the morally absolute concept of the inherent worth of every individual.

From the natural law standard established by Locke and others, anyone would be hard pressed to declare modern authority anything but illegitimate. This gigantic sprawling system has tentacles in every aspect of our lives, applying pressure and wielding arbitrary authority to guide the social, economic, and political machinery of the nation.

This excessive and overbearing authority has grown as a consequence of the utilitarian demand for action in the face of suboptimal circumstances – John Stuart Mill's requirement for moral action – leading to involvement in all aspects of life where improvements can even be *imagined*. This has inevitably led to restrictions on liberty and other natural rights in an effort to prevent not only negative outcomes for others, but even for ourselves.

Along these lines, the social contract has become a widely misused concept that has been twisted to become culturally synonymous with the idea that citizens must submit to all demands of society. This inversion is antithetical to Locke's ideas of the social contract, where he illustrated a trade, a delegation of a small portion of natural rights to an authority that could then better secure the rest. Instead, Mill's view of utilitarianism as a precursor to rights has reversed the concept, popularizing ideas that rights are not natural, and are simply the product of authority – valued for their utility instead of inherent morality.

In the modern age, adherents of natural law are often split on the concepts of legitimate authority, with classical liberals aligning with the views of John Locke, supporting small and more reasonable limited government, while anarchists in the tradition of Proudhon, Goldman, and Spooner believe that the nature of authority itself is a violation of the inherent rights of human beings.

In the end, in a choice between continuing down the path of increasing utilitarian application or returning to the protections of natural law and individual rights, the choice seems clear. We need to embrace natural rights, a system that values the inherent worth of individuals, not just as a statistic to be calculated as a part of a collective.

11

The Greatest Good

Since the very beginning of human debate over right and wrong, the principles of natural law have remained a significant part of philosophical conversation. The ideas have been reflected in legal codes since the time of Hammurabi around 1750 BCE, persisting through to today, almost 4,000 years later.

For much of this history, beliefs about human nature and morality were common in philosophical circles, although natural law was not explicitly recognized by authorities and governments. As we saw, rights such as legal equality for citizens, property rights, and religious tolerance appeared across many of the major empires and cultures of the past, including the Roman Republic and later Empire, throughout ancient Greece, and again through the Islamic Golden Age around the 7th century CE.

Although the specifics of these ideas varied according to time and place, with the Enlightenment they took on a more concrete shape, coalescing into the concept of natural rights, protections owed to every person by virtue of their very humanity.

The Enlightenment era consolidation of principles under Grotius, Hobbes, Locke, and others explored the theory from a wide range of angles, including international law, rights of nations, secular natural law and religious tolerance, individual rights, political and social contract theory, and the rousing ideas of citizen consent and the rights to revolution. These ideas and the acceptance of natural rights spread like wildfire through Western nations and became the battle cries of revolutions, standing up against injustice and illegitimate authority.

Both the American and French Revolutions at the end of the 18th centuries were the direct result of these Lockean ideas on individual natural rights and the illegitimacy of coercive and arbitrary authority. Both movements encoded these natural rights into their founding documents, declaring the rights of the people as the ends, to which government was simply the means. This idea was also clearly put by English historian, writer, and politician Lord Acton in his 1877 address to members of the Bridgenorth Institute, quoted below.

> *Liberty is not a means to a higher political end. It is itself the highest political end.*

Although the French Revolution quickly cannibalized its founding ideals, the movement that claimed "Liberty, Equality, Fraternity" had a lasting impact on Europe and the world, setting a precedent with its challenge to monarchy and the feudal system, and greatly popularizing the ideas of abolition and women's rights.

The American experiment was much more successful, enshrining natural rights in the Declaration of Independence and the U.S. Constitution, natural rights that remain the basis for many modern movements of equality and liberty for all.

These documents and rights were the backbone of movements to end slavery, pursue women's rights, and uphold religious tolerance around the world, proclaiming that all humans are of equal worth, a universal moral standard that transcends borders and ideological barriers.

These concepts of natural rights and the inherent worth of humans were also influential in the anarchist movements across much of the 19th century and afterwards, with Proudhon, Spooner, Tucker, and Goldman all sharing many of these foundational principles, though they often differed in conclusions.

Overall, the belief in inherent rights for all people is simple and powerful, striving to protect life and liberty for everyone, primarily through restrictions on authority and the empowerment of those who are governed. These universal ideas are still as relevant today as they were in ancient Mesopotamia thousands of years ago, echoing their timeless message for us to decipher. You, the individual, matter. You are the greatest good. You are the moral means that should not be compromised for a chance at some greater end. It isn't a call for selfishness, for a lack of concern for your fellow man, just a recognition that human civilization and everything humanity has achieved is the result of our natural tendencies towards voluntary cooperation, stability, and mutual respect.

As we have seen throughout this book, the uncompromising recognition of natural rights allows us to treat every individual as their own end, and in doing so, both individuals and society prosper.

12

Restoring Natural Order

In retrospect, it is easy to see how false intuition and dreams of a better world have led us here, and it is no small task for each of us to look at our own beliefs and overcome our inner bias – drilling down to hit moral bedrock. But, as we sit back and consider the long road behind us from the perspective of natural law, it does raise one daunting question.

How do we return to our moral origins in natural law – reversing the course of the most powerful utilitarian decision-making engines the world has ever seen?

That is certainly a question that is difficult to answer, perhaps as utopian in nature as utilitarianism itself. But at the very least, it provides us with a framework through which to view the world around us, a moral barometer we can use to begin evaluating policy, action, and especially our own convictions.

While the clichéd proverb might tell us that "A journey of a thousand miles begins with a single step," I would suggest that it in fact starts with looking inward, and deciding which moral landscape we are stepping into. With the concepts outlined herein as a guide, we can adopt the universal and moral principles underlying natural order and human connection, the first and greatest of many steps forward.

To that end, it cannot be overstated how much of an essential role both introspection and empathy play in the embrace of moral decision-making and moral action. As the ancient maxim inscribed in the Temple of Apollo at Delphi once said,

Know thyself.

And while introspection can also serve us well in many other areas of personal life, the rational exploration of our assumptions, desires, and intentions can certainly help us more closely align with the universal principles of natural law. This process of inner reflection helps us explore many different aspects of moral behaviour, not only to examine the choices we make, but how we make those decisions, what our motivations are, who is being impacted, and even if we have a right to make the choice in the first place.

Evaluating the honest motivations behind our preferences and decisions is no easy task, but it can help us avoid the pitfalls of cognitive bias and develop a more consistent and robust moral framework. For example, are we embracing a policy, entitlement, or law simply because we expect to personally benefit as a result? This approach to morality is more of an alignment of convenience than a principled stance, using morality as a smokescreen to hide expectations of beneficial consequences – a utilitarian decision by any measure.

While the recognition of natural rights is intrinsically moral regardless of intention, even when advocating for natural law we should be mindful of focusing on means rather than ends. Otherwise, what happens when moral action is no longer convenient or beneficial – would we discard natural law for a new moral paradigm?

We should also be cautious of the inverse, ignoring or overlooking immoral action because we are not immediately affected. Acceptance of natural rights is inseparable from the fundamental understanding that they are universal and apply equally to all people, not just ourselves. As

Thomas Paine wrote in his *Dissertation on First Principles of Government in* 1794,

> *He that would make his own liberty secure must guard even his enemy from oppression; for if he violates this duty, he establishes a precedent that will reach to himself.*

The question of what obligations natural law places on an individual in this capacity has also been widely debated, with Locke and others believing that there is a moral duty to preserve the rights of others. Although demands for action fall outside of the mandates of natural law, there is certainly a strong case to be made for mutual enforcement of the natural rights within society.

The question of how we should make choices under the guidance of natural law is relatively simple, and it starts (and ends) with the following axiom: *the natural rights of others are inviolable.* This simple rule places a requirement on every action we take, not to maximize outcomes regardless of cost, but to respect the autonomy and self-determination of others who might be affected. While it is considerably easier in our own lives to avoid actions that encroach on others, this premise also applies to those we sanction, or who act on our behalf, including authority.

Unlike the democracies of ancient Athens, modern democratic systems make it quite a bit more difficult to oppose an authority's immoral actions. In essence, representatives are seen to inherit the moral authority of those they represent – taken as a de-facto assumption of consent to further action. This form of governance flies in the face of Lockean ideas on consent of the governed, where people are able to withdraw consent at any time, and authorities that violate rights are deemed illegitimate.

So how do we, as participants in a system where our moral approval is taken for granted, make moral choices? Unlike the utilitarian requirement to engage in action with preferable consequences, natural law simply requires you to avoid action that violates rights. In the case of representative democracies, this could even be seen as a call to avoid participation entirely – abstain from bringing legitimacy to systemic violations of natural law.

Many people would undoubtedly argue that this is not an actual solution, and will not lead to change, but through the lens of intrinsic right and wrong, moral action is both the solution *and* the goal. That being said, political renunciation is only one path towards avoiding immoral action.

In a more concrete and moderate sense, applying natural law can take the form of active opposition to policies or action that would violate the natural rights of others. This includes violations of property rights through the requirement for taxes that extend well past reasonable levels, policies that dabble in unequal treatment across various criteria, laws that restrict personal choices, and the implementation of victimless crimes, alongside many, many others.

From this perspective, we should also remember that modern laws and moral behaviour are only loosely connected, and the relationship between the two should not be taken for granted. To see a clear example, we only need to look back a few hundred years to when owning slaves was legal – a "legal" blatant violation of natural rights.

As we have seen often in recent decades, the rejection of utilitarian policy is especially necessary in times of crisis, and other situations where we are particularly susceptible to the *affect heuristic* – or emotional decision-making. The utilitarian view that action is mandatory in the face of suffering commonly leads to the erosion of natural rights, and often fails to solve the problem anyway.

It's also important to clarify the distinction between wanting to help and wanting a solution to be mandated by authority. Natural law does not suggest we ignore the suffering of others, only that we don't use force to compel solutions – a preference towards voluntary interaction and charity over the application of authority. The idea was succinctly put by Frédéric Bastiat in his work *The Law* in 1850, as follows.

> *Socialism, like the ancient ideas from which it springs, confuses the distinction between government and society. As a result of this, every time we object to a thing being done by government, the socialists conclude that we object to its being done at all. We disapprove of state education. Then the socialists say that we are opposed to any education. We object to a state religion. Then the socialists say that we want no religion at all. We object to a state-enforced equality. Then they say that we are against equality. And so on, and so on. It is as if the socialists were to accuse us of not wanting persons to eat because we do not want the state to raise grain.*

In essence, we should avoid using the government in order to enforce solutions to problems at the cost of liberty, not that we should avoid solving problems altogether. The most crucial idea presented by Bastiat is not that collective services are bad, groups can still self-organize and build their own systems of support and services – simply that they should not be mandatory.

Outside of the codification of natural rights, supporting the heavy-handed application of laws, even for the benefit of society, not only imposes our values on others, but removes their autonomy and self-determination.

Overall, while our earlier question remains unanswered, at the very least we can do our part to engage in moral action. Promote the voluntary exchange of ideas instead of mandates, advocate for the protection of every person's natural rights, and accept that values and choices are unique to each person – even when we don't agree.

Conclusion

Over the course of this book, we explored the evolution of these two influential ethical systems, observed the real-life policies that have grown from them, and examined them for flaws. In short, we have laid bare these two theories and found one of them wanting.

Utilitarianism rests entirely on the premise that qualitative experience can be accurately quantified and compared, a claim amounting to the fact that we can achieve the impossible on its way to a moral utopia. Among its many other flaws, this foundational premise has been found to be false, and the consequence is the invalidation of its own moral structure.

On the other hand, the natural laws derived from human nature have been shown to truly help us reach towards a more equitable and just society, despite their focus on moral actions instead of moral goals. They provide the groundwork for every one of us to live our lives to the fullest, free from arbitrary authority, ideological persecution, and coercion. These most basic principles in the form of individual rights have given us a baseline, one on which we can build our own compatible cultural, religious, or ideological belief systems.

"Liberty becomes a question of morals more than of politics." – Lord Acton

Although the ideas of liberty, natural rights, and legitimacy of authority are often considered strictly political or economic concerns, like Lord Acton believed, we can clearly see that they are actually the foundations of moral behaviour.

With Western society having spent the better part of a century moving towards more and more utilitarian ideals, the resulting cracks in social stability, happiness, and trust in authority are larger than ever before. The ever-increasing size, reach, and power of authority has broken the promises of the American Experiment, throwing away the essential principles of liberal democracy, natural law, and individual liberties.

This subversion of Enlightenment ideals and the dwindling of individual autonomy was meant to bring about a better world. After all, how can a system whose sole purpose is a greater good result in anything else? But in return for this grotesque and demanding social contract, we've received nothing but unfulfilled promises. The outcomes that we assumed would be the obvious result of utilitarian and collectivist goals have never materialized – a one-sided trade by any measure.

Although a societal return to the values of natural law seems like an overwhelming, even utopian goal, the first step is to take stock of our own values and convictions and do our part to engage in moral action. If there is only one single thing that you take away from this book, I would have it be this:

Your natural rights are paramount, and YOU are the greatest good. But so is your neighbour, and your colleagues, and even the strangers you pass on the street.

When I first started writing this, I didn't have an explicit goal in mind. It was largely a journey of discovery in order to better understand the radical differences in perceptions of moral behaviour in Western society. Throughout the process, it evolved into an exploration of how we reached this point in history where seemingly simple concepts like rights could be perceived so differently across moral and ideological divides.

Although I have expanded my own understanding of the origins of modern morality in writing this book, I don't expect everyone who has read along to reach the same conclusions or walk away with the same sentiments. I hope that despite the differences in our beliefs, our reasoning and our conclusions, everyone has gained some value from this work, and hopefully we will all look at decisions, actions, society, and life through a new or at least more thoughtful lens.

Thank you for joining me on this journey.

References

[1] Colon, D. (May 31, 2022). DOT announces multi-agency study to 'reimagine' the Cross Bronx Expressway. *Streetsblog NYC*. https://nyc.streetsblog.org/2022/05/31/dot-announces-multi-agency-study-to-reimagine-the-cross-bronx-expressway

[2] Fetherston, H., Calder, R. (2020). Australia's health tracker by area: smoking summary report. *Mitchell Institute, Victoria University*. https://www.vu.edu.au/mitchell-institute/australian-health-tracker-series/poorest-australians-seven-times-more-likely-to-smoke

[3] Wilkinson, A., Scollo, M., Wakefield, M. et al. (2019). Smoking prevalence following tobacco tax increases in Australia between 2001 and 2017. *The Lancet*. Volume 4. Issue 12. E618-E627. https://www.thelancet.com/journals/lanpub/article/PIIS2468-2667(19)30203-8/fulltext

[4] Frontier Economics. (2020). Impact of the national living wage on businesses. *ADR UK*. https://www.adruk.org/our-mission/our-impact/impact-of-national-living-wage-on-businesses/

[5] Berche, P. (2022). Life and death of smallpox. *La Presse Médicale*. Volume 51. Issue 3. 104117.
https://www.sciencedirect.com/science/article/pii/S0755498222000100
Also published here: https://pubmed.ncbi.nlm.nih.gov/35143880/

[6] CDC. The USPHS Untreated Syphilis Study at Tuskegee. *CDC.gov*. https://www.cdc.gov/tuskegee/index.html

[7] EPA. (2020). Trends Report. *EPA.gov*.
https://gispub.epa.gov/air/trendsreport/2020/documentation/AirTrends_Flyer.pdf;
https://www.epa.gov/air-trends/air-quality-national-summary

[8] EPA. (2011). Benefits and Costs of the Clean Air Act 1990-2020. Second Prospective Report. *EPA.gov.* https://www.epa.gov/clean-air-act-overview/benefits-and-costs-clean-air-act-1990-2020-second-prospective-study

[9] EPA. (2011). Benefits and Costs of the Clean Air Act 1990-2020. Final Report. *EPA.gov.* https://www.epa.gov/sites/default/files/2015-07/documents/fullreport_rev_a.pdf

[10] EPA. Air Trends. *EPA.gov.* https://www.epa.gov/air-trends/air-quality-national-summary

[11] Wolpaw Reyes, J. (2007). Environmental policy as social policy? The impact of childhood lead exposure on crime. *The B.E. Journal of Economic Analysis and Policy.* Berkeley Electronic Press. Volume 7(1). https://www.nber.org/papers/w13097

[12] Lobell, D., Burney, J. (2021). Cleaner air has contributed one-fifth of US maize and soybean yield gains since 1990. *Environmental Research Letters.* Volume 16. Number 7. 4049. IOP Publishing Ltd.
https://iopscience.iop.org/article/10.1088/1748-9326/ac0fa4

[13] Ibid.

[14] Boehnke, K., Litinas, E., Clauw, D. (2016). Medical cannabis use is associated with decreased opiate medication use in a retrospective cross-sectional survey of patients with chronic pain. *The Journal of Pain. Volume 17. Issue 6.* 739-744.
https://www.sciencedirect.com/science/article/pii/S1526590016005678

[15] Ogborne, A., Smart, R. et al. (2011). Who is using cannabis as a medicine and why: an exploratory study. *Journal of Psychoactive Drugs.* 32(4). 435-443.
https://www.tandfonline.com/doi/abs/10.1080/02791072.2000.10400245

[16] Wen, H., Hockenberry, J. (2018). Association of medical and adult use marijuana laws with opioid prescribing for Medicaid enrollees. *JAMA Internal Medicine.* 178(5). 673-679. https://www.bmj.com/content/361/bmj.k1514.full

REFERENCES

[17] Bachhuber, M., Saloner, B., Chinazo, O. et al. (2014). Medical cannabis laws and opioid analgesic overdose mortality in the United States, 1999-2010. *JAMA Internal Medicine.* 174(10). 1668-1673.
https://jamanetwork.com/journals/jamainternalmedicine/article-abstract/1898878

[18] California Department of Justice. (2018). California Criminal Justice Data Reports. *oag.ca.gov* https://oag.ca.gov/news/press-releases/attorney-general-becerra-releases-2017-california-criminal-justice-data-reports

[19] Kerstein, S. (2021) Cannabis Tax Revenue Update. *lao.ca.gov.*
https://lao.ca.gov/LAOEconTax/Article/Detail/687

[20] Williams, D., Falcone, E., Fugate, B. (2021). Farming down the drain: Unintended consequences of the Food Safety Modernization Act's Produce Rule on small and very small farms. *Business Horizons.* Volume 64. Issue 3. 361-368.
https://walton.uark.edu/initiatives/supply-chain-research/posts/researchers-examine-food-safety-laws-unintended-consequences.php

[21] Sommers, D., Baicker, K., Epstein, A. (2012). Mortality and access to care among adults after state Medicaid Expansions. *The New England Journal of Medicine.* Vol. 367. No. 11. https://www.nejm.org/doi/full/10.1056/NEJMsa1202099

[22] Sterling Thermal Technology. (Updated April 28 2023). The biggest power plants in the world. *sterlingtt.com.* https://www.sterlingtt.com/2022/03/01/biggest-power-plants-world/

[23] Three Gorges Dam. In Wikipedia.
https://simple.wikipedia.org/wiki/Three_Gorges_Dam

[24] Gan, N. (July 31, 2020). China's Three Gorges Dam is one of the largest ever created. Was it Worth it? *CNN style.* https://www.cnn.com/style/article/china-three-gorges-dam-intl-hnk-dst/index.html

[25] Ibid.

[26] USGS. (November 17, 2016). Before and after the Three Gorges Dam for the Yangtze River. *usgs.gov*. https://www.usgs.gov/news/science-snippet/earthview-three-gorges-dam-brings-power-concerns-central-china

[27] Ibid.

[28] Awad, E., Dsouza S., Shariff, A. et al. (2020) Universals and variations in moral decisions made in 42 countries by 70,000 participants. *PNAS*. 117(5). 2332-2337. https://www.pnas.org/doi/10.1073/pnas.1911517117

[29] Burnstein, E., Crandall, C., Kitayama, S. (1994). Some neo-Darwinian decision rules for altruism: weighing clues for inclusive fitness as a function of the biological importance of the decision. *Journal of Personality and Social Psychology*. 67(5). 773-789. https://psycnet.apa.org/record/1995-09360-001

[30] Krekula, L., Forinder, U., Tibell, A. (2018). What do people agree to when stating willingness to donate? On the medical interventions enabling organ donation after death. *PloS One*. 13(8): e0202544.
https://journals.plos.org/plosone/article?id=10.1371/journal.pone.0202544

[31] Wilson, T., Gilbert, D. (2003). Affective forecasting. *Advances in Experimental Social Psychology*. Volume 35. 345-411.
https://citeseerx.ist.psu.edu/document?repid=rep1&type=pdf&doi=05c8943ac31a31a2d738236bc6cd5567c8c00f04

[32] Hines, L., Freeman, T., Gage, S., et al. (2020). Association of high-potency cannabis use with mental health and substance use in adolescence. *JAMA Psychiatry*. 77(10); 1044-1051. https://jamanetwork.com/journals/jamapsychiatry/article-abstract/2765973

[33] Johannes, N., Vuorre, M., Przybylski, A., (2021). Video game play is positively correlated with well-being. *Royal Society Open Science*. 8:202049.
https://royalsocietypublishing.org/doi/full/10.1098/rsos.202049

[34] Pew Research Center. (2013). The global divide on homosexuality. *pewresearch.org*. https://www.pewresearch.org/global/2013/06/04/the-global-divide-on-homosexuality/

[35] Pew Research Center. (2020). Americans' views of government: low trust plus some positive performance ratings. *pewresearch.org*.
https://www.pewresearch.org/politics/2020/09/14/americans-views-of-government-low-trust-but-some-positive-performance-ratings/

[36] Hannikainen, I., Miller, R., Cushman F. (2016). Act versus impact: conservatives and liberals exhibit different structural emphases in moral judgement. *SSRN*.
https://papers.ssrn.com/sol3/papers.cfm?abstract_id=2727363
For a different study with similar results, see:
https://pubmed.ncbi.nlm.nih.gov/33615911/

[37] Philanthropy Roundtable. Statistics on U.S. Generosity. *philanthropyroundtable.org*. https://www.philanthropyroundtable.org/almanac/statistics-on-us-generosity/

[38] Paarlberg, L., Nesbit, R., Christensen, R. (2018). The politics of donations: Are red countries more donative than blue countries? *Nonprofit and Voluntary Sector Quarterly*. Volume 48. Issue 2. 283-308.
https://journals.sagepub.com/doi/abs/10.1177/0899764018804088?journalCode=nvsb

[39] Hariri, A., Mattay, V., Tessitore, A. et al. ISerotonin transporter genetic variation and the response of the human amygdala, *Science*. Volume 297. Issue 5580. 400-403. https://www.science.org/doi/abs/10.1126/science.1071829

[40] U.S. Bureau of Economic Analysis. (2023). United States government spending to GDP. *tradingeconomics.com*. https://tradingeconomics.com/united-states/government-spending-to-gdp

[41] Moffitt, R., (2015). The deserving poor, the family, and the U.S. welfare system. *Demography*. 52(3); 729-749.
https://www.ncbi.nlm.nih.gov/pmc/articles/PMC4487675/

[42] USDA. A short history of SNAP. *Food and Nutrition Service usda.gov.* https://www.fns.usda.gov/snap/short-history-snap

[43] Toossi, S., Jones, J. (2023). The food and nutrition assistance landscape: fiscal year 2022 annual report. *USDA Economic Information Bulletin No. 255.* https://www.ers.usda.gov/webdocs/publications/106763/eib-255.pdf?v=3411.3

[44] SSA. (2023) Annual statistical report on the social security disability insurance program, 2022. *SSA Publication No. 13-11826.* https://www.ssa.gov/policy/docs/statcomps/di_asr/2022/di_asr22.pdf

[45] TPC. (May 11, 2023). Historical highest marginal income tax rates. *taxpolicycenter.org.* https://www.taxpolicycenter.org/statistics/historical-highest-marginal-income-tax-rates

[46] USDA. Snap: characteristics households fy 2018. *Food and Nutrition Service usda.gov.* https://www.fns.usda.gov/snap/characteristics-households-fy-2018

[47] Pew Research Center. (2012). A comparison of results of surveys by the Pew Research Center and Google consumer surveys. *pewresearch.org.* https://assets.pewresearch.org/wp-content/uploads/sites/5/legacy-pdf/11-7-12%20Google%20Methodology%20paper.pdf

[48] Pew Research Center. (2020). Americans' views of government: low trust plus some positive performance ratings. *pewresearch.org.* https://www.pewresearch.org/politics/2020/09/14/americans-views-of-government-low-trust-but-some-positive-performance-ratings/

[49] Saad, L. (November 25, 2019). Socialism as popular as capitalism among young adults in U.S. *Gallup.* https://news.gallup.com/poll/268766/socialism-popular-capitalism-among-young-adults.aspx

[50] Jow, L. (2015). Willams Institute researched played role in same-sex marriage decision. *UniversityofCalifornia.edu.*

https://www.universityofcalifornia.edu/news/williams-institute-research-played-role-same-sex-marriage-decision

[51] American Psychological Association. (2015). Obergefell v Hodges. Amicus brief. *apa.org.* https://www.apa.org/about/offices/ogc/amicus/obergefell

[52] Hartig, H. (September 25, 2020). Before Ginsberg's death, a majority of Americans viewed the Supreme Court as middle of the road. *Pewresearch.org.* https://www.pewresearch.org/short-reads/2020/09/25/before-ginsburgs-death-a-majority-of-americans-viewed-the-supreme-court-as-middle-of-the-road/

[53] Pew Research Center. (September 19, 2023). Public trust in government: 1958-2023. *Pewresearch.org.* https://www.pewresearch.org/politics/2023/09/19/public-trust-in-government-1958-2023/

[54] Ibid.

[55] NORC. (June 29, 2022). Bipartisan dissatisfaction with the direction of the country and economy. *apnorc.org.* https://apnorc.org/projects/bipartisan-dissatisfaction-with-the-direction-of-the-country-and-the-economy/

[56] Pew Research Center. (June 6, 2022). Americans' views of government: Decades of distrust, enduring support for its role. *Pewresearch.org.* https://www.pewresearch.org/politics/2022/06/06/americans-views-of-government-decades-of-distrust-enduring-support-for-its-role/

[57] US Inflation Calculator. (2024). Consumer Price Index Data from 1913 to 2024. *CoinNews Media Group.* https://www.usinflationcalculator.com/inflation/consumer-price-index-and-annual-percent-changes-from-1913-to-2008/

About the Author

Driven by a lifelong passion for moral philosophy, J.A. Mitchell has always been fascinated by the foundations of moral decision-making in modern society. From an early age, he was exposed to a wealth of conflicting ideas and contrasting philosophical viewpoints. Raised by Christian parents who were on the periphery of the anti-establishment movements of the 1970s, J.A. Mitchell himself grew up in Atlantic Canada, during the late punk era under the influence of bands like Bad Religion and NOFX – opposing forces which both provided a strong foundation for his anti-authoritarian views.

While his own religious beliefs didn't stick, they did help to infuse a deep sense of empathy for different beliefs while navigating diverse philosophical ideas across religious and political spectrums. With feet in conflicting worlds, over time it became increasingly clear that many people generalize, misrepresent, or even misunderstand the fundamental views and beliefs of those they disagree with. This insight led him to explore the concepts at the root of moral theory, aiming to better understand where modern misunderstandings were really coming from.

His first book, *You: The Greatest Good*, is an attempt to examine society's moral roots through the balanced lens of both classical and contemporary thought.

www.ingramcontent.com/pod-product-compliance
Lightning Source LLC
Chambersburg PA
CBHW030543080526
44585CB00012B/239